CRASH LANDING

CRASH LANDING

Surviving a Business Crisis

Richard O. Jacobs

Glenbridge Publishing Ltd.

Library of Congress Catalog Card Number: LC 90-84800

International Standard Book Number: 0-944435-12-2

Printed in the U.S.A.

*Dedicated to the people at Park Bank who had the
courage and strength to crash land.
These are the lessons we learned, which I now
pass on to others.*

Now I know that there are three classes of people in the world. The first learn from their own experience — they are wise. The second learn from the experience of others — these are happy. The third learn neither from their own experience nor from the experience of others — these are fools.

> Og Mandino, The End of the Story

Table of Contents

Part VI — Doing the Right Thing

Foreword

Many books and articles have been written in the past few years dealing with the governance of United States corporations and financial institutions — all of which have shed some insight into the success and failures of these entities.

The 1970s and 1980s were replete with examples of management and board failures. These failures have been the focus of shareholder and stockholder suits and have contributed to the disembowelment of many companies by raiders, often resulting in the loss of hundreds of thousands of jobs and market shares to foreign competition. The failure has also precipitated a hue and cry from shareholders, stakeholders, and regulators, at the federal and state levels and in the halls of Congress, demanding accountability and asking "where was the board of directors?"

Richard O. Jacobs's account is one man's experience as a director who later became CEO of Park Bank in Florida. In an impassioned portrayal, Jacobs describes the events that led to the failure of Park Bank of Florida, then the seventh largest bank failure in the United States. It is but one example of a failure of management and a board of directors to recognize the early warning signs: "the black hole of impending disaster."

Jacobs takes us through his personal travails, his in-depth analysis of events, reflections, and insights combined with personal anecdotes and quotes from Lao Tsu, Aristotle, Santayana, Thoreau, and others. He is to be lauded for his soul searching to determine what he and the board of directors could (or should) have done differently.

While conveying much personal pain, the book will prick the subconscious and conscience of those of us who serve as CEOs and directors. It points out human frailty, the consequences of unbridled egos, and the pied piper mentality that may afflict managements and boards and become the root causes of "black holes." It identifies the steps to be taken to avoid such "holes."

While everyone may not agree with all of Jacobs's conclusions, *Crash Landing* has to be one of the more intuitive and thought-provoking business books of our time. It should be mandatory reading for those responsible for the governance of America's corporations.

John M. Nash, President,
National Association of Corporate Directors

Preface

This book is based upon my personal experiences. Thus, it has been written from the male point of view. I wish that I could speak from global understanding, but I cannot. I do believe, however, women — historically more expressive, more open, seemingly more willing to accept the emotional elements of life's experiences — may well be the stronger of the sexes in surviving troubled times, and, therefore, in coping with crisis trauma. Men, often less holistic and egocentrically wrapped up in work-defined self-images, may well be the greater losers when things go wrong.

This view seems supported by the work of Judy B. Rosener of the University of California, reported in her 1990 *Harvard Business Review* article entitled "Ways Women Lead." She describes women leaders as being more transformational than men. Transformational leaders are at the heart of any crisis turn-around.

I hope that further research into the varying effects of crisis on the sexes, as well as their varying crisis leadership roles, will be encouraged by this book and that, ultimately, each will gain from the strengths of the other.

A book about life's difficult lessons can only be crafted from personal experience with support and encouragement from a wide circle of understanding and insightful friends as well as a devoted family. *Crash Landing* has certainly been no exception. All who have contributed have my undying gratitude.

Several who had experienced the pain of Park Bank's failure, including directors Gary Froid and Bill Zemp, and officers Paulette Gross, Steve Jeatran, Susan Dawson-Johnson, Howard Schmidt, and Grant Hunt, provided advice and suggestions at various stages of the manuscript. So did my attorneys, Chuck Ruff and Jim Murray, and long-time banker friend, Neil Savage.

My sister, Cathy Schley, was exceedingly helpful. A former English teacher, she had come to Florida to spend a Christmas vacation with us and ended up spending untold hours proofing early chapters. And Royce Haiman, a professional writer and editor, helped me shape the initial draft of *Crash Landing* with an energy and professionalism that became contagious.

Reviews by friend and business colleague, Bob Lee, encouraged the disciplined detail and focus I needed during the early going. Invaluable commentary and ideas came from a number of friends, including Jack Murray, Lois and Stu Gurske, Pat and Don Baldwin, Bill Simon, Tom Riden, Jim Gillespe, Karen and Bob Saltz, Barry Solo, Bob Forlizzo, and psychologist Ray Bowman.

Professor William R. Boulton, from the University of Georgia, led a team of business school professors in the preparation of a case study about Park Bank. The experience I gained through participating in his interview process and by observing him diagnose issues was more than helpful; it was a business analysis course in and of itself. Professor Boulton and his team offered a refreshing and encouraging contrast to the negative observations about business schools and their professors I make in the Introduction to this book.

The support and encouragement I received from my family, during the crisis and its aftermath, was never-ending. Without them, this book could not have happened. The kindest thing that I can say about myself during the darkest days of the Park Bank crisis is that I was hell to live with; yet, my wife, Joan, children Julie and John, and John's wife, Denise, never lost faith or faltered in their love, support, or friendship. And during the writing process, Joan became my most steadfast reviser and astute evaluator.

I would like to thank especially Shirley Linde, who served as my consulting editor.

Shirley, an author of some two dozen books, patiently introduced me to the professional world of publishing. She read and critiqued drafts and redrafts of this manuscript (each one thought by me to be "final"). Thank you, Shirley. Your dedication and expertise are a credit to the publishing industry.

Introduction

We get very little wisdom from success, you know.
William Saroyan

1

In a narrow sense, *Crash Landing* is a case study about a business failure: specifically, the 1986 collapse of Park Bank of Florida, at the time the seventh largest bank failure in the United States.

But, in its broader sense, *Crash Landing* is about leading a business during the most perilous of times — during crisis — when there is no visible end to trouble, when there is no solution that works.

It's about what you do next when the "right executive stuff" turns out to be the "wrong executive stuff."

It's about painful lessons, the tough "how to" knowledge that arose from the wreckage of Park Bank.

And it's about emotions. Emotions dominate crisis and, therefore, the events described in this book. For crisis management is, after all, the leadership of people during the most turbulent times — during times when hopes are shattered by broken dreams, when good intentions are thwarted by fears, when exemplary efforts are crushed by catastrophe. Living through crisis is like bivouacking on a battlefield. The bombardment never ends, dominating every thought, overwhelming every feeling.

As a lawyer confided to a reporter for the *National Law Journal* about his law firm break up, "First, it's unthinkable. Then, it's thinkable. Then it's all you think about."

Yes, the thought of experiencing crisis is unthinkable.

Until you experience it.

I know. I experienced it.

At Park Bank. As its CEO.

Inside the Park*

Ironically, I had not set out to be CEO when I and eight businessmen acquired Park Bank in November 1977 and became its board of directors. I had a successful, growing law practice on Florida's west coast that was keeping me busy.

Five years after our purchase, however, as the banking industry entered into the early stages of deregulation, Park Bank started to experience growing pains. Park had expanded from its nine original investors to several hundred stockholders, and from one office with $8,000,000 in assets to eight offices with $170,000,000 in assets. And Harold Kelley, Park Bank's CEO, pulled by outside pressures, was no longer effectively leading the bank.

In a December 1982 strategy meeting, Park Bank's board of directors decided that John Kearney, a CPA who was one of the original nine investors, and I should become more involved in the bank — at least for a while — as Park recruited additional executives, installed new systems, and prepared for deregulation. I approached my law partners (our firm represented the bank) for a leave of absence for a few months — "certainly not over six" — so I could become more active in shaping the bank's direction.

John Kearney replaced Harold Kelley as Park's chairman and CEO. Kearney was to oversee the bank's lending and finance functions and the installation of its new computer systems. I, as president, planned to focus

---

*Throughout this book, examples from the Park Bank experience will be italicized in sections entitled "Inside the Park." Inside the Park was the name of Park Bank's monthly employee communications letter.

on the challenge and opportunities deregulation presented Park Bank as a young, growing community bank.

During the first few months of 1983, as Park Bank's spectacular growth continued, I familiarized myself with the bank and organized several deregulation activities, including Park's Private Banking and International Divisions and its investment advisory subsidiary. In its outward appearances, Park Bank seemed to be on track. However, in late 1983, the Federal Deposit Insurance Corporation (FDIC) examined Park Bank and was critical of its rapid loan and deposit increases, its lending practices, and control systems.

More shocked at getting a bad report card than with the reasons behind it, Park Bank's board and management underestimated the significance of the FDIC's findings. After reviewing the FDIC criticism, Park's chairman admonished his agreeable boardroom audience that the regulators simply hadn't caught up to Park's ingenuity — Park was growth oriented, but creatively careful. A few screwdriver adjustments, the board envisioned, were all that were required to tighten up the ship.

So the bank tightened up its loan management and monitoring systems, and its efforts seemed to produce solid results. A June 1984 regulatory check-up ratified the board's perception that progress was being made.

But in late 1984, I became convinced that Park Bank was not solving its fundamental problems — that the bank was giving its troubled loans one-minute fixes. In addition, like Kelley before him, Kearney's own outside business interests had become a major distraction to him. He was unable to concentrate on the bank. Changes in Park Bank's leadership had to be made. Park Bank had to focus on long-term resolutions of its problems. I tried to convince Kearney, but to no avail.

I took my attempt to initiate leadership change to the board; I was met with an iron curtain of resistance. But ultimately, in early 1985, after an emotional, behind-the-boardroom-doors struggle, I was able to convince Park Bank's board, with the result that John Kearney resigned as Park's chairman and CEO.

That effort proved to be the most difficult task I have ever undertaken. The magnitude of the controversy between myself and John Kearney, and then later in Park's boardroom, never got into the press. The St. Petersburg Times *reported matter-of-factly that "personal financial problems dragged Kearney away from his bank responsibilities. Meanwhile, he and Jacobs clashed over the seriousness of Park's problems and how to deal with them, several directors say. . . . Last May, Kearney severed all ties with the bank, and Jacobs took full control."*

At the time I stepped in as CEO, Park's lending and growth problems looked solvable. I still hoped that my position as Park's CEO would be temporary. My goal was to stabilize the bank and recruit a professional banker as CEO; unfortunately, Park Bank was already too deep within its Black Hole. The momentum of the bank's decline accelerated so rapidly that recruitment was impossible. So was the bank's ability to survive.

In an emotionally wrenching ceremony held in our bank lobby on Friday, February 14, 1986, after the bank's teller lines had closed for the weekend, I turned Park's bank charter over to the FDIC and Florida's Division of Banking. Park's staff who had worked so desperately to save the bank during those last few months stood by, teary-eyed. There was nothing more that could be done. Park Bank had run out of capital — it had experienced engine failure in outer space and had crashed.

2

On my wall hangs a plaque entitled "Winners and Losers." It reads:

The Winner is always a part of the answer.
The loser is always a part of the problem.
The Winner always has a program;
The loser always has an excuse.
The Winner says, "Let me do it for you;"
The loser says, "It's not my job."
The Winner sees an answer for every problem;
The loser sees a problem in every answer.
The Winner sees the green near the sand traps;
The loser sees the sand traps near the green.
The Winner says, "It may be difficult but it's not impossible;"
The loser says, "It may be possible but it's too difficult."

The winners-losers plaque had been displayed on office walls throughout Park Bank's headquarters — the message about winning and losing stood as Park Bank's theme.

Park Bank had soared high before its crash. It was the talk of the business world — the fastest growing community bank in Florida, for a time the fastest growing bank in the United States. The bank's award-winning advertising boasted about Park's prowess, describing where Park Bank was headed and how it was going to get there. Bold and brash, Park Bank had been full of the entrepreneurial spirit.

There was little doubt among Park's directors that the bank would end up as the leader in community banking innovation. Park's board felt it had identified a well-defined market niche; a niche that would withstand and prosper in the face of the expected heavy competition from the regional banks and the money center banks soon moving into Florida.

This "winner's" attitude at Park Bank before its crash was not the exception. In fact, the winner's attitude permeates corporate cultures and the philosophical teachings at business schools. Despite the high number of business failures in any given year, the subject of failure — the ultimate business crisis — is ignored. In late 1986, the year of Park Bank's collapse, William E. Blundell wrote for the *Wall Street Journal*: "A rhetoric of success enshrouds the American corporate scene like a cloud of rosy mist. Business pays a horde of gurus to infuse it with upbeat, motivational messages. . . . We don't hear much about the highest rate of business busts since the Great Depression. Failure clearly is not getting the attention it deserves."

The subject has also been largely ignored by business schools. While preparing material for this book, I approached a well-known business school professor, hoping to gain his guidance.

I told the professor about Park Bank's collapse. I explained that there were many lessons learned: about leadership and teamwork experienced under unrelenting stress; about motivating a troubled and frightened staff; about retaining customer confidence; about managing cash flow when there is no cash flow; about communicating never-ending bad news to employees, regulators, stockholders, and the public.

I explained that I thought a book about the fundamental principles developed from these first-hand experiences would furnish valuable lessons, not only for students, but also for executives and boards of directors — those with companies in trouble and those trying to avoid trouble.

But the professor was not enthused. Of more use to his students and his business courses, he said, was the expansion strategy of Chase Bank of New York — the winner of the FDIC auction of Park Bank.

I remained convinced, however, that my professor friend was wrong. In today's troubled world, a CEO's and board of director's focus must include the hazards affecting company survival; there is no choice but to anticipate crisis. My feelings were vindicated a few months later when I spoke in Palm Beach, Florida, to two hundred members of the Young President's Organization. The members were strong, ambitious leaders, presidents of their companies before they reached age forty.

As I spoke of my struggle at Park Bank and of the pain of Park Bank's failure, I could sense their kinship, a shared awareness of their own potential for going too far too fast, of miscalculating their way into disaster. They knew the threat was there. Always. They lived with the clear understanding that among the success-companies of today are the disaster stories of tomorrow.

The cost of business collapse has become too significant to permit its message to be buried by an unrealistic focus on the opportunities found among the bones of business failures as my professor friend proposed.

In addition to Park Bank, 143 other banks failed or were bailed out by the government in 1986. The year 1986 was not particularly exceptional for the 1980s. During the entire decade hundreds of commercial banks collapsed and hundreds more of thrift institutions became insolvent, thrusting the federal government into a massive rescue effort. The billions of tax dollars required from the American public to fund the cost of the 1980s financial institutions industry crash has become *the* issue of the 1990s. The estimates place the cost at $2,000 for each man, woman, and child.

But, it turns out, financial institutions have not been the only troubled businesses the 1980s witnessed. In 1986, the year of Park Bank's failure, Dun & Bradstreet reported that more than 61,000 businesses failed, an increase of 7 percent from 1985. In 1987, failures increased another 5 percent. Business failures have continued to increase since then. Few companies and but a handful of industries, have been immune.

As the decade of the 1990s emerges, the bank and thrift crises of the 1980s have spread to insurance companies and other financial institutions.

And the strength, as well as the world-wide competitiveness, of vast segments of American industry — airlines, automobiles, computers, consumer goods, oil and gas, steel, financial services, and real estate, to list a few — saddled with mountains of debt and unrealistic projections left over from the leveraged buy-everything excesses of the 1980s, are pummeling in the wrong direction.

The great corporate buyout boom of the 1980s has fast become the workout boom for the 1990s. Divestitures, bankruptcies, reorganizations, and business collapse are now the way of life for many in corporate America.

Alvin Toffler wrote in *Powershift*: "As we move further into a period of economic and political turbulence, punctuated erratically by technological breakthroughs and disasters, we can expect crises to crowd in on one another." And they are.

3

And each crisis, each business collapse, brings with it its aftermath, more devastating than the downfall itself. The adverse effects, like radiation from an exploded atom bomb, linger for years. The pain of the crisis aftermath is in part related to financial disaster. However, the truly tragic suffering is tied up in dreams gone awry. For when the dreams are destroyed, the spirits of those involved can be destroyed as well.

Avoiding spiritual destruction is far from easy. Just as the momentum of success can carry one to euphoric highs, the momentum of failure can drag one into the depths of despair, distorting perspective, adversely affecting health, and seriously stressing relationships within families and among friends.

Park Bank's downfall was no exception. During Park's aftermath, each new day was worse than the last. There was never-ending publicity, lawsuits, investigations, and innuendoes. There was anguish and emotional shock from financial ruin. There was humiliation and loss of pride from personal failure. There was guilt from losses suffered by friends who had become investors because of their faith in the founders of the crashed business. There was stress from the uncertainty about starting over late in life.

When one is spiritually weighted by despair, it is easy to compound the negative effects of crisis and its aftermath — to bury all possibility for understanding by condemning one's self or by shifting blame to others.

That is unfortunate, for man's perceptions, not the events themselves, foretell his destiny. Whether a business disaster provides the training ground for the future, or the burial ground for the past, is determined by the set of the mind.

There is an old Viking maxim: "Things that don't kill you outright make you stronger." Some people never recover from business tragedies. Yet, others, like the Vikings of old, grow stronger during crises. For them, catastrophes furnish learning experiences which set the stage for higher orders of accomplishment and satisfaction.

4

In 1967, on my thirty-sixth birthday, my brother-in-law presented me with a gift certificate for an introductory flying lesson. I had gone back to law school in my early thirties, had just graduated, and was starting my legal career in Florida. He thought it was also time I opened myself up to some other new experiences.

I remember the excitement and fear as I took off in the student seat of the low-winged Piper Cherokee aircraft with my instructor on that warm summer day. When the weather's right, high flying is a joy. It's a euphoric feeling climbing in wide, slow circles, the sun's rays playing among the big cumulus clouds.

One day several years later, after I had advanced to multi-engine aircraft, my flight instructor and I took off for an emergency procedures review from St. Petersburg's downtown waterfront airport. We were over the end of Runway Six, at three hundred feet, Tampa Bay passing beneath us. The weather was balmy, and I looked down at the top of a sailing ship's tall mast, its sails extended in a brisk breeze.

Suddenly, the right engine sputtered and stopped. I was shocked. I knew that, when least expected, a good instructor will switch off an engine's gas line; but, according to FAA regulations, we were too low for practice. Was this the real thing? After seconds, which seemed like forever, I reacted as I had been trained, stepped hard on the opposite rudder-pedal, lowered the nose of the twin-engine Piper Seneca, and feathered the propeller, bringing the plane under control for an emergency landing.

"I guess the engine didn't read the FAA regulations," my instructor said, quietly laughing. Then, as we came around, he leaned toward me in earnest, "You've got to be ready — always ready; you don't get a chance to pick your time and place."

That was a lesson I will never forget.

Sometimes high flying turns into low flying, good weather into bad, and euphoria into pain.

Crash landings — even in companies — don't follow scripts.

5

The study of business crash landings is in its infancy. Much is yet to be learned about handling ourselves and our companies during those inevitable danger periods that disrupt and threaten the foundations of our enterprises. The entire subject is in need of careful research and open discussion by those who have suffered through Black Hole experiences, if history is to offer any comprehensive lessons.

This book is one lesson for the future, learned painfully on the rim of Park Bank's Black Hole. Part I provides insight into the deep emotional feelings involved in the last day of Park Bank's business life. It also provides background about the spirited Park Bank culture, the culture that set the stage for disaster.

Part II explores the blinders that make an approaching Black Hole so difficult to see. Part II cautions us that though the Park Bank-type experience can be viewed by the participants as unique, in reality, its ordeal reflects fundamental, universal encounters experienced in various ways by all of humankind.

Part III describes the crisis environment, called the rim country, and its rim people. Part IV guides us through a most important task: the management of the self during troubled times. Then, Parts V and VI explore the roles of the CEO and the board of directors of a company finding itself on the rim of a Black Hole.

The rim country tests the spirit and will, taking each to the brink. It demands from leaders of those trapped in that unholy environment a willingness to act decisively in the face of uncertain outcome. Rim leadership is investment of the total self without holding back. It involves the setting of an example, the providing of spiritual guidance, the bonding of people together as a team, encouraging and permitting them to perform beyond their known abilities.

Rim leadership is also the reorientation of the self toward a deeper, internalized understanding of the meanings of success and failure.

Crisis management deals with what are, in retrospect, but brief periods of instability. But, as in flying, it is how we handle these critical times that makes the difference. Reading about crisis is not the same as surviving through it; but, being forearmed may help you traverse the rim of some future business Black Hole suddenly looming along your way.

Part I

Inside the Park

Who the Lord loveth, the Lord teacheth early how
to take a setback.

Peter Drucker

Chapter 1

Today We Die

*The setting of a great hope is like the setting of the
sun. The brightness of our life is gone.*
                                                H. W. Longfellow

It was Valentine's Day, Friday, February 14, 1986, 4:30 P.M., in St.
Petersburg, Florida. Linda, my secretary, opened the door to my office.
Her face was drawn.

"It's Lou."

I knew I would not like the call. I picked up the phone and talked to
investor Louis Farris who was calling from his office in Texas.

The call was short. The regulators had rejected Lou's final offer to
capitalize our ailing bank. Park Bank's life was over.

The FDIC had given us until today to solve our problem. But Lou's
offer, our solution, was rejected. Now officials from Florida's Division of
Banking were going to close us down. At 6:00 P.M. tonight.

Wearied from the strain of the last several months, I turned slowly
toward my secretary. "Linda, call the managers. It's time for them to
inform the staff."

We had developed a procedure for this moment, though we had hoped it would never come. Our managers would bring their people together in small groups and inform them of what most in their hearts already knew.

We needed to prepare them for the events of the next few hours. There would be panicky customers. There could be, but must not be, a run on the bank. Then there would be the bank's closing, followed by a long night of work for the FDIC. Everyone would have to keep performing.

We were going to crash. It was finally here. The regulators would arrange for the FDIC to take over Park Bank as the court-appointed receiver, after hours, when there would be no customers around. The FDIC would move fast. While FDIC auditors were doing their nighttime work, FDIC officials in Atlanta would auction off the bank's assets to the highest bidder. By Saturday night, a new bank would occupy the space where we had just died.

Park Bank was on the West Coast of Florida, in a growth area. It would be no problem to get a bid. A high bid would protect the depositors. An out-of-state bank winning the bid would mean our people would have a good chance at keeping their jobs. In the right scenario, only the investors lose; but, if the bid were to come in high enough, there might even be something left over for them.

I stared out the window. For a moment it was as if I were in another world. I felt the drain of energy from the final letdown. But I could not stop. Tired as I was, I had to keep focusing.

Had we done all we could? Were we prepared for the crash? Most of all, our people — would they hold together?

I rose from my desk and walked slowly around my office. I had spent so much time there; its surroundings were more familiar than those where I lived. Now it was my last day. I had to pack up my things and leave. Tomorrow someone else, probably a banker from New York, would sit in my chair.

I became aware of the silence.

I walked out of the office, across the bridge to the adjacent parking garage.

I was alone.

I had to prepare for the six o'clock meeting with the staff and the regulators. The plan was to assemble in the main bank lobby on the second floor. A representative from Florida's Division of Banking would read the governor's proclamation declaring our bank insolvent. The FDIC would outline its closing procedure, asking employees to work that night so the bank could be secured.

And I was to say a few words.

Say a few words.

What do I say? To people who had dedicated their entire beings to a cause now lost? To people who struggled to save an institution we all felt was so important to our community, an institution that was now going to crash?

I leaned heavily on the railing surrounding the parking level, and looked out over Tampa Bay.

I took a deep breath and fought back the tears.

I reflected back on the last several months. We had flown into a Black Hole. We could not escape.

Black Holes — where universes collapse. Carl Sagan and Isaac Asimov write about such things — voids in the ethers of outer space that have such magnetic pulls, such swirls of power, that, once in their grasp, there is only death and destruction. Even light cannot resist. The power of the Black Hole is such that as one is drawn deeper into its inner core, the force of its gravitational pull increases; the ability to resist, to escape, diminishes. The pull and weight of it all becomes unbearable. Then there is nothing.

I was standing in the center of a Black Hole. Right here on earth. In our home town. It was our collapsing bank. For more than eighteen exhausting months we had kept our hope, our hearts, fastened on survival. But now it was to end.

Now, our dream was to die among the ashes of what would never be.

Today, our last day. I wondered how Wainwright felt during the last day on Bataan. I wondered how Lee felt when he surrendered to Grant.

In mid-January, I had met with the FDIC in Atlanta. It was clear that Park's time was up. Before the meeting, no one had wanted to face the inevitable fact that the death of our business was at hand. After the meeting, we knew we would have to pull off a miracle. Each of us sensed the futility of the effort, but we kept going.

On Wednesday, two days ago, I had met again with the regulators, asking for their help. Park was being courted by Lou Farris. Lou wanted regulatory assistance for his buyout. We got little encouragement. How I wished Park Bank had been bigger, like Continental Illinois or Chrysler. We needed the kind of help they got, but we didn't have the clout to pull it off. For banks our size, the FDIC had a simple goal: protect the Federal Deposit Insurance Fund. Bidding the bank nationally, they felt, would produce a premium price and the Fund would be safer. I agreed on a takeover procedure with the regulators if we could not consummate a sale by Friday. Everyone knew it was unlikely. I flew back to St. Petersburg with little hope.

That night I had called an emergency management meeting to review the crisis plan we had developed to use, if our "what if" became a reality on Friday. As I walked out of the meeting, a reporter who had followed Park closely was on the telephone. Too tired to talk, I told Linda that I would write out a brief statement to give to him. He understood.

After preparing the press statement, I went home. I wanted to be alone so that I could compose some final message, some lasting communication to our staff. I wanted to be ready to send it out on Friday night if that was to be our final day. I could not leave without something personal from me to them, to thank them and let them know how much they had done.

So I wrote:

Sometime ago I wrote an article for Inside The Park *entitled "Winners and Losers." By now most of you have seen plaques carrying that message throughout the bank. It has been our theme, our way of life.*

On this, the last day of our corporate life, it is time to revisit that message.

"Winning-Losing" expresses one's attitude toward life. That attitude deals with life as a whole, not success or failure as to any one happening. Actual success or failure in regard to any particular event is often beyond the will of the participant. Fate and circumstances . . . can determine a particular success or failure.

In this broad perspective, a true winner is not afraid of life. Winners do suffer failure — it's called the "agony of defeat." But winners rise again.

It is this willingness to face up to and deal straight on with what is out there before us that sets winners apart from losers. No excuses. No short cuts. No blaming others. Just stretching out. Doing.

Monday is the celebration of Lincoln's birthday. A long time ago he said, "If I were to try to read, much less answer, all the attacks made on me, this shop might as well be closed for any other business. I do the very best I know how —

the very best I can; and I mean to keep doing it to the end. If the end brings me out all right, what is said against me won't amount to anything. If the end brings me out wrong, ten angels swearing I was right would make no difference."

And Lincoln said another thing: "When you have a running elephant by the hind legs, there comes a time when you have to let go." Yes, Lincoln knew when to let go. That is also a vital part of the attitude of winners.

And now it is time for us at Park to let go.

Always remember the value of what you have given. Contributing is truly the mark of the ultimate winners in life. A winner, in the end, gives more than he takes; a loser dies clinging to the illusion that winning means taking more than you give.

You have been winners. I thank you for that. And so does everyone connected with Park Bank. I wish today I could have visited with each of you. I could not. But our paths will cross again.

Thursday, yesterday, I continued meeting with potential investors. I was getting last-minute calls. The constant publicity about our problem stirred up bargain-hunting buyers. But it was too late; there was not enough time to put together a new package.

At 5:00 P.M. Thursday, our board held its final meeting, authorizing me to proceed with the regulators on Friday if our miracle did not occur. Management met and worked out the last-minute details needed to implement our crisis procedure. We all agreed that if we had to crash, we would do it with as little damage as possible.

That was now history.

Wednesday's pen was down. Thursday's hopes are gone. Today is Friday.

And it is Valentine's Day. Quietly, envelopes are being stuffed with my last message. My last message! Hardly a Valentine!

My mind traced through the events of the day. I had been up since 6:30 A.M. and had jogged. Jogging was always therapeutic for me. Pounding the streets worked better than anything to drive the tension out of my body and to clear my mind. The stress drove right into the pavement. A run helped even today; but it was tough; my feet were very heavy. And my back, my weak point where it all settled, ached from the tension. But I knew I couldn't show it; everyone needed me to be okay. My health had become a barometer of our endurance.

At 9:00 A.M. this morning, our lawyers had met secretly with the lawyers from the Division of Banking to organize the last moments. The meeting was held away from the bank, at the St. Petersburg Yacht Club, to avoid being spotted by constantly patrolling TV cameras and reporters. At noon, I had taken the senior officers to lunch, a last good-by. Spirits were up outwardly, but voices cracked, tears filled saddened eyes.

6:00 P.M. . . . at 6:00 P.M. tonight, what can I possibly say?

Finally, I stretched as tall as I could, took another deep breath and returned to my office to prepare for the last stage of our long descent into our Black Hole. In an hour there would be no more Park Bank.

Inside my office, Linda gave me a letter from Louis R. Cohen that had just arrived. A few days earlier, Lou had left his law practice to become Deputy Solicitor General of the United States. Until that time he had been one of the lawyers who worked closely with us during the last trying months. Lou wrote:

Dear Dick:

Having now left the law practice for awhile after 17$\frac{1}{2}$ years of it, I wanted to write to say how much I enjoyed spending a good chunk of the last $\frac{1}{2}$ year with you and how sorry I am that we could not achieve the consummation you so devoutly wished. . . .

You may remember that in Book II of the Aeneid, *as Troy is burning and Aeneas is trying to quench the flames, the ghost of Hector appears and tells Aeneas to flee, saying, "If Troy could have been saved by mortal hand, mine would have done the job." Like Hector and Aeneas, you could not overcome what the gods had decreed, but it was a valiant effort, worthy like theirs of being recorded. . . .*

You may also remember that Aeneas, leaving Troy with his father on his shoulders and his son at his side, looks around for a new project to work on and decides to found Rome. I have every confidence that your next project will meet equal success.

I stood by the window. I looked out. It was 5:55 P.M. I turned, and walked down the long stairs from the third floor to the lobby of the bank. I was ready.

As I walked, I thought of Aeneas and I pondered on an ancient thought of Seneca, "Death is punishment to some, to some a gift, and to many a favor."

What would it be for us?

Chapter 2

Picnic in the Park

*You can be victimized by your imagination if you
imagine yourself astonishing the world.*

                                        Fred Prohé

It started out as a fun thing for us to do: buy a bank and build it into
the leading independent bank in St. Petersburg, Florida, one of the most
exciting growth areas in the nation. Nine of us tried to do that.

Dr. Peter Dawson, a dentist who exuded civic pride, decided he
wanted to help rebuild sleepy, downtown St. Petersburg into what everyone said it should be — a progressive city. So Peter started to buy up some
of St. Petersburg's downtown real estate with the idea of constructing a
modern, high-rise office building.

While he was in the middle of his land assemblage, his banker decided
that St. Petersburg, and downtown growth, were incompatible. Without
any advance warning, he told Peter that his bank would withdraw its
funding of his project. It didn't matter that Peter had committed hundreds
of thousands of dollars in anticipation of bank financing.

Taken aback, Dr. Dawson asked his bank's president, "What do we do
now?"

The president shrugged. "You're very bright. I'm sure you will think of something!"

As Peter and his CPA advisor, John Kearney, left the meeting, Peter said, "Never again!"

And John said, "What we need in St. Petersburg is a bank that will take care of business. Let's buy one!"

Within a few months, John Kearney, with the help of banker Harold Kelley, had found a small community bank with $8 million in assets on the outskirts of St. Petersburg. Kearney organized a group of St. Petersburg businessmen to buy the bank: Gary Froid, a leading life insurance man; Bill Zemp, one of the top advertising men in Florida; the Vineyard brothers, Phil and Vernon, former owners of the largest McDonald's franchise in Florida; Frank Byars, the owner of one of the best known tourist attractions on Florida's West Coast Gulf Beaches; Harold Kelley, former president of a local bank; and I, head of a prominent law firm on Florida's West Coast. Of course, the group also included Peter Dawson, the dentist, and John Kearney, a leading Tampa Bay CPA business consultant.

The objective: establish a bank that could understand, and be responsive, to the requirements of local businessmen. Regional banks had begun to acquire many of the local banks. Dr. Dawson was not the only person who had become frustrated with banking; others had felt the pain of having their local banking needs "second-guessed" hundreds of miles away in Atlanta or Miami.

The group bought the bank in November 1977. It was terrific. Everyone brought in customers. Director think tanks sprouted strategy. Ingenious marketing and advertising plans were developed, touting the directors' leadership roles and their understanding of local businesses. Creative banking and very responsive banking were Park's objectives. Less than seven years later, the bank had grown in response to all the enthusiasm from its original $8 million in assets to more than $500 million.

Sheer Bliss

In the spring of 1984, in celebration of growing to that half billion dollar mark, the board authorized a memorial book as a toast to the legend being created. Park's ad agency responded and produced an award-winning marketing piece entitled *Still Practicing What We Preach*. The book was a testimonial to Park's remarkable record. The preamble said the book was about "our philosophy, how we do business, the factors we feel have sparked and sustained our growth."

The up-beat *Still Practicing*, however, brushed by one aspect of Park Bank's recent past as if it were insignificant. In the first quarter of 1984, Park Bank had received its first bad report card from the FDIC. The report card, for the year 1983, criticized Park's rapid growth and liberal lending policies; however, a follow-up examination by Florida's Division of Banking, held in the late spring of 1984, had indicated that the bank had gotten control of its growth and loan portfolio.

The board was convinced that Park Bank was back on track, if it had ever been off. As everybody knew, shortly before the FDIC examination had taken place, the board had already started to build up the bank's systems and staff. Park's original CEO, Kelley, who had suffered personal problems, had been replaced. A lot of top-notch people had been recruited. What was the worry?

In July 1984, *Still Practicing* was published and was sent to Park's customers and stockholders, a proud statement of what community banking — Park Bank style — was all about. It glittered, not only with what it said, but with its reproductions of many of Park's award-winning ads, which reflected the entrepreneurial spirit *par excellence*.

Park's advertising had always reflected its mission and spirit as perceived by the board. Park's spirit bolstered its employees and officers and charged up its directors; nothing was impossible. Making money the Park Bank way was fun, exciting. As director Frank Byars said in an ad: "If something can be imagined, it can be accomplished. Imagination is the soul of the entrepreneur. It's the one quality that separates leaders from followers."

Everybody at Park Bank was a believer in those days. The introduction to *Still Practicing* said it all: "We're proud of that growth not because we proved the skeptics wrong (they said there was no room for an independent bank in an age of giants), but because we proved ourselves right. We still believe (and always will) in that grandest, most noble of American spirits — the entrepreneur. Maybe it's because we see so much of ourselves in that spirit, or maybe it's because we didn't see enough of it in our community, that we've dedicated ourselves to the entrepreneurial spirit — to supporting it with our experience, our enthusiasm *and* our funds."

With that kind of spirit, with that kind of community feeling, and with all those smarts, what could ever go wrong?

Nothing. It was a picnic in the Park.

The best of picnics! Here's how Park Bank's picnic was memorialized in:

Still Practicing What We Preach.

There are no aging photographs. No ancient parchment charters. No sacred relics that the typical bank proudly displays in its lobby as testament to a long distinguished history.

Park Bank of Florida is seven years old.

Seven years old. *Yet in the course of its short history, the bank has literally revolutionized the financial services industry on the West Coast of Florida. From a modest eight million dollars in initial assets in 1977, the bank has grown to over half* a billion dollars in total assets in 1984.

Don't let the figures fool you. To the casual observer, such spectacular growth would indicate a bank that is extremely aggressive, smarter than the guy down the block, and overly generous in customer incentives. Dig a little deeper, however, and you discover something much simpler and much, much more profound in its implications:

We cut through the baloney.

Unlike many banks that have positioned themselves somewhere between God and your best friend, Park Bank has never waltzed around the fact of exactly what it is: A tool. A tough, sophisticated financial organization with the talent and instincts *to get things done for its customers.*

When the bank was founded in 1977, this wasn't a particularly popular position to take within the banking community. We were viewed as an upstart, a maverick; "that little bank out on 66th Street" with little more to sell than the experience of our directors. In fact, the only people we appealed to were exactly the kind of people we were trying to appeal to.

We are not for everybody, nor have we ever attempted to be. There's a saying in the market that only two types of customers are attracted to Park Bank: those who've made it, and those who want to. That's a fair description; we've never been big on free toasters, and the quality of our deposit base reflects it. . . .

Right up front we established ourselves as a business and professional bank, with little tolerance for red tape and bureaucratic nonsense. . . .

We also promised hard-nosed reality.

Our directors have never *been figureheads. They are among the most successful business and professional people in the Southeast, and Park is probably one of the few banks in the country where that kind of "real world" experience gets out of the boardroom and down to the customer level where it can do us both some good. As one director put it, "the whole point of starting this bank was to get closer to the customer, to give him the benefit of our own mistakes and successes in business, and hopefully steer him around some expensive pitfalls." When the big banking chains started missing the point that this is a "hands on" business, it created a void and we moved right in. . . .*

Very early on, we recognized that the business and professional customer wasn't one customer, but many *customers — he was an investor, a depositor, a saver, a spender, a borrower, a cash manager, a builder and protector of assets. The competition wasn't just other banks. It was the Merrill-Lynchs, the Prudentials, the major non-banking financial corporations who've been successfully dividing up the traditional banking market in the interest of specialization. We vowed to bring the customer back — and we have.*

As you can see from our ads, we've addressed virtually every major area of financial concern for the business and professional customer. Even in the early days, before deregulation, we were competing successfully for the investment dollar — and giving our customers FDIC protection, to boot. Historically, we've paid among the most competitive rates in the market and there's no secret how we did it. When you lend smarter, you can afford to pay higher. Keep in mind, though, that we've never offered higher rates simply for the sake of deposit acquisition. . . .

In 1983, six years after "that little bank out on 66th Street" opened its doors, we've accomplished exactly what we set out to do: The Park Private Banking Group, initiated in the fall of 1983, now allows us to offer our clients a highly confidential, totally personalized, single source of complete asset management, including personal financial forecasting, capital management services, discount brokerage services, retirement planning, personal business trust services, investment advisory services (through Park Capital Management, Inc.) and traditional banking services. We've also established the International Division and the Corporate Banking Division and are continually investigating new opportunities to go well beyond banking to "take care of business" (to quote our credo).

In short, Park Bank has gone from being an alternative to becoming the solution. And we'd be the first to tell you we've had a lot of help doing it. . . .

The conventional view of the shareholder is that of being a source of capital. Period. We view our shareholders, however, as being a source of support, and that's a very big distinction. *There's always been an implied partnership at work here, a joint mission to make Park everything that it can be — to expand its scope, broaden its services, strengthen its clout as a financial tool for the business and professional customer. On our side, we've promised to proceed in a safe and sound manner, provide a superior long term return on capital, and hopefully enhance the investor net worth.*

On their side, our shareholders have shown tremendous enthusiasm and confidence, continually provided us with insightful suggestions based on their business experience, and given us a free rein to meet the bank's operational needs as we've seen fit:

- *Physically we've grown at the average of one new office per year, with the bank now operating eight full service offices and three loan production offices, forming a triangular network south from Pinellas County to Sarasota to Naples/Ft. Myers and back to Tampa.*

- *We've designed, built, equipped and staffed one of the most sophisticated data processing centers in the country, affording us not only more efficient (and profitable operations), but allowing us to bring on line the myriad of computer-based systems necessary for Private Banking and providing total financial services.*

- *We've actively recruited and hired the highest calibre financial professionals in the financial industry, increasing our ranks from 60 in 1977 to over 350 in 1984.*

Much has been accomplished, and our shareholders have been there with us every step of the way. Park is, in every sense, their *bank: A business and professional bank dedicated to the business and professional customer; staffed, directed and owned by professional people.*

Our commitment to our employees — and theirs to us — has likewise been that of a close partnership. Over the years, the profession of banking has become increasingly staid and formulized, with long lists of corporate do's and don'ts positively strangling individual initiative and creative thinking. Park Bank was founded, in large measure, as an alternative to that situation. Creativity in our forward planning is our lifeblood, *our specialness to the market, and we do more than value individual thinking — we engender it. We've always attracted the best and brightest talent at every level of operation, offering more opportunities for personal and career development than any other area financial institution.*

. . . None of our growth and success, of course, has occurred in a vacuum. We are very much a "community-minded" bank, and not just in the conventional sense of the term. Banking, more than any other form of commerce, has the power to promote or hinder the economic health of the community.

A bank with overly conservative lending policies stifles progress. One that's too liberal does nothing to nurture quality businesses and professional practices, which are the key to sound, stable growth and prosperity for the community at large. It takes an enlightened bank to know the balance; one that channels not only money, but experience, understanding, and practical know-how to make that money work in the way it was intended to. It's no coincidence that we are Pinellas County's leading commercial lender, funding a substantial portion of new development. We are also a major supporter of downtown re-development providing both construction funding for new office buildings and preservation of historic ones, as well as providing meeting facilities at our own Park Place for builders, developers, architects and executives interested in re-locating in the downtown area. . . .

We know the West Coast of Florida business community inside and out. We know the opportunities and the problems. The whole modus operandi *of this market and its industries. With this kind of experience, you can be fast, flexible and very sound in your lending. . . .*

So there you have it.

A half-billion dollars worth of growth based on a no-nonsense commitment to customers, shareholders, employees, and the community. No wonder we've grown.

With that kind of support, how could we not?

Then, No Picnic in the Park

On January 22, 1985, barely six months after *Still Practicing What We Preach* was published, John Kearney resigned as Park Bank's CEO.

On April 13, 1985, nine months after *Still Practicing What We Preach* was published, I, as Kearney's successor, painfully reported to the *St. Petersburg Times* that Park Bank reported losses of $5.37 million for the year ending December 31, 1984, and that we would not make a profit for 1985, adding, "We recognize that we've grown too fast and that some of our loan procedures were too liberal. . . . We outgrew the skill level of our people as well as some of our internal controls."

In a lengthy interview with the *Times*, I said that our problems were the result of our enthusiasm:

We got caught up in the enthusiasm of what we were doing. We were becoming a dominant bank in Pinellas County. We were excited by that, but in retrospect, we were too liberal in our lending. There is no question about that.

Our number 1 priority is to slow down and put our house in order. We have to sit back and evaluate where we stand, take a breather, and basically go through a year of belt-tightening.

After discussing our new computer systems and recent management recruiting, I assured the reporter: "We are now prepared with stronger senior management, a stronger financial position and enhanced operations capabilities."

I concluded, "When you have problems, you have to step back and look at what you are doing. The first step is to look inside the bank at your people. What I'm trying to do is set a moral, upright tone. We want to be disciplined and conservative. We know we have an image problem. What we are doing is making sure our house is in order and developing internal confidence. Everything else will take care of itself."

Unfortunately, everything else would not take care of itself.

There was to be no more picnic in the Park.

Part II

Why We Fail to See Black Holes

In a human situation, the waters are usually muddy
and the air a little foggy.

William Barrett

Chapter 3

Black Hole Blinders

*For the most part we do not see and then define, we
define first and then see. And these preconceptions,
unless education has made us acutely aware, govern
deeply the whole process of perception.*
                                                            Walter Lippmann

During mid-1987:

The American warship, Stark, was on peacetime duty in the Persian
Gulf. Observers on the Stark saw an Iraqi fighter plane circle and turn
toward the ship, flying low, skimming over the waves. Within seconds, the
Stark was in flames, its hull penetrated dead center by a French rocket that
was part of the weaponry of the Iraqi. Thirty-seven young Americans died
in the wreckage. An investigation ensued; reports indicated that the
commander on the bridge of the Stark did not perceive that his ship was
in any present danger, and despite what could have been recognized as
early warning signs, the attack took the Stark by surprise. *Why didn't the
commander of the Stark react to what, in the clear light of hindsight, were
obvious signs of danger?*

Edgar Rosenberg, husband of Joan Rivers, committed suicide. Miss Rivers was quoted as saying she missed all the warning signs before her husband's death. She asked, *"Why didn't I pay attention to the signs? Why didn't anybody?"*

Nathan Pearson, chairman of the Mellon Bank Corporation, informed angry stockholders at the annual meeting that he and other outside directors were "shocked and surprised" when they learned that the Mellon Bank had severe loan problems. The bank had just reported a $59.8 million quarterly loss. An outraged stockholder asked about the board members, astute business persons in their own rights: *"Where were the directors when the warning signs went up?"*

Inside the Park

During that same mid-1987 period, while enduring a tense moment in a lawyer-filled conference room located in a not-too-friendly law firm representing disgruntled Park stockholders, I was cross-examined in deposition about Park Bank's demise: "Mr. Jacobs, is it fair to say that Park Bank's directors were shocked when the regulators presented them with the adverse results of their examination?"

I slumped in my chair and sighed deeply. My answer was a slow, simple, "Yes."

At that moment I felt very stupid — embarrassed. I could not help but remember the old saying: "To the blind, all things are sudden."

How had I and eight other bright, experienced, successful business-men missed what in retrospect were very obvious early warning signs that Park Bank was on a direct course for a Black Hole?

Why Don't We See Danger Approaching?

Danger of attack, potential for suicide, practices that led to business collapse — each clearly visible in hindsight. Is there something in our psyche or ways of life that so blurs our vision that our ability to recognize and interpret early warning signs of disaster go awry? The answer is a resounding "yes."

Why? In part it's because we are human and in part it's because we operate in environments that make detection difficult. In the business context, the interrelationship of innate humanness and environment can defer recognition of crisis signs for months or years — until "momentum effect," the unyielding pull of the business Black Hole, has built such a force that recovery is impossible.

Unlike many crisis-causing events (such as the St. Helens' volcanic eruption and the *Stark* attack) which occur rapidly, most business crash-causers kill slowly, as if the business was a frog immersed in water brought lethargically to a boil. Occasionally a company will suffer an episodic crisis event, such as the unexpected death of its CEO, or experience the short-term crisis tension associated with a hostile takeover attempt; but for the most part, business crises come on gradually, over months or years, and then explode — suddenly, all at once, everywhere. It is during the gradual periods of crisis, when data are most fragmented and fraught with ambiguity, that interpretation is most difficult.

What makes detection of warning signs of potential business crisis so difficult? It's a layering of the following:

- *Boardroom Blocks.* Ultimate corporate strategies and interpretative decisions are shaped in boardrooms far removed from the source of information about early warning signs. Directors' sensors aren't usually well-enough honed to interpret the messages contained among the fragments of data that reach them until it's too late. That is because they're part time participants in the corporate governance process; they operate from summarized, pre-interpreted data; and they suffer from groupthink and other decisional pressures that distort meaning and the opportunity for careful analysis. Boardroom Blocks are the subject of chapter 5.

- *Masters of the Universe.* CEOs with the wrong executive stuff, those most likely to fly their companies into Black Holes, suffer from one or both of these massive blind spots: the illusion they have *mastery over all life's events* and the illusion they are blessed with *immunity from bad luck*. Either illusion is sufficient to blind the holder to his potential for crashing in a Black Hole. Both are usually fatal. Masters of the Universe are the subject of chapter 4.

- *Black Hole Blinders*. Each of us sets up interpretive defenses that prevent our seeing trouble signs that disagree with our personal version of the world. The reasons behind our seemingly self-destructive action — clothing ourselves with Black Hole Blinders — are the subject of this chapter.

Trouble Signs: Dangerous and Missed Worldwide

Make no mistake about it: the potential for calamity caused by our proclivity to miss and misjudge trouble signs is monumental and worldwide, frequent and catastrophic.

For example, during the last six months of 1990:

- The international community of political analysts found itself victimized by its collective failure to foresee the "profound changes that have shaken the world in the latter part of 1990." Analyst Max Jakobson reflected: "None of us diplomats, journalists, scholars, or spies was able to draw the right conclusion from the mass of information available to all. . . . Indeed, political leaders have been inclined not to believe what they actually saw happening."

- In his article, "Trump's troubles are linked to bank irresponsibility," Hobart Rowen, writing about Donald Trump's fallen star and increasing financial woes, observed: "Trump's mystique was such that the banks couldn't visualize that he'd ever be in trouble."

- A series of investigations into defects crippling the $2.5 billion Hubble space telescope revealed that Hubble's flaws could have been discovered. The *Los Angeles Times* reported that data revealing the optical system errors were readily available but "were not recognized or fully investigated at the time." In another article, Senator Gore observed "I think there's an attitude in NASA not to believe negative tests."

- A former football player for Notre Dame claimed widespread steroid use at the University and that its highly respected coach,

Lou Holtz, "had to have known" about it. Holtz denied any knowledge, and evidence appears to support Holtz.

• Reporting on the Japanese drive to dominate the worldwide computer technology business, Jeff Shear quoted Charles H. Ferguson of MIT's Center of Technology in *Insight* magazine as saying that for Apple Computer it's "all over but the funeral." An Apple executive rebutted, arguing that the Japanese "can't compete with us because they can't clone us." The article concludes that Apple's solution (proprietary systems that can't be copied) is the likely source of its early demise: the industry has moved from closed systems to open systems, and Apple risks being left behind.

• A Special Report prepared on the 25th anniversary of the Vietnam War from *U.S. News & World Report* indicates that early-on during the war, then Defense Secretary McNamara wrote a secret memorandum to President Lyndon Johnson stating the war could not be won. *U.S. News* reporter Joseph L. Galloway notes: "The danger was visible at the time, to those willing to see." President Johnson ignored McNamara's warning and continued the military build-up. General Vo Nguyen Giap, now retired from the Vietnamese army, observed recently in Washington: "In Vietnam, your commanders never realized that there are limitations on power, limitations on strength. . . . What I have learned was that the most intelligent of men can do the stupidest of things."

• The *Wall Street Journal* criticized General Motors new Saturn car. "GM has learned the wrong lessons from the Japanese" its article concludes.

• As the Iraqi crisis built in the Middle East, several articles examined the early missed signs of the potential for war. Jessica T. Mathews, writing a related article entitled "America still hasn't learned its energy lessons," first reflects back on the 1973 embargo and the 1979-80 oil cartel price increase, and then ponders "whether three oil crises were enough to learn the energy lesson."

- Chrysler's legendary guru, Lee Iacocca, was severely criticized for his company's diminished strength, faltering competitive position, and shaky survival prospects. A Chrysler consultant told reporters Warren Brown and Frank Swoboda: "Iacocca's worst enemy has been his ego. . . . On the one hand, it drove him to heroic steps to save the company. On the other, it clouded the judgment he needed to keep Chrysler going."

During the same six months, additional articles pointed out: that the 1990s hotel industry suffers from a glut of over-capacity brought about by missed early warning signs; that purchasers and marketers of Milken's junk bonds failed to check out the problems underlying his theory that low-grade bonds are high-grade buys; that Russia's *glasnost* is turning into Russia's "last hurrah" because, for years, its leaders have ignored the warning signs.

The stories of missed and misinterpreted trouble signs are ongoing; only the variations change with time.

Principle of Defective Observation

Our seemingly unconscious penchant for blinding ourselves from reality and signs of approaching trouble can be summarized by what I have come to call the *Principle of Defective Observation:*

> *Our human observation is defective because each of us finds it necessary to interpret events we encounter and data we receive in ways that enhance our self-image and stabilize our perception of the universe.*
>
> *To that end, we search out and embrace information supporting our peculiar worldview. We exclude, refuse to gather, and refuse to recognize conflicting data.*
>
> *Our interpretations lead us to block out potential signs of trouble that threaten or are inconsistent with our self-image and worldview and to assign wrong interpretations to the signs we identify so as to minimize their importance.*

We do this, each of us, for very human reasons related to the defense of our personalities and our attempt to provide ourselves with a secure, stable universe. The net result is that our internal observation systems fail to endow experiences and data with the appropriate relevance and meaning. When it comes to trouble signs, our interpretive defenses provide blocks so that evidence reaching us doesn't convince us fast enough that trouble is on its way.

Factors Underlying the Principle of Defective Observation

Summary

Factors underlying the Principle of Defective Observation are:

- *Data.* Most of the data available to provide us with clues and information are fragmented, scattered, and meaningless by themselves. Thus, stray signs are easily ignored or overlooked.

- *Reality Construction.* Data requires interpretation for it to have meaning. The process of interpretation is defined as "reality construction" or, as Peter Drucker describes it, "the process of endowing data with relevance." The process is not objective.

- *Interpretive Defenses: Background Factors and Other Sources of Bias.* We each construct our own reality not as it is, but as our backgrounds, thinking styles, hopes, fears, drives, prejudices and other influences shape it for us. We seek interpretations that make us comfortable with our preconceptions. In a sense, we first arrive at conclusions and then search out information to support our predetermined versions of reality.

- *Commitment.* The depth of our commitment to a cause also shapes our prejudices and, therefore, our interpretations. Overcommitment can be as disastrous as no commitment, and each can provide a misleading twist or turn.

- *Cultures and Traditions.* Reality construction takes place within an environment architected by cultural influences and traditions. These give body to our interpretations and conclusions, further defining events and data in non-realistic ways.

Data and Relevance

The daily scatterings of facts and events that filter in isolation or incomplete combinations through our sensory systems in and of themselves offer scant hope for interpretive meaning and rarely any warning of potential disaster. Data take on meaning when apparently insignificant bits and pieces are sorted through (synthesized) to detect those that are strategic. Only when strategic facts are isolated do data become relevant, providing a basis for reasonable and meaningful inferences.

In the corporate environment, synthesizing bits and pieces of data into meaningful information patterns is particularly difficult. Facts are scattered throughout the organization's divisions and branches among people who rarely communicate with each other. Employees isolate their attention on their own activities. The isolation minimizes and lack of intra-company communication increases the likelihood employees will be unable to recognize a larger significance within the data coming to their attention.

Corporate Decision-Makers Rarely See Raw Data

Initial signs of crisis rarely come directly to corporate CEOs or members of the board of directors. Staff persons and department heads generally screen and summarize data before sending it to the top. In the process, they apply their own interpretations, deciding what to exclude, what to include and what included data mean. Thus, the decision-maker is left to apply his interpretations of information to pre-existing interpretations without the benefit of all of the raw data.

Reality Construction

Fragments of data, though endowed with relevance, have no useful meaning within a business or other environment until interpreted. *Reality construction* is the process by which a decision-maker supplies meaning to otherwise ambiguous data. Through his interpretations, the decision-maker architects his very personal version of reality. Danger lies in that the decision-maker's version of events may be at remarkable variance with — and when it comes to interpreting potential trouble signs, less threatening than — the authentic world.

How is reality apt to be constructed? Psychologists tell us that people have a bias to assemble interpretations in ways that enhance the images they have of themselves. For most people, images are optimistic. In fact, Tom Peters and Robert Waterman, authors of *In Search of Excellence,* concluded that most of us are "exuberantly, wildly irrational about ourselves."

The meanings people give life's experiences are designed to support their self-images and sustain their individuality and integrity. People are selective, blocking out evidence that contradicts and choosing evidence confirming their psyche. A CEO or board of directors member is no exception. Each interprets experienced events based upon his self-image and particular worldview. His reality construction, distorted for better or worse, is how he views his business environment and forms the basis for his decisions.

The process a decision-maker uses, psychologists say, is one of negotiation. The decision-maker negotiates with reality, producing his own reality construction that, in his mind at least, resolves the conflicts between his theory about who he is and the way life is actually proceeding. The negotiation process can involve making elaborate excuses as well as assigning the wrong reasons to the events occurring, thereby avoiding true understanding and creating distorted forms of reality construction in the face of threatening signs of failure or crisis.

Interpretive Defenses.

Interpretive defenses block out unsatisfactory or unpleasant data and repress conclusions that would be emotionally disturbing. The defenses thus interfere with one's ability to recognize potentially threatening, or conflicting, signs or information.

We may create less threatening, or more optimistic, versions of data that are disturbing or potentially damaging, or we may set thresholds of crisis awareness so high that we simply don't acknowledge the less dramatic precursors of crisis until disaster has reached overwhelming proportions. The result of unconsciously setting high recognition thresholds is that people on the brink of potential disaster have trouble identifying crisis warning signs, while those not involved have no trouble at all in seeing its indicators and cannot understand why those involved remain oblivious.

A CEO or other decision-maker setting up interpretive defenses blinds himself to the signs of danger visible to others whose advice he is unwilling to heed until it is too late.

We Have Different Backgrounds

The decision-maker's interpretations of summarized communications are further complicated because language has its own private meaning. CEOs or directors who rely on literal meanings of language can easily be trapped if they assume that their suppositions and words are used in the same way by others. There are private meanings of language influenced by varying experiences and backgrounds that have gone into the preparation of the communications presented to the decision-maker, and they can lead to assumptions about the state of things that are not true.

Because each person interprets what he sees and hears from a perspective shaped by experiences from his particular background, people can arrive at dissimilar interpretations of the same data and events. Childhood experiences, early successes and failures, health problems, influences of parents and mentors, worldliness of experiences, fears and traumas, each come to provide us with expectations about the meanings of encounters and events, influencing our interpretations, positively, negatively — or, sometimes, but rarely — realistically.

We Use Different Thinking Styles

Another reason danger signs go unnoticed is that individual interpretations are shaped by personal thinking styles. Each thinking style reflects a different approach to problem identification, problem analysis, and problem solving. Differences in thinking styles among people are not widely appreciated, and it is easy to fall into a trap of assuming that others think just like we do. Yet, each of us is different in the way we think and, therefore, different in how we interpret and evaluate the meaning of events and facts.

In their book, *Styles of Thinking*, psychologists Allen F. Harrison and Robert M. Bramson conclude that people are — in various combinations — analysts, realists, pragmatists, idealists, and synthesists.

The *idealist* has high standards and ideals, exhibits strength of character, and maintains values. He is usually willing to listen and accept input

and advice from others. On the negative side, the idealist is often unrealistic, missing unpleasant, near-term economic realities or facts.

The *pragmatist* is a person concerned with whatever works right now.
He usually proceeds piecemeal through complex problems. On the negative
side, he is short-term oriented and often may miss the implications of his
strategies.

The *analyst* is a person who seeks a logical "best" solution in a given
circumstance. He concentrates on facts rather than feelings. On the
negative side, subjective data are often ignored, or he may limit a data
search to facts and figures that support his theory about his one best
solution, ignoring possibilities and data that would point in other directions.

The *synthesist* is a person who sees connections between issues and
things, who digs beneath underlying assumptions, looking at problems
from a variety of viewpoints. On the negative side, his abstraction and
speculation may be carried to extremes, and he may miss the obvious.

The *realist* is a person who focuses on what can be heard, seen, and
touched. On the negative side, he sometimes suffers from tunnel vision,
does not listen to others, chooses quick fixes, and misses the problems
created by his quick fixes.

By not understanding these varying thinking styles and the influence
background experiences have on interpretations, we fail to realize the full
import of early warning signs of trouble. As Peter Drucker explained in
People and Performance, "It is no accident that the old story of the blind
men meeting up with an elephant on the road is so popular. . . . For each
level of management sees the 'elephant' — the business — from a
different angle of vision. . . . Each level needs its particular vision; it could
not do its job without it. Yet, these visions are so different that people on
different levels talking about the same thing often do not realize it — or,
as frequently happens, believe they are talking about the same thing, when
in reality they are poles apart."

We Use Shorthand Communication

Another block to recognizing danger is that people often talk in
shorthand communication. When familiar words are heard in an accustomed
context, they portray an assumed state of being. The shorthand communi-

cation is a form of non-probing "I'm okay-you're okay" exchange used by each of us in our personal and business conversations to save time and energy. When the words used sound "okay," we conclude the situation is "okay," and that nothing more is required of us — thus our energy can be expended elsewhere.

Within companies, the meaning of shorthand communication is developed, in part, from a company's shared meanings and specialized language; and to the degree people within the company share a common culture, their use of shorthand communication should elicit a similarity in meaning.

However, over-reliance on shorthand communication can lead to miscommunication, because the symbolic communication implies more than it reveals. Subtle nuances are missed by the listener who fails to probe the impressions. He stops listening when images expressed by the words he hears soothe him into complacency, and danger signs, which could surface if he were to probe are easily missed.

We Are Influenced by Corporate Cultures and Traditions

Corporate culture is the company's system of shared values and knowledge (often passed on through stories and myth about the company and its founders) that serve as frames of reference, helping people define situations as they encounter them. The corporate culture determines what people recognize as a crisis or an early warning sign. Counter-culture signs are ignored.

Corporate cultures represent the norms by which people within the corporation govern and judge themselves and their encounters. Cultures create and reinforce beliefs that the way things are being done are the right, if not the only, way things should be done. Cultural beliefs, like the beliefs of individuals about themselves, distort interpretations of events, favoring those that are supportive and blocking out those that are threatening.

Cultures, like Park Bank's, that are bound by predominantly "elitist" value systems (that is, value systems that honor the superiority and importance of the company) tend to be the most blind to the presence of counter-culture crisis warning signs. Indicators of potential trouble ascertainable from data that, if properly interpreted, would contradict corporate elitist cultures are discounted by the people within the organization. Thus, potential trouble signs, which conflict with can-do cultural interpretations go undetected, or are viewed as temporary interruptions.

If a company is hide-bound by traditions that have been passed on within the company from generation to generation, those traditions can sometimes mold themselves into rigid, archaic, bureaucratic rules, doctrinaire thinking and frozen assumptions lasting long after reasons for their existence have disappeared. Forcing changes in companies that have "always done it that way" can be more difficult than within up-beat, growth companies accustomed to some form of daily chaos.

Corporate cultures and traditions also define what kind of events will in fact be a crisis for a particular company. Researchers Wilkins and Dyer observed that what is a shock, and therefore a crisis, within one organization will not be a shock to another. They conclude: "As a result, we would be hard pressed to define a priori what constitutes a crisis for all frames of reference. Rather, we need to understand how participants interpret events."

We Are Affected by the Level of Our Commitment

The more committed the executive management is to the corporation's culture, tradition, and value system, the more likely the company will miss crisis warning signs. A very strong commitment to a company's system makes any thought of the need for change in the company's procedures or objectives unthinkable. The highly committed executive is thus more likely to misinterpret negative events.

Another vision and action block that is related to commitment is sometimes found in the use of Management-by-Objective programs (MBO programs), which can influence executives to develop job descriptions and objectives that leave little room for discretion and little motivation to reach beyond the tasks developed for the position.

Rewarding or punishing executive performance measured against pre-set objectives developed in an MBO program ignores the need companies have to develop managers who are willing to risk using their curiosity and peripheral vision, both essential in early crisis detection. The interdependence of managers and the subtle, nonobjective requirements that exist in the penumbra surrounding every management job may go unattended while an executive scores well on his MBO objectives.

Thus, management planning systems that over-concentrate on objective, short-term goals, and executive compensation and promotion systems emphasizing those performances, can further blind executives, hindering their abilities to detect any potential crisis lurking in the periphery of their business lives.

After Warning Signs Are Recognized . . .

Signs of potential crisis, even after they are recognized, can be misinterpreted or minimized. Management has great difficulty recognizing itself as the source of the company's problems. Admitting such a possibility is tantamount to self-indictment. Thus, under the circumstances, management looks for outside causes to assign to internally induced events. Executive decision-makers seek explanations for setbacks that will not damage self-esteem. In a sense, executives negotiate with reality to reinterpret data in more harmonious ways. The process may involve minimization — categorizing trouble as temporary or controllable — or it may involve using scapegoats — placing the blame on other people or events, usually outside the company.

Park Bank's board and management, of course, both minimized and misinterpreted the significance of the FDIC examination, and also used the regulators' "lack of understanding" as a scapegoat. We comment on Park's defective observation at the end of this chapter.

The misinterpretation process can also involve an overly optimistic estimate of recovery signs. We also had that experience at Park.

Inside the Park

In May 1985, shortly after our management changes were made, we thought we had Park Bank turned around. We thought we had bottomed out and were on the rebound. Our new loan officers, in particular, had put their shoulders to the rudder to turn our course away from the Black Hole. One of our largest troubled loans was restructured after enormous effort. Several small loans were also turned around. A mid-year checkup by the state regulators looked positive. We were ecstatic. We were on our way home!

For the first time since the crisis became visible, our public reports would show a reduction in potential problem loans. When I talked to the press about our first quarter results in mid-May, I proudly said, "The turnaround has definitely occurred. . . . We've pretty well discovered all the potential problem loans."

But I was wrong. We were all wrong. The light we saw at the end of the tunnel was not our way out; it was a train — and it was coming right at us!

A banker who had been through it before told me, "When you think you are at the bottom, you're not — you might be half way there; but you're not there."

Leatherwood and Conlon observed in the *Academy of Management Journal* that, ironically, when blame can be placed on others, there is a greater tendency for management to accept the existence of crisis-causing problems. Therefore, changing courses of action in response to crisis may more often depend upon the availability of scapegoats or other face-savers than upon the nature of the crisis itself. However, when courses of action instituted in response to the now-admitted trouble are directed at the scapegoat targets rather than the real causes of trouble, the result is increased trouble. The root problem remains unsolved, and the wrong solution will have its own day of reckoning — it, too, must be solved.

The Jobian Assignment of Causation

Humankind's propensity for assigning causes creates bizarre interpretations and, therefore, reactions in the face of failure. In that regard, the Old Testament story of Job has particular meaning. After Job suffered the loss of his family, his health, and everything he possessed, his friends, Bildad, Eliphaz, and Zophar, became convinced that Job's sufferings and failures were inflicted by God as his punishment for wrongdoing. Job's story ends with God telling his friends that they were wrong: Job had not been punished for wrongdoing. However, the view that troubled times and failures are punishments meted out to atone prior malevolent acts has survived in various forms through the ages.

At its core, however, the Book of Job is not about the source of suffering or failure. Rather, the Book of Job is about man's journey *through* the experience of suffering and failure — about how man's life is shaped, not by the suffering or the failure itself, but by the way he interprets and copes with his experiences, including his suffering and his failures.

Unfortunately, our culture has too frequently adopted the attitude of Job's friends: when man-made disaster occurs, someone must have done something wrong — really wrong. Perhaps that attitude is a reaction to the unflappable egoism of the many fallen leaders who are symptomatic Masters of the Universe, the subject of the next chapter. Whatever the reason, when a business fails, assumptions of wrong-doing involving those at the helm commonly follow.

Inside the Park

A painful glimpse into the Jobian assignment of cause, as it applied to me, appeared in a St. Petersburg Times *article written during the aftermath of Park's collapse:*

"Two opinions of the 54-year-old Jacobs have emerged since the fall. Many Park Bank employees and board members say he was legitimately trying to save the bank from its fatal end. According to that version, the problem was that he didn't take control of the bank from Kearney and Matthews soon enough.

"Unhappy shareholders propose a different view. They have difficulty believing that Jacobs. . . was unaware of what was happening."

A result of the Jobian view about business failure is that business postmortems are rarely performed. Those maneuvering through failure's aftermath have to spend too much time defending themselves, or their egos, against further ruin. There is little opportunity for them to reflect or to contribute true understanding. The result is that ultimate knowledge on the subject of business failure is meager.

Thus, we rarely define root causes and history continually repeats itself.

Bad News Messengers as Scapegoats

Historically, the whistle blower, the person who finds signs of trouble in his company and reports them, has been treated poorly, experiencing retaliation, financial loss, and stress when he has spoken out. Clyde Farnsworth reported in the *New York Times* the advice of one whistle blower: "Don't do it unless you're willing to spend many years, ruin your career and sacrifice your personal life."

The courageous acts of whistle blowers are rarely rewarded. More frequently, they are treated as the enemy and end up losing their jobs. In response, states have recently promulgated laws designed to protect whistle blowers.

Since the discoveries of whistle blowers are, in effect, indictments of management and corporate cultures, it is little wonder that attitudes about whistle blowers block upward communication and the ability of companies to discover crisis signs at an early stage.

The Invisible Turning Points: the First Early Warning Signs

By definition, "crisis" is a *turning point*, a decisive moment, in the life of a business that can lead, or does lead, to disaster. Thus far in this chapter we have discussed the visible early warning crisis signs and blocks that impede their timely recognition or correct interpretation. Ultimately, the visible signs reflect themselves on the bottom line of boardroom reports or make the headlines: the Exxon oil spill, the J&J Tylenol tampering crisis, Wall Street's junk bond fiascoes and related bankruptcies, and the thrift crisis are but a few of the available examples.

Sadly, however, by the time crisis signs are visible on the bottom line or in the press, it is usually too late: the "momentum effect" of events has driven the troubled company over the rim of its Black Hole.

There are, however, "invisible" crisis signs. Visible crisis signs are rarely the destroyers of business; rather, for the most part, they reflect earlier, undetected, fundamental flaws vividly clear in hindsight, but *invisible* to the decision-maker at the time. Perhaps a combination of examples, from inside and outside Park Bank, will illustrate the point. We start at the South Pole, far from the subtropical Florida location of Park Bank.

At the turn of the century British explorer Robert Scott lay in his tent, trapped by a deadly blizzard, his mission to reach the South Pole lost forever. His pained, freezing hands scratched out his final words:

The causes of the disaster are not due to faulty organization, but to misfortune in all risks that were undertaken. . . We are weak, writing is difficult, but for my own sake, I do not regret this journey. We took risks, we knew we took them; things have come out against us, and therefore we have no cause for complaint, but bow to the will of Providence. Had we lived, I should have had a tale to tell of the hardihood, endurance, and courage of my companions which would have stirred the heart of every Englishman. These rough notes and our dead bodies must tell our tale. . . .

Inside the Park

Near the end of Park Bank's life, in one of those dark moments that last forever, I stood next to the window of my office, peering out over Tampa Bay, absorbed in my thoughts. I felt about our looming Black Hole as Scott had written about his final days. I pondered similar questions: Had the Park Bank experience been an unfortunate encounter with risks fate threw against us? Had Park's plan been wrong? Had Park's plan been "right," its execution "wrong?"

I had no answer that day. But I knew what had gone against us:

- *The Federal Reserve had sought to break the back of inflation, pushing interest rates to all-time highs, curbing Park's margins, reducing loan collateral values, placing Park's interest-sensitive real estate projects in jeopardy.*

- *Florida's real estate market had become glutted, driving real estate values down, adversely affecting Park's collateral margins and hindering its ability to liquidate properties in amounts sufficient to cover its loans.*

- *Park's ability to raise capital, necessary for it to maintain reserves and fund operations and projects underway, was derailed by an SEC regulatory quagmire.*

- *As deregulation penetrated Park's market area, banking became highly competitive, making non-community bank alternatives available to better credit risks, shrinking the community bank market for quality loans.*

- *The west coast of Florida had been devastated by hurricane Elena, severely damaging several partially completed Gulf Beach projects financed by Park Bank.*

- *A key developer, heavily financed by Park, suffered a heart attack, leaving his projects and our largest loan unattended.*

- *Several members of Park's board began to spend time away from St. Petersburg. In the process, those directors, relying frequently on attendance at board meetings by telephone and on written reports based on loan officer's hope and pride rather than on analytical substance, lost sensitivity to Park's sliding status and crumbling environment.*

- *Park's chairman, John Kearney, experienced trouble with his own real estate projects. As his troubles grew, his attention and ability to concentrate on Park's problems floundered. Despite his inattention, Park's board continued to be mesmerized — one director describing Kearney in* Florida Trend *magazine as a "Pied Piper." The combination of his troubles and his insufficient attention confused Park leadership and the thrust of the bank's direction.*

- *After Park's management changes had been forced, momentum effect took over, driving Park Bank toward its Black Hole; publicity became unbearable and emotionally burdensome; litigation drained liquidity; competition bore in relentlessly; and worst of all, the FDIC's regulatory system, designed, supposedly, to minimize loss from troubled banks, worked against Park Bank, encouraging potential buyers to wait for Park Bank to reach near-death, forcing the FDIC to provide bail-out money.*

I went to my desk and listed all that had gone against us. I came up with fifteen events — turning points — each beyond our control.

I had planned to detail the list of Park's uncontrollable turning points in our next 10K annual report securities filing; but the next 10K was never published. Park failed before its due date.

Sometime later, after Park's crash, I had the opportunity to study Scott's heroics in depth. Early historians had attributed his death to unexpectedly bad weather. Movies have pictured his courageous risking in face of it.

But later analysis drew a different conclusion. Scott had not died because of outside, uncontrollable, unforeseeable events and circumstances, as his final words depicted — though those events and circumstances did in fact occur. Rather his death resulted from fundamental flaws related both to his fallacious assignment of causes behind the events he experienced and to the ways he exercised his judgment in response to them.

Writer-explorer Jared Diamond wrote:

- Scott died 11 miles from his supply depot. He had been advised to establish the depot closer to the South Pole. He ignored advice and said, "I'm not going to defy my feelings for the sake of a few days march."

- Scott brought three motor sleds to carry supplies, but only one extra cylinder. One sled sank and the other two each blew a cylinder. Had he brought another cylinder, he could have moved his supplies closer to the Pole — close enough to have reached them during his final hours.

- One of his crew members, Apsley Cherry-Garrard, was illiterate when it came to polar navigation. Scott passed off Garrard's inability as unimportant, saying, "There is not one chance in a hundred that he will ever have to consider navigation on our journey." As Scott lay freezing to death in his tent, Cherry-Garrard was immobilized at Scott's supply depot, afraid to search for Scott because he could not navigate over the polar ice fields. Had Garrard been able to navigate the polar wastelands, he could have rescued Scott.

Diamond pointed out that Scott's disaster was rooted in his psychological inability to comprehend, or accept, that any potential for disaster lay in his decisions and actions. Blinded by excessive egoism about his abilities, convinced he was master of life's events, he proceeded in the face of unreasonable risks, spurned the advice of others, and, unwilling to accept ultimate personal responsibility, designated outside events and other people as scapegoats.

Scott's decisional processes ignored what Peter Drucker identifies in an article entitled "The Effective Decision" as the essential boundary conditions for an effective executive decision: an effective executive decision can be made only after those involved in the decisional process first set up the specifications — the boundary conditions — that any decision must satisfy if it is to work successfully. Drucker wrote:

> *Above all, clear thinking about the boundary conditions is needed to identify the most dangerous of all possible decisions: the one in which the specifications that have to be satisfied are essentially incompatible. . . . This is the decision that might — just might — work if nothing whatever goes wrong. . . .*
>
> *Decisions of this sort are usually called "gambles." But actually they arise from something much less rational than a gamble — namely hope against hope that two (or more) clearly incompatible specifications can be fulfilled simultaneously. This is hoping for a miracle; and the trouble with miracles is not that they happen so rarely, but they are, alas, singularly unreliable.*

Scott's decisions were, as Drucker put it, worse than gambles. They were based upon the possibilities of miracles. Scott refused to accept the possibility that his plight was the product of his decisional processes.

Scott ran into bad weather, worse weather than normal for that time of the year. Why, as Diamond observed, hadn't he considered the possibility of unseasonable weather in his decision-making?

Scott ordered his supply ponies to trek across thin ice in the face of advice to the contrary. Why did he believe his ponies would not fall through thin ice?

When Scott wrote from his snow-inundated tent, he wrote about his adversity as if the gods had turned against him, unexpectedly and unforeseeably, and beyond his control. Dead bodies, he said, must tell his story. They did.

***Inside the Park* (continued)**

Reflection about Scott and Drucker's admonitions provides a sober-
ing review of some of Park Bank's early policy decisions and the oppor-
tunity they provided for those involved to assign erroneous causes to the
events in Park's life.

- *Yes, the Federal Reserve raised interest rates "unreasonably" —*
  to all-time highs. But who made the decision to concentrate Park
  Bank's primary lending activities in interest-sensitive markets like
  real estate? Was Park Bank's management and board unaware
  that governmental anti-inflation action was a realistic possibility?
  Did Park, by relying on continued inflation to support collateral
  values and results, violate what should have been its boundary
  conditions for good decisions?

- *Yes, the "hurricane gods" visited Florida's Gulf beaches, devas-*
  tating several projects at the most inopportune of times. But who
  made the decision to concentrate a large share of Park's lending
  activities on financing beach projects?

- *Yes, Park's board and management did not fully comprehend or*
  accept the conclusions of the 1983 FDIC examination. But why did
  management and the board, without an independent evaluation of
  its loan portfolio and policies, draw the conclusion that Park was
  on track, that its real problem was that the FDIC did not under-
  stand the bank?

- *Yes, Park's growth outstripped its systems and the skill-levels of its*
  people. But who made the decision to grow rapidly in the first
  place?

Did Park's decisional process itself, like Scott's, result in reality
distortion, assignment of scapegoats and misinterpretation of its disinte-
grating events?

All of the executive actions leading to Park Bank's state of affairs described above reflected decisions arrived at by Park Bank's leadership, its executive officers, and board of directors. And, like Scott who found himself dying at the South Pole, Park found itself crashing on the rim of its Black Hole. Scott's failure to comprehend the impact of decisions made in clear weather set Scott up for a deadly blizzard. Failures of its executive management and board of directors to comprehend the effects of its growth and lending policies made during Florida's boom-times flung Park Bank into its Black Hole. Those kinds of failures are strategic failures, policy failures, decision-maker failures.

Flawed policies and strategic decisions are the decisive moments in the life of the business, the turning points that months or years later explode as crisis. Only in retrospect, after the explosion, are the signs clearly visible.

Inside the Park

The principles described in this chapter were major factors in the downslide of Park Bank. In particular, Park Bank's elitist culture unquestionably had a blinding effect on those inside the Park and, in particular, on the formation of its policies.

Park Bank's director of human resources, brought in as one of Park Bank's management changes, was interviewed in 1989 by Professor William R. Boulton from the University of Georgia for a case study he was preparing. In the interview she said, "Park Bank had a real strong culture. There was a mindset that they were doing it the right way. . . . They believed that if we had just continued to let them run it the way they were, they would become the biggest bank in the universe."

Park Bank's culture was clearly upbeat. Working in the Park was euphoric, challenging, an opportunity that had to be experienced. The motto of the bank, reflected in each of its ads, was "Taking Care of Business." The central theme of the bank was that it was finding solutions to customers' problems. One of Park Bank's advertisements quoted its board chairman as saying, "Our bank is doing things that should have been done years ago. We're aggressive, creative, and certainly more flexible in our financing than just about any bank I've seen anywhere.

With the right mentality and the right bank, there is no limit to what a businessman can do."

Another of Park Bank's directors described in his testimonial ad that: "By helping the businessman cut through the red tape, we're really giving him the freedom to fulfill his potential. . . . Quite simply, we're organized to help make people successful."

The mindset in Park Bank's loan committees evidenced the same intentions. Rejecting what was viewed as the typical banker's approach — "Why should we make this loan?" — loan committees focused on "How can we make this deal work?"

Another director's testimonial ad also described Park's zest for making deals: "Too many good ideas have been killed by under-capitalization, usually the result of tight lending policies. We're not afraid to take reasonable, calculated risks at Park Bank."

It should not be surprising, given Park Bank's upbeat, elitist environment, that the adverse observations of the FDIC in its 1983 examination were, at first, given inadequate attention. When Park Bank's chairman called a special meeting and told its board that Park Bank's problem was merely that the FDIC's understanding had not caught up to Park and its futuristic avant-garde philosophy, no one in his agreeable boardroom audience objected or seriously doubted him.

Park Bank was Meredith Willson's "Hawkeye-Iowa," its chairman the "Music Man." The board played 76 trombones, and the lenders tooted 110 cornets right behind!

We had constructed a false reality blinding us to trouble signs. Our blindness during Park Bank's picnic days further became painfully evident to me when, three years after Park Bank failed, I was deposed in the FDIC suit against the directors and the bank's advisors. As I testified about internal bank documents — some authored by myself — I was again chagrined, as I had been a few months earlier in depositions for the stockholders' suit. I could not believe that we had been so naive, so caught up in our hype. We simply discounted any evidence that our skyrocketing growth, high deposit costs, and concentration in real estate lending was risky. One memo from me, for example, suggested that the FDIC was being unfairly tough on Park and other small banks in its examination process because it wanted to force mergers and consolidations of finan-

cial institutions during pending deregulation, thus making the FDIC's job easier. I felt so strongly that we were right that I suggested that we lobby our position in Washington.

The company's response at each stage of a crisis depends upon the interpretations of the signs available to the CEO, his management group and the board of directors. Is what management and the board see unimportant, or is it critical? Is it temporary or permanent? Threatening or nonthreatening? Internally caused or externally caused? In most circumstances, the view will be muddled and grey, the choices unclear — and, unfortunately, the interpretations unconsciously biased.

More determining of the outcome of most business crises than prompt detection and correct interpretation of visible signs, however, are the long-term effects of the company's strategies and policies. The ultimate effect of a strategy or policy can ferment for years before flaws become visible. By the time the negative effect is evident on the bottom line of the company's reports it's usually too late.

It is imperative for each of us to always be aware that there is risk, real risk, that recognition and the right interpretation of early warning signs, visible or invisible, might not be made in time on warships like the *Stark*, in the closest of relationships, or within executive suites or boardrooms.

Chapter 4

Masters of the Universe

"The great act of faith is when man decides he is not God."

Oliver Wendell Holmes

W. Somerset Maugham's classic novel, *The Razor's Edge*, about Larry Darrell, a ravaged war veteran questing life's meaning among the monasteries of Tibet, includes a conversation between a friend of Darrell and Maugham. The friend asks Maugham how she can convince Darrell to abandon a dangerous effort doomed to fail.

Maugham was pessimistic: "You won't succeed."

Why?

Maugham became philosophic. "You see, he's enthralled by one of the most powerful emotions that can beset the human beast. . . . Self-confidence is a passion so overwhelming that beside it even lust and hunger are trifling. It whirls its victim to destruction in the highest affirmation of his personality. The object doesn't matter; it may be worthwhile or it may be worthless. No wine is so intoxicating, no love so shattering, no vice so compelling."

Psychologists say being possessed with an abundance of self-confidence is healthy. It can increase feelings of control and stability as well as happiness and productivity. Recent work by researchers Shelley Taylor and Johnathan Brown has gone even a step further. In his article, "Dash of unreality may be good for us," Daniel Goleman reports Taylor and Brown's conclusions that living under a modicum of illusion and false hopes coupled with a modestly inflated self-regard may actually aid psychological health.

As healthy as some inflated feelings about self-worth may be, many executives have been unrealistic about being unrealistic! Peters and Waterman reported in their book *In Search of Excellence* that, when it comes to leadership ability, 70 percent of executives see themselves as among the top 25 percent of business leaders and only 2 percent see themselves in the bottom 50 percent. Peters and Waterman conclude that most of us are "exuberantly, wildly irrational about ourselves."

Optimistic self-confidence, blended with a sliver of pretentiousness, can produce the right executive stuff — like *The Right Stuff* Tom Wolfe wrote about when he described those primordial drives that propel test pilots like Chuck Yeager and astronauts like John Glenn into the unknown reaches of outer space and boost the endorphins of manliness and courage to all-time highs.

Unfortunately, an overabundance of self-confidence can also produce the wrong executive stuff. Professor Eugene Jennings's research (reported in Roy Rowan's *The Intuitive Manager*) tells us that executives with the wrong executive stuff are most likely to possess one or both of the following characteristics: the "illusion of mastery of all life's events" or the "illusion of immunity to bad luck."

When an otherwise healthy amount of self-confidence is twisted by one of Jennings's illusions, those delusions, which consume the "Masters of the Universe" Tom Wolfe wrote about in *The Bonfires of the Vanities,* take over. Wolfe's story is about a Wall Street Master of the Universe bond broker, Sherman McCoy, and a supporting cast of characters who think they, too, have the "right stuff." Unfortunately, their total absorption is with their egocentric, deluded selves.

Egocentric self-delusion can take on different forms. Larry Darrell believed that he was the master of life's events; he could not fail in a situation where failure was a certainty. Sherman McCoy's self-indulgence consumed his life as if his horn of plenty would flow forever; he thought he was immune to bad luck.

When actions are dictated by the illusion that one has the skills for mastering the events of life itself, or that one has been blessed with perpetual good luck, self-confidence becomes intoxicating, compelling, and finally, as Maugham says, destructive.

Self-confidence can express itself as positive self-regard, accelerating one toward his or her highest goals; or excessive, unbridled self-esteem can also blind the possessor to reality, dragging him over the edge of the Black Hole.

When Is a CEO's "Stuff" the "Wrong Stuff"?

Leveraging Leaders

When my experiences at Park Bank are reflected against a background of the research available, certain conclusions about the behavioral characteristics of Black Hole-bound CEOs emerge.

My conclusions support Professor Jennings's findings that business leaders with the wrong executive stuff do suffer from the illusion that they are masters of all of life's events or that they are immune from bad luck. But that conclusion can be drawn one step further: I believe that those twisted illusions ply disaster because leaders burdened with the wrong executive stuff leverage their companies to propel their self-esteems to intoxicating highs. They become "leveraging leaders."

The gain sought by a leveraging leader is not just financial. Greed, so often asserted as the sole driving force behind business abuse, is more likely to be a subordinate factor. The leveraging leader's sought-after reward is predominantly psychological: the power and control he considers necessary for self-esteem. His quest, however, is distorted, often leading to both his, and his company's, Black Hole crash.

Leveraging leaders manage their companies to preserve their illusions. Early-warning crisis signs that conflict with those illusions are ignored or twisted because the leveraging leader's ego refuses to accept the possibility that he might fail or have bad luck.

Leveraging leaders are not always obvious. They disguise their motives, and they don't all work in the same way. I have organized leveraging leader types into six categories. The characteristics of each will take on meaning as you relate these observations to your own experiences.

- *Risk Junkie.* Oblivious to bad luck, he is blind to crisis signs because risk taking, not risk avoidance, is the objective. He leverages his company to support his risk-taking habit.

- *"I-can-hit-it-with-a-broomhandle" Philosophizer.* He is oblivious to crisis signs because he believes that business leadership aptitude is unconnected with specific business knowledge. His illusion of mastery is based upon past successful experiences and his generalized knowledge which he believes have universal application; his lack of specific knowledge about his business makes his decisions risky and prevents him from identifying early warning signs of trouble.

- *Boredom-Burnout Victim.* He has become the consummate risk-taker because he is burned out and bored. His decisions are made without adequate thought and little projection as to their effect. He can't see signs of approaching crisis because he is inattentive. He remembers that, at one time, he mastered life's events; that illusion keeps him going now.

- *Hold-Tighter-Hero.* He won't admit to the presence of crisis signs after his decisions turn sour because, psychologically, he can't let go of his bad idea. His continued obsession causes his company to divert even more resources, risking its future needlessly.

- *Myopic Manager.* He risks the future for the present. He misinterprets and underestimates the long-term damaging effect of his policies. For him, short-term performance carries the illusion of long-term luck.

- *Gatsby Grabber.* He has a give-it-to-me-now personality and places his personal enjoyment and status ahead of the needs of his business. He is blind to signs of danger that interfere with his personal cravings. His horn of plenty knows no bounds even though it hurts the company.

Risk Junkies

T-People

We Americans praise highly the risk takers, the doers, innovators, experimenters, entrepreneurial spirits, those who live life to the hilt. Society looks up to them, makes heroes out of them.

Popular business writings also enhance the attractiveness of the cult of the risk taker. In *Tough-Minded Leadership*, Joe Batten attributes Apple Computer CEO John Sculley as describing risk takers as "the people you'll lose against." Tom Peters quotes MCI executive Dick Liebhaber in an *Academy of Management Executive* article as saying: "We don't shoot people who make mistakes; we shoot people who don't take risks."

Who belong to the cult of the risk takers? University of Wisconsin psychologist Frank Farley calls risk takers *Type T* — thrill seekers — people who need "the uncertainty involved in risk taking."

What distinguishes Type T personalities? The intensity with which they pursue their goals and their self-confidence. They are goal driven and convinced of their invincibility.

Of course, every business involves risk, and a successful businessman learns to measure and select the right risk. Solid, well-grounded risk taking involves identifying the factors that influence success or failure, their probabilities for occurrence, their cost, and the effort required to influence risks in a positive way. Successful risk taking looks more daring than it is. When risk taking is done right, it involves thoughtful analysis and careful decisions, not blind movements that ignore the potentialities for failure.

Successful risk takers are not irrational fools, acting as if they were immune to life's events. As a psychologist said, "The ones who succeed don't jump off the bridge until they know the parachute works."

But they do jump, and occasionally a parachute doesn't open even when it should. The willingness to take those leaps of faith is characteristic of even the most prudent risk takers.

In the spring of 1988, 39-year-old Prince Charles of England was skiing in Switzerland with Major Hugh Lindsay and other friends on Wang Mountain near the Austrian border. The prince, ignoring avalanche warning signs, led the skiers off the marked trails. Suddenly, the mountainside gave way and cascades of snow buried them. Major Lindsay was killed; the prince barely escaped.

In an article entitled "The Avalanche Death of a Friend Has Prince Charles Grieving — And England Pondering His Love of Risk," Bonnie Johnson wrote: ". . . Charles has never been known for playing it safe. There is a feeling in England that he relishes the role of a man of action, testing the limits of a life that seems bounded on all sides by public functions."

One skier was quoted as saying, "The perception of danger was something we often talked about. We found that danger acceptable."

Is Prince Charles a T-Type person who unnecessarily extends his risk taking? T-Types are addicted to risk, risking just for the sake of it, consumed by action. Hyatt and Gottlieb, authors of *When Smart People Fail*, describe people who enjoy living on the edge as risk junkies. "When risk junkies are successful, they are the Midases of industry: everything they touch turns to gold. We — they — believe their success will never end. The trouble is, when these people fail, they fail big."

Because risk seeking is their life, risk junkies are blinded to signs of potential trouble. Potential trouble is what they seek. For them trouble isn't trouble; it's the source of their addicting highs. Eventually the results spell disaster for their businesses.

The T-Type personality characteristics of a CEO prone to test the rim of the Black Hole just for the sake of it are not always easy to identify. "Too much" can look quite brilliant in the beginning. Thus, it's easy to minimize the importance of personality quirks, visible in the periphery of a person's life, which should be telltale indicators of "T" characteristics.

I-Can-Hit-It-With-a-Broomhandle Philosophizer

A few years ago, my then teen-aged son John was taking a golf lesson from Bob Toski, one of the all-time greats among golf instructors. John was lining drives with his 3 iron far down the fairway, aiming over a stake Toski had driven into the ground. Acting the proud father, I asked Bob about John's golf clubs — Should I get a new set of clubs for John? If so, what kind? Toski grinned, put his hands on his hips, and looked up at me: "Hell no, when you're good, you can hit it with a broom-handle!"

That philosophy, the *I-can-hit-it-with-a-broom-handle* philosophy, is unfortunately prevalent among top business decision-makers. The philosophy is based on the idea that, at the CEO level, business principles are basic, of universal application: a CEO who can run one business can run any business. Business fundamentals and business experience are enough.

When Lynn Townsend, Lee Iacocca's predecessor at Chrysler, nominated John Riccardo, an accountant, his successor in 1976, he said, "At this level of management, it doesn't make a difference what your background is. We don't design or build cars at this level. We set objectives and policies and monitor the progress."

Of course, the results were a disaster.

David B.Sicilia, reviewing the movie *Tucker: The Man and His Dream* in Harvard Business Review, cites the same faulty thinking for the fall of Preston Tucker, the post-World War II automobile entrepreneur: "History demonstrates that the essential ingredient for entrepreneurial success is a thorough understanding of your business — an understanding Preston Tucker never developed."

The hit-it-with-the-broom-handle theory fails to distinguish the principles of corporate leadership from those that relate to corporate management. Running a business, or managing a business, is not the same as leading a business. Particularly a troubled business.

John P. Kotter, of the Harvard Business School, differentiated leadership and management in *The Leadership Factor*. He wrote that management is based upon generalized principles involving budgeting, organizing, planning, controlling, and the like, and that managers' skills are based upon universal principles rather than business-specific information. Leadership, however, is not generalized. Leadership in today's complex business environment is data-specific.

The differentiation should not be ignored: professional managers may be able to rely on principles that have universal application; leaders, however, require massive amounts of specific knowledge about the company, its industry, and the situation.

Tomorrow's CEO, says Peter Drucker in *Harvard Business Review,* will manage like a symphony orchestra conductor, directing musicians who are specialists in their fields. Like the conductor, the CEO will have to have comprehensive knowledge about both the orchestra's score and the parts played by each instrumentalist.

Good golfers may be able to hit the ball with a broom-handle; but the right tools are necessary if they want to shoot par. When it comes to corporate leadership, specific knowledge and relevant experience are, likewise, required to shoot par — in fact, to merely stay on the course.

Boredom-Burnout Syndrome

A person experiencing *boredom-burnout syndrome* is often exhausted, dulled, unobservant, and unresponsive. Boredom-burnout can attack anyone, but high achievers are prime candidates. The typical victim has high personal expectations and high performance standards; he has thrown his entire being into his business and his project.

CEO burnout usually happens after a long, exhausting, intense period of business activity, when the CEO can push himself no farther. Although his symptoms might be physical fatigue, his exhaustion is mental, like a soldier who has been on too many missions.

He goes through work motions long after he has lost his effectiveness, thinking that his old skills are still performing. He puts things off. He scapegoats. He has no reserves, no ability to spring back. He neither recognizes, nor admits, that his capacity to lead is gone. He is too fatigued to stretch into the future. He loses his ability to observe and so misses early signs of trouble. The result is that he places his company at risk.

Hold Tighter Heroes

Escalation Dilemma

There are two sides to risk taking: knowing what is worth trying, and knowing when to let go. Kenny Rogers sings in *The Gambler*, "You've got to know when to hold 'em; you've got to know when to fold 'em."

Some CEO's hang on to a pet project forever; they don't know when to "fold 'em." Instead of cutting losses when their idea doesn't work out, they push on, continuing to invest more energy and money into the project — all the way to the bottom of the Black Hole. They suffer from *escalation dilemma*.

An escalation dilemma occurs when the CEO's pride, fear of change, or insistence that his project is symbolic of everything his company stands for (or all of the above) blind him. He refuses to let go of his idea, he equates it with his self-efficacy; he escalates his efforts and his company's. His doomed project can suck corporate resources for years, diverting them from other, worthier projects.

Why do escalation dilemmas occur? In part, because business projects rarely die a sudden death. They bleed slowly. Early trouble signs occur a little at a time and are ambiguous. People with escalation dilemma interpret ambiguous signs as favorable signs, don't admit to danger, and instead, provide additional resources for the troubled project.

Inside the Park

One of the most difficult problems loan officers and loan committees have is determining the right course of action for troubled loans, particularly when the borrower involved is a "good customer."

How long should the bank support the borrower? How long should the bank advance funds or extend payments? Faced with possible losses, a little more time, a few more dollars into the project, reworking the loan, hanging on until the economy turns all sound logical.

I remember a particularly troubling real estate subdivision project. The developer had a heart attack; the project drifted while he recovered. When he returned to work, we considered restructuring his loans, extending payments, reducing interest rates, carrying the project out for years. Park Bank had worked with the developer for several years, and though he was worn out by his health problems, he seemed determined to come back. Emotionally we wanted to help him. We also calculated that if the project stopped, Park Bank could lose millions, reducing our capital, and adversely affecting our recovery progress.

Park Bank would incur a sure loss if it didn't restructure the troubled loan. A restructuring would take the project off the current delinquency list, something we desperately wanted, and if projections were accurate, reduce our loss exposure. However, several years would be needed to work with the developer's limited resources, a risk that increased our exposure if everything did not work out exactly right. In effect, the restructuring could save the present, but at a higher risk to the future.

We called in a consultant; he helped us see that the developer did not have the stamina to carry the project through. His health might turn again

at any time, his optimism, and our hope, notwithstanding. An increased
time period to complete the project increased the bank's risk of future loss
through several years of real estate cycles.

We helped the developer find a buyer, took a measured loss, and went
on to other projects.

Hero Effect

Escalation dilemma becomes increasingly dangerous when it is bolstered by what Michael M. Miller and Patricia Bellew Gray call the *hero*
effect. During the tenure of chairman Roger Smith, General Motors, Miller
and Bellow wrote, had been victimized by his efforts to bring about his
hero effect. They observed: "Objectivity in decision making is often
further compromised by the hero effect. An immensely dynamic chief
executive decides on a flawed course of action; blinded by his charisma,
subordinates either cannot see faults in his plan or are reluctant to say the
emperor is naked."

Troubled and criticized during his tenure because of his failed efforts
to reshape General Motors, the now-retired Smith had implemented a
major public relations campaign to improve his then tarnished, but initially
bright, image. At the start of his General Motors chairmanship, Smith had
been touted as one of the new heroes of American business — one of the
two men (the other being Iacocca) who had revitalized the U.S. automobile industry.

But then General Motors, thought by some to be invincible, fell like
a dinosaur under its own bureaucratic weight and Roger Smith's vision,
distorted by hero effect. General Motors's profits plunged 70 percent
during the fourth quarter of 1986 and for the first time since Henry Ford
sold his Model T in 1924, Ford Motor Company's annual profits exceeded
those of General Motors.The latter incurred monumental operating costs,
the highest in the American automotive industry. Its car designs were no
longer attractive, and its product lines were not sufficiently differentiated
to encourage customers to trade up within the various General Motors
lines.

CEOs can be good at *Impression Management (IM)*; that is, influencing what others think of them. Possession of IM skills coupled with

hero effect makes it tough to own up to a bad deal. A CEO with IM skills, also blinded by hero effect, looks for ways to avoid ego damage, to manage the impression others have of him in a positive way when a project goes wrong. If troublesome elements can be blamed on outside factors or other people without damaging his fragile ego and image, he may be able to let go and stop the escalation; otherwise, he is apt not to back away, he holds tight and escalates his company's investment in his gone-bad project.

For CEOs steeped in IM and swayed by hero effect, stopping escalations may depend more upon what kinds of scapegoats are available than upon the CEO's ability to accept truth.

Escalation Dilemmas and Government Agencies

Bureaucratic government agencies can also be swayed by the illusion of infallibility. Shortly after Park Bank's crash, the Federal Home Loan Bank Board (then, the savings and loan industry regulatory agency) required Financial Corporation of America (FCA) to recruit a new CEO. In return, the Board promised financial support for FCA's subsidiary savings and loan association (S&L) which was experiencing a costly run on deposits.

The Federal Home Loan Bank Board based its decision to pump money into the troubled thrift on the idea that large companies, particularly large S&Ls, simply don't fail. Since FCA was too big to fail, there was, the Board reasoned, no risk to the government. Millions of dollars of losses later, FCA was described by David B. Hilder in the *Wall Street Journal* as the largest insolvent thrift in the country.

The *Journal* lamented that the Bank Board's action was illusory, merely deferring losses to another day. The Federal Savings and Loan Insurance Corporation (FSLIC), then on the verge of insolvency itself, ended up covering the excessive FCA's losses from its own troubled insurance fund. A former FSLIC examiner called the situation sad: "We weren't even close to having the type of information we needed."

Data about FCA, which could have given some insight into its situation, wasn't gathered or analyzed. That decisional process, premised on the infallibility of the decision-maker, blocked the Board's ability to give significance to data that conflicted with its already-architected version of reality.

The Slow Decline

There is another kind of escalation dilemma — the slow decline. In this kind of dilemma, investment simply continues in an obsolete, nonperforming project or business — the continuance of the same old thing long after it has lost its usefulness. The result is a slow fading away of the business. Psychologist Harvey Hornstein says, "People get comfortable with decline. When you live with dragons for a while, they don't look so bad close up anymore. You persist because it is infinitely more terrifying to leap into darkness." A course of action can seem comfortable but, in the end, be disastrous.

How Corporate Culture Promotes Escalation Dilemmas

The effects of escalation dilemma and hero effect are skewed by our cultural bias favoring persistence. Iacocca became a hero to business because he persisted. He turned a big loser into a big winner, at least initially. Miller and Gray wrote that: "The heroes of business are not people who cut losses early and ran, but those who stuck to their guns and turned big losers into big winners. 'When the going gets tough, the tough get going,' says an old saw — which conveniently ignores that a lot of them then go right into brick walls with their heads down. And so too often management simply hangs on and goes down with the ship."

Inside the Park

I am painfully reminded of another plaque I hung carefully in my office after I took over as CEO in 1985. John Taylor of the St. Petersburg Times *referred to it in an article: "Richard Jacobs has a new plaque hanging on the wall of his office. It is inscribed with an Oriental proverb: 'We are continually faced by great opportunities brilliantly disguised as insoluble problems.' If Jacobs, chairman and president of Park Bank of Florida, gets frustrated in his battle to turn the troubled bank around, he need only gaze at the nearby plaque for inspiration."*

I still have my plaque with its Oriental proverb. But I have also learned that there are some problems that simply must be accepted for what they are, no matter how contrary to my nature the idea may seem.

Myopic Managers

In the 1988 Touche-Ross study of *Ethics in American Business,* businessmen, professors, and professionals agreed that one of the chief sources of undue pressure on American business ethics was management's increased concentration on short-term profits. Professors Mitchell and Scott call our preoccupation with maximization of short-term gain a "deadly obsession," pervasive in society and government alike.

Concentration on the short run at the expense of the long run is more than a threat to business ethics; it is a risk to business itself. Excessive concentration on short-term objectives — aptly labeled by *Wall Street Journal* reporter Ralph Winter as *myopic management* — can be another pathway to company failure. Management needs to consider both the short run and the long run. A management problem is not solved if immediate profits are taken at the expense of the long-run health of the company.

It is not always easy. There are factors that pressure CEOs to ignore tomorrow. A hostile takeover threatening loss of executive jobs, short-term executive performance bonuses tied to stock values, stockholder's drive for current yields — all combine to drive executive management to focus on the "next quarter's profits." These short-term considerations, however, sap management energies and drain corporate capital. The net effect is that companies risk their futures for immediate gains.

Ralph Winter cautioned: "U.S. companies are damaging their future vitality, and even viability, through reluctance to undertake long-term investments and new product development."

Evidence available from the patent office supports Winter's observations. The Patent Office reported that almost half of the 89,385 patents issued in 1987 were granted to foreign applicants, especially the Japanese. Since 1987, there has been no improvement in the trend. The number of foreign patents has doubled over the last 20 years. One Patent Office spokesperson said American companies are falling behind international competition because "U.S. industry plays a game of takeover and restructure."

We noted in chapter 3 that as the '90s decade began, Chrysler chairman Lee Iacocca found himself uncustomarily criticized, his company in trouble. Chrysler, it seems, became the victim of myopic management.

After Chrysler's spectacular recovery from disaster, Iacocca chose to ignore R&D expenditures, and instead, used millions of dollars of Chrysler's cash to redeem Chrysler stock and to acquire unrelated businesses (later unloaded at losses). Chrysler depleted its cash reserves and ended the 1980s with noncompetitive product lines. In the process it lost market position to Toyota and Honda and, perhaps, its long-term vitality. Predictions are that Chrysler will not survive as a major factor in the automobile business unless it attracts a financially strong partner.

The biggest factor behind myopic management may be the pressure of today's investors wanting an immediate payout instead of a gain in the price of the stock values several years down the road. Institutional shareholders — mutual funds, pensions, insurance companies, and foundations — driven by near-term objectives, dominate stock markets, accounting for 90 percent of stock trades on any given day. Institutional fund managers are compensated for performance — short-term profits derived from the investments they recommend. Their clients want quarter-to-quarter improvements with regard to their own portfolio objectives. The pressure for immediate profits is riveted on the roofs of the companies in which institutions invest. Any pause in profit growth, regardless of reason, is resisted. Goldman Sachs partner, Leon G. Cooperman, told professors Mitroff and Mohrman, authors of "The Slack is Gone: How the United States Lost its Competitive Edge in the World Economy," that "I don't think any company can afford a long-term investment today unless its management own 51% of it."

Short-term management strategies assume everything will always go well — that every plan and projection will be met. They ignore investments required to shape the company's future, leaving the company stripped of its staying power, flexibility, opportunity to innovate, and ability to withstand potential shock waves associated with rapid change, competition, or inevitable crises.

The Gatsby Grabbers

F. Scott Fitzgerald's *The Great Gatsby* is about a man, Jay Gatsby, who epitomizes the person driven by his cravings for social status and position. A Gatsby Grabber character combines his self-assurance and romantic hopes with his fixation about the magical powers of wealth-bought status. Status, not the money itself, is the driving force of the Gatsby Grabber. Marilyn Monroe may have described the Gatsby Grabber best when she pined, "I am not interested in money, I just want to be wonderful."

Soft-spoken, nattily dressed Ivan Boesky of Wall Street insider-trading fame told the graduating class at the University of California's Business School before his indictment that "Greed is all right. Greed is healthy." Boesky has been likened by Adam Smith in *Esquire* to Gatsby. The Gatsby Grabber complex also has shown up in the lifestyles of high-flying bankers who have been the subject of the 1980s governmental investigation resulting from the collapse of the thrift industry, such as the "indulgent and opulent" modus vivendi of Donald R. Dixon, the former chairman of the now insolvent, Dallas-based Vernon Savings and Loan. William Adler and Michael Binstein wrote in *Banker's Monthly* magazine that Dixon used Vernon's expense account and jet for European pleasure trips, that Vernon provided him a $10 million yacht for entertainment and a $2 million beach house in California. His S&L paid out more than $800,000 in house maintenance in a single year. The thrift also lavished him with a $900,000 art collection, a $56,000 wine collection, and a $157,000 gun collection. Dixon was the toast of the town. He also left his thrift ruined.

Concerned with the showmanship provided by their riches, the Gatsbys of the world find no place for anything that interferes with their grand designs. Companies are rarely able to finance the pace of their self-gratification.

Inside the Park

When I began to question the leadership of John Kearney as Park's chairman in late 1984, I learned firsthand how difficult and emotional it can be to convince a board of directors, particularly when they are long-time business friends, to listen to trouble.

Not surprisingly, at one point, I wanted to give up. I spent a weekend, emotionally exhausted, listing reasons why I should resign and reasons why I should continue. I filled a yellow pad with reasons why I should walk away — relief from stress, escape from possible lawsuits, time to do what I wanted. I had written down only a few reasons why I should hang on — feelings of responsibility were at the top of the page. But I questioned whether or not I had any responsibility; after all — where were the board members?

On a Sunday in December 1984, I called my lawyer and told him I was going to resign. "I know you will be relieved. I know you want to get away from this mess," he said. However, I was not relieved; I tossed all Sunday night. Monday morning I changed my mind. I had to follow through. I could not back down.

Was my change of heart from feelings of responsibility? Or was I, too, seeking to be the Master of Life's Events, blinded to the possibility of my own bad luck or failure?

A year later, when a director from another bank asked me, "Why did you do it? Why did you stick your neck out?"

I reflected, "I thought I could do it. I just didn't recognize — maybe I didn't want to recognize — the magnitude of Park's problems until it was too late."

Some Final Observations on the Broomhandle Philosophy and Intuition

Inside the Park

In the fall of 1986, I gave a speech before the Young President's Organization on Park Bank's crisis. During the question and answer period following the speech, one businessman in the audience asked me, "Before you finally made your move to replace Park Bank's senior management, why was it so difficult for you to recognize that the bank was headed for trouble?"

I reflected for a few moments, then said, "Because I didn't go with my gut!"

When I finally recognized the crisis signs, my gut, my intuitive right brain, started asking questions. But I lacked the knowledge and experience my feelings needed for solid support. The evidence presented by men I believed more versed in banking was at odds with how I felt, so I didn't go with my gut.

A person can approach problems from his left brain, the so-called logical side. Our training in school, particularly business and law schools, stress the value of logic and analysis; so for many, the left brain is dominant. For the left-brain dominant, the feeling is that analytical thinking is all that is required. The result is closure to the possibilities of intuitive insights.

Intuitive skills, though seemingly mysterious, are not metaphysical gifts, as broomhandle philosophers would have us believe. In fact, psychologists now recognize that the intuitive mind is an experienced mind, that intuition and expertise are aspects of the same kind of judgment. *Psychology Today* reported that Nobel laureate Herbert Simon, professor of psychology at Carnegie Mellon University, has concluded that intuitive people share an essential trait: *expertise*. Intuitive people are intuitive precisely because they have focused their attention and become knowledge-rich and masters at what they do.

Jay A. Conger writes in *The Charismatic Leader* that intuitive people "spend a lot of time reading and gathering information, and then synthesize it until they come up with an idea." The intuitive person is able to make well-grounded "real-time" decisions because mammoth amounts of diverse, on-point information are stored in his mind. When confronted with questionable data, he tests it against his wealth of knowledge and experience, sorts out the unimportant, synthesizes it, and visualizes a coherent whole.

Inside the Park (continued)

If I had had more experience as a banker when I went down to Park, would I have been more confident in my intuition? Would I have stood fast to my premonitions about what we were doing? When interviewed by the Tampa Bay Business Journal, *I told reporter Joe O'Neill that after I left my law firm and started to work on deregulation problems at Park Bank, I eventually began to sense that Park was plagued with other problems. Frustrated because I did not move fast enough in face of what ultimately occurred, I said: "I think honestly if I'd had more experience I would have spotted the problems maybe six months sooner."*

Does intuition that is not backed up by experience come out as naiveté? In that same article, O'Neill also wrote, "Dick Jacobs, insiders say, was probably too trusting of senior management when he came on board, and too much damage had already been done by the time he moved over from the law firm."

How about the gut-level experiences of other CEOs? After interviewing several of America's top corporate executives, Harry Levinson and Stuart Rosenthal reported in their book, *CEO*: "The single note of self-criticism struck by all leaders was that they hadn't followed their intuition and instincts as assiduously as they should have."

Chapter 5
Boardroom Blocks

You don't need a board of directors at all. It is a
rubber stamp. . . . [I]f the company is not doing as
well as it could, then what? What can the board of
directors do about it?

Harold Geneen

Myth and Reality in the Boardroom

State laws governing corporations provide, in one form or another, that "the business of the corporation shall be managed by a board of directors."

Management literature, however, provides limited guidance about the roles boards of directors are to play when leading and managing their corporations. Peter Drucker's *People and Performance: The Best of Peter Drucker on Management* makes no reference to boards of directors at all. Neither does *Leadership*, written by Pulitzer Prize winner James MacGregor Burns. Harold Geneen, former chairman of ITT, devotes a chapter to boards in *Managing*, but he views boards as less than useful, especially in tough times.

In contrast to the paucity of business literature about board governance, legal libraries are filled with information pinning responsibility for corporate mismanagement on boards of directors. Transforming CEOs, like Iacocca and Geneen, are heroes in today's corporate culture when companies fly high. But when corporations wind up in Black Holes, it's the boards of directors who are faulted for the carnage and suffer the ultimate liability for the pain and loss. The directors, legal literature is clear to point out, should have recognized the early warning signs.

No wonder the position of outside corporate director has been described in *Business Week* as "The Job Nobody Wants." Appointment to the position of director is no longer a prestigious salute to one's community status. Rather, directors, insured under D&O liability policies, have become deep-pocket targets for disgruntled, litigious stockholders, creditors, employees and regulators. In 1987, the National Association of Corporate Directors advised its members that a director's lawsuit, on the average, costs six years and $470,000 in legal fees — a heavy price for the one-out-of-five directors sued. Particularly when less than 5 percent of the suits ultimately go through trial.

Banking and financial institution directors — chosen, ironically, for their community status and business-attracting ability, not for their knowledge about banking or finance — are held to higher standards than directors of regular business corporations. In a bank director liability case, a Kentucky court held: "The community has a right to assume that the directorate does its duty. They invite the public to deal with the corporation, and when anyone accepts the invitation he has the right to expect reasonable diligence and good faith at their hands, and if they fail in either, they are responsible for the result."

The ABA (American Banker's Association) advises bank directors that neither "ignorance nor inexperience may be pleaded as an excuse." Furthermore, the ABA points out, entrusting management to bank officers who mismanage the affairs of the bank will not excuse bank directors from liability.

Inside the Park

After Park Bank failed, one of Park's directors was asked by a reporter about the bank's demise and its causes. He responded, "If you take a position on the board of directors of a bank and your area of expertise is not the loan area, then you have to trust the people who have

*banking experience. It's one thing to raise concerns in that kind of
environment when you're an expert. It's another thing to pinpoint [those]
concerns."*

*The board make-up at Park Bank was typical of most community
banks. Park's outside board came from dentistry, insurance, advertising,
law, real estate, fast food franchising, resorts, and accounting. All the
directors had been involved in relatively small, entrepreneurial businesses
and professional practices of the type Park sought to serve.*

*Only one of Park's original directors had extensive real estate
experience — the principal lending area of Park Bank. Only one had been
a professional banker, although most had had prior experience on bank
boards. The majority of those latter experiences was obtained, however,
on the board of a local affiliate of a regional bank chain where the
significant decisions were made at a distant home office.*

Despite the law cases and hard-nosed advice from organizations like
the ABA, there is little practical evidence that boards of directors do, in
fact, plan corporate strategies and manage companies, as required in state
statutes of incorporation. After supervising a study about director activity,
Professor Myles L. Mace reported in *Harvard Business Review*: that
". . . the generally accepted roles of boards, e.g., selecting top executives,
determining policy, measuring results, and asking discerning questions —
have taken on more and more the character of a well-established myth."

The Mace study was written in 1972. More recently, in 1989, Professor
Jay W. Lorsch, author of *Pawns or Potentates: the Reality of America's
Corporate Boards*, observed that a lot has happened since the Mace study.
Today, directors are less figureheads, more independent. However, after
surveying directors among the Fortune 1,000, Lorsch concludes that
though the legal mandate for directors to manage is clear, "problems arise
when [directors] try to act upon that authority." The problems come from
the managerial and human issues found in boardrooms. Thus, while
today's boardroom may be approaching textbook form, substance continues
as an issue yet to be resolved.

One of the unresolved boardroom issues, unfortunately for the health
of corporate America, is that directors seldom know when their companies
are on the rim until it is too late. Charles Schwab described the dilemma

well when a member of Bank of America's board: "I'm the last to know of critical developments."

In addition, directors are poorly positioned to do anything about trouble when it occurs. ITT's Geneen says that the fault for directors' nonperformance lies less with the personalities of individual directors than with the system of directorship, which makes "it virtually impossible for any individual director to fulfill his responsibility adequately."

Why Boards Don't See Early Warning Signs of Black Holes

The individual backgrounds of board members and the process of boardroom activities make it difficult, if not impossible, for directors to recognize warning signs of an approaching Black Hole in time to chart changes in the course of their starship.

There are several reasons:

- Outside directors are unfamiliar with the business and lack deep understanding about the personalities who run the business.

- Outside directors operate under the fallacious assumption that the I-can-hit-it-with-a-broomhandle philosophy works in the board-room.

- Information disseminated to board members does not lend itself to critical evaluation or inquiry because it is presented in a summarized, optimistic, fragmented format.

- Board members' analytical and interpretative styles are shaped by individual backgrounds and experiences. Thinking styles, honed in other places, can be inappropriate for the business at hand.

- Boardroom procedures are influenced by the psychology of group decisional processes.

An Unfamiliar Environment

When a business leader agrees to serve on the board of another company, he finds himself thrust into an unfamiliar environment. He may be the CEO of his own company (about 2/3 of outside directors are), but the world of the corporation on whose board he sits is a world that belongs to others — to friends or business associates perhaps, but not to him.

Beyond boardroom meetings, golf games, and a few cocktail parties, the outside board member has little contact with the operating leaders and managers of the business. The outside director may be a business or golfing buddy with a corporate executive, but he is most likely a stranger when it comes to judging his buddy's abilities to recognize Black Holes.

Lacking specific knowledge and information about the business, its leaders and managers, the director's decisional processes become distorted. Inquiry can only be superficial; innuendoes and subtleties are easily missed. Heavy reliance is placed on management's interpretations because other versions are not available.

Geneen summarized the board's dilemma: "The management team has reviewed and rehearsed what they are going to say so that they can make orderly, coherent presentations to the board, putting the best possible face on the facts. Directors come in only once a month. What do they know? What have they got to back them up — intuition, feelings, gossip overheard, or a report in the media? If one stubborn director continues, he is likely to be embarrassed by what he doesn't know. If he persists, he is casting himself in the role of a troublemaker, and no one likes to be a troublemaker. So what does he do except sit back in his chair, taste his coffee, and desist?"

A Fallacious Philosophy

Just like CEOs, outside directors often are proponents of the I-can-hit-it-with-a-broomhandle philosophy. Subscribing members believe their keen business instincts have universal application and supersede any requirement for specific company knowledge. As harmful as that philosophy is to CEOs when they deal with their own companies, it can be disastrous for outside directors who spend, on the average, fifteen days each year on corporate business.

There is simply no substitute for boardroom knowledge and information about the business that the board members are charged with managing. Without it, pontifications from their talent and experience, no matter how brilliant they sound, come out as hit-it-with-a-broomhandle philosophy bad hunches.

A natural result of director unfamiliarity (in addition to over-reliance on the CEO and management for interpretations of information) is over-reliance on today's intuitive substitute, the computer forecast. Unfortunately, the director who relies on computer-driven forecasts can be as misled as the director who relies on his uninformed intuition.

After analyzing three decades of business forecasts, Steven P. Schnaars, author of *Megamistakes: Forecasting and Myth of Rapid Technological Change*, wrote that 80 percent of business and product forecasting had been "completely off base." The reason, he says, is that the "people who made [the forecasts] have been seduced by technological wonder. . . . They fall in love with the technology and ignore the market. . . ." A deification of the projection, detached from the potential fallibility of its underlying assumptions and the unpredictability of reality, then occurs.

Inside the Park

When interviewed by Florida Trend *magazine's John Craddock, John Kearney described his various enterprises, including his computer software (cash flow forecasting) company and consulting services. He reflected: "I have an intuition about what is going to happen. And often I can figure out what you really want to do — which may not even be what you think you want. I can tell you whether you can turn those dollars into millions. I can project ahead for years. . . ."*

I now ponder — Did we on Park Bank's board adopt his deification of the projection process?

Careful analysis of the applicable factors involved in the computer forecast — the selection of appropriate assumptions — is critical. Assumptions cannot be chosen without careful analysis or by one who lacks broad-based experience. Any project forecast "works" if its suppositions were selected to "make it work."

Technology-driven cash flow forecasts were used to justify billions of dollars of leveraged buy-out junk bonds issued during the 1980s. Yet a high percentage of the LBO projections flopped. A rash of bankruptcies has been the result. Cash flow forecasts may justify a client company's ability to meet highly leveraged debt service in the minds of investment bankers, but in the reality of the business world, high leverage continues to be a disaster.

The inevitability of the cash flow projection, its linear reality, its precisely mathematical, irrefutable conclusion, is the source of its own fallibility. Life is simply not linear, it is chaotic.

Financial institutions easily fall into the forecast trap when they rely too heavily on cash flow forecasts in their loan underwriting and minimize other criteria. Necessary forecast assumptions — demographic and population trends; future interest, vacancy, or rental rates; construction costs; construction time-frames; product demand; competitive factors; and uncertain world events — can rarely be predicted with sufficient accuracy. Easily overlooked can be the adverse affects of unknown competitive projects, unseasonable weather, product liability claims, radical interest and inflation rate fluctuations, or regional or worldwide economic factors.

Heavy emphasis on the validity of the forecasted numbers can also shift attention from, and diminish consideration of, the company's most important inquiry — the skills and character strengths and gut-level abilities of its people to bring off the project as projected.

Inside the Park

Substituting computer analyses for careful thought turned out to be a major source of Park's loan problems. Caught up in the technology of John Kearney's state-of-the-art forecasting software, Park's lenders and loan committee paid too little attention to lending's not-so-intangibles — the borrowers' skills and abilities to perform.

Computer studies are only as good as their assumptions. And once written, computerized conclusions are difficult to refute — but rarely fulfilled. Park Bank's were no exception.

Presentation of Board Information

Director decisions are traditionally based upon information that is summarized, optimistically formatted, and fragmented. Boardroom information is, therefore, incomplete. Management presents the information in formats that make boardroom approval easy and routine.

The board's meeting agenda, also set by management, typically avoids consideration of matters that could have an adverse impact on the company — often because management doesn't recognize the existence of potential problems.

Incomplete information handicaps the board's ability to grasp the situation and ferret out appropriate questions. Thus, board members are unable to analyze committee or management reports in critical detail and, therefore, to challenge the inappropriate.

Information supplied by executive management can be overly optimistic, influenced by the executives' attitudes and biases about the strength of programs and strategies. Pros and cons are often minimized; the information presented typically ignores the possibility that programs may be off target. Recognized problems are described by management as external (i.e., related to the environment or economy), temporary, easily solvable, or of little significance.

The fragmentation of managerial responsibility varies from business to business. If the business is decentralized, there may be difficulty in obtaining a meaningful overview about the interrelationships between product lines, divisions, geographic locations, and subsidiaries. Specialized or divisional managers practice "turf protection," focusing on their particular responsibilities. Consequently, signs of potential problems are not recognized as having any overall business effect. Those managers, sensing isolation, take care of "their own." They are unaware or unconcerned about the rest of the company or about the Black Hole that could develop from their myopically directed efforts. Trouble signs are misinterpreted, rarely passed on, and, as a result, their fragmented reports to the boardroom have little relevancy or meaning.

Backgrounds and Thinking and Speaking Styles.

Further complicating the boardroom processes are the assumptions each board member takes into his job as a director. He views and evaluates boardroom proposals framed by his own experiences. His perspective, based upon that experience, may not be adequate for the task before him. Unique characteristics of the business may not be fully appreciated since he views what is going on within the company from his own experiences.

Most people assume that their own thinking styles and ways of approaching problem solving are similar to those with whom they interact. In addition most boardroom communication is done in shorthand, monitoring only superficially the health of the company. Outside directors, rushing from their own hectic worlds into the boardroom worlds of others, have scant time or enthusiasm to accomplish much more.

Information that the company's bottom-line is "up" or "solid" is quickly interpreted in the boardroom to mean that there are no emergencies today. Since their energies are required elsewhere, the directors demand no further inquiry; they are satisfied with the monitoring results and move on to other areas.

The shorthand communication used in boardroom meetings has another danger; it carries less meaning than in personal relationships. The amount of time board members and executive management spend together isn't enough to develop sensitivities to nuances of speech and to acquire shared meanings. Management's explanations to directors' perfunctory questions are, for the most part, hollow assurances of status, not facts. Such hollow assurances permit early signs of potential trouble to pass unnoticed.

The bottom line is that a board member is required to make quick superficial judgments in meetings with colleagues who are, likewise, making quick, superficial judgments — all based on the advice of people barely known.

How Groups Approach Decision Making

An understanding of group decisional processes is vital to an understanding of why boards miss trouble signs.

Importance of Majority Position

Group decisions, researcher Glen Whyte has written, are highly predictable; they tend to follow the option supported by the majority of its members at the outset. Group members strive for decisional uniformity because members desire harmony. Lack of member expertise on the issues also contributes to uniformity; silence and acquiescence by the less informed supports dominant members.

Risky Options

Whyte also pointed out that groups, such as boards of directors, faced with a decision framed as a choice between losses more often choose the risky option. Faced with a decisional quandary, groups (bank boards in particular) tend to choose the option that avoids certain immediate loss in favor of an alternative that holds a greater loss potential but "just might" work. The group simply ignores the risk, choosing the option that holds out some hope.

For example, a bank board considering a delinquent, under-secured loan will evaluate the bank's loss potential by comparing (1) the loss involved if the troubled loan is called and the inadequate collateral is foreclosed now, against (2) the bank's future loss if the loan is restructured, thus allowing time for increased product demand, improved borrower management, inflation, interest rate changes, or simply luck to bail the project out. Of course, if the reworked loan fails to accomplish the bank's objectives, the additional investment by the bank will increase the losses.

In quantitative terms, if the board is faced with deciding between a certain $1 million immediate foreclosure loss and a potential $1.5 million refinancing loss that is perceived to be only 60 percent certain (a $900,000 present value), the board tends to choose the risky refinancing option with the 40 percent bailout opportunity. The bank's risk is increased in absolute terms by $500,000 in the process.

Risks, of course, are easily underestimated. The risky choice rarely works and the bank's loss, if the second alternative is selected, will most likely be $1.5 million (or, if pressured by escalation dilemmas, even more).

Escalation Dilemmas

A board's tendency to select risky options is related to the concept of escalation dilemma discussed in the preceding chapter. When faced with a difficult or declining situation, boards, like individuals, are likely to put increased effort and additional resources into existing situations rather than seek new, innovative approaches. What is in fact a risky option is not viewed as risky because the board is merely authorizing an extension of previously approved activity.

Professor Barry M. Straw of the University of California and Jerry Ross from the *Institute Européen d'Administration des Affaires* (France), writing for Science magazine, have concluded that escalation dilemmas — "decisional pathologies" — are more likely to occur in situations where there is a long lag time between investment and return. In those cases, they say, "shortfalls in revenue or outcomes may not be monitored closely or cause alarm, since losses are (at least initially) expected to occur." That description fits the dilemma surrounding project loan workouts.

Inside the Park

In retrospect, during the early stages of Park's problems, Park's loan workout decisions were oriented toward risk.The escalation dilemma, the Peter Drucker's it just-might-work syndrome, was in effect. Faced with sure losses, time and again Park Bank approved project-continuation alternatives: refinancings, loan extensions, capital injections, putting people on the boards of the troubled companies, venturing distressed properties with a bank subsidiary. In one case, Park's board members bought a troubled $500,000 loan from the bank at its face value and attempted to rehabilitate the project with the developer.

Each troubled loan was analyzed. Computerized workout projections demonstrating best case, worst case possibilities were spewed out. During those early workout days, Park's management and board rarely demanded loan repayments that required the bank to recognize a sure, measured loss. The optimistic projection, the plan that "just-might-work" if things went right, was selected.

In the end, the restructurings rarely helped and never worked in accordance with the optimistic projections.

When Park's troubled loans were realistically faced, the losses exceeded all estimates of the loss exposure involved. The sad result was that the original troubled loan and the reworked loan both produced adverse results. For example, in the case of the $500,000 loan bought by the board, the board increased its investment in the project to almost $650,000 and lost the entire investment.

For Park Bank and its board, it was, as Neil Diamond sang, "a lesson too late for the learning."

Groupthink

Boardroom shortcomings are further accentuated by groupthink, the collective pressures brought upon the decisional practices of individual group members by the group itself. Groupthink causes a deterioration of mental efficiency, reality testing, and moral judgment. A group's drive for consensus tends to override its desire to appraise alternative courses of action.

Negative Groupthink Pressures

Researchers call the the group's tendency to make risky, unwise decisions the "risk shift phenomenon."

Fred Luthans, wrote in *Organizational Behavior*, that negative groupthink pressures lead board members to:

- believe in their own invulnerability, causing them to have unwarranted optimism and take excessive, unreasonable risks;

- rationalize early warning signs of trouble, causing them to misinterpret data in a nonthreatening way;

- have unquestioned belief in their inherent morality, blocking their abilities to recognize questionable stances on issues;

- stereotype opposition as unpopular, evil, weak, or stupid;

- insist on a level of loyalty that is unquestioning of the group's values and perceptions;

- provide group self-censorship in regard to any deviation from group consensus;

- create an illusion of unanimity, treating silence as consent.

Boardroom Protocols

Corporate boardroom protocols also add groupthink pressures and impede sound decision-making both during normal times and in crisis. In *Pawns or Potentates,* Professor Lorsch calls the protocols the "norms of delicate behavior and undiscussability." They include: the CEO's use of private discussions with individual directors prior to meetings to gain consensus and avoid give-and-take discussions within meetings; the unwritten rule that the CEO is not to be criticized in board meetings; the understanding that a director does not assert himself over fellow directors or contact fellow directors outside meetings; and directors speaking as if they measure their considerations in terms of responsibilities to stockholders rather than their other constituencies. Lorsch concludes: "With so many topics publicly undiscussable, boards often react too slowly when issues arise and allow small, management problems to fester and grow into major crises."

Sources of Groupthink Pressures

Research indicates two principal sources of boardroom groupthink pressures: the operations within the boardroom and the corporation's culture.

A principal source of operational groupthink pressures is the common board practice of operating by consensus — the unwritten rule that board agreements should be unanimous. However, the decision to act by consensus squelches any opportunity for open dissent or realistic consideration of alternatives. Unpopular, deviant, or alternate views are ignored or suppressed.

Another potential groupthink source is found in today's trend toward the use of a wide variety of board committees, such as audit, compensation, nominating, and strategic planning. The purpose of committees is laudable: to increase the expertise of committee members about whatever the committee charge is. The problem, however, is that board members rarely question or debate committee reports. Most reports are accepted without discussion. The board members engage in decisional coasting, relying on the committee members instead of their own minds.

Inside the Park

When we organized ourselves as the board of directors of Park Bank, we discussed dissent, open discussion, and how we would vote. We decided that we would always have open discussions. Any board member could say anything. But when we voted, we would vote together; we would decide things as a team, as one. We operated by consensus.

My research concludes that Park's boardroom experience was not that unusual, despite today's trends toward increased director independence. Boards of directors, even when dominated by outside board members, tend to operate by consensus. Members commit to working things out together. Board members are pressured by groupthink and boardroom protocols to be team players, to support management, and to bet on the CEO. In most cases, even when boards have independent nominating committees, the CEO nominates the slate of directors. Usually the slate runs without opposition. Therefore, there is a strong tendency for board members to support the views of the CEO.

Rarely are board members willing to become aggressive and run the risk of being branded troublemakers. Fewer directors yet are willing to admit any lack of knowledge about boardroom issues. Their silent consent is taken as an affirmative vote.

When is a board most vulnerable to groupthink?

I discussed this problem with Professor William R. Boulton at the University of Georgia's Business School. I said that one of the problems we had on the Park Bank board was that the members knew each other too well. His reply startled me. "Not so," he said. "If board members had known each other as well as you thought they did, there would be no reason to operate by consensus."

The dangerous stage for boards, Boulton believes, is the in-between stage, when they know each other pseudo-well but are not close enough to talk freely. During the pseudo-well stage no board member wants to offend any other member.

Psychiatrist M. Scott Peck calls a group characterized by pseudo-well friendship a "pseudo-community." At this stage, the group attempts to avoid individual differences at any cost. The group thus ignores and avoids problems and troublesome issues. Dr. Peck says groups are ineffective until they free themselves of such behaviors.

Groupthink Pressures from Corporate Culture.

Businesses in an exciting start-up stage tend to have cultures that Yoash Wiener has described as "elitist-charismatic." Corporate cultures bound by elitist values stress the importance of the company and its status, producing a species of corporate nationalism. There are strong feelings of pride among employees and perceptions of corporate superiority. Charisma builds on the employees' identification with the values of their corporate leader. Persons in elitist-charismatic organizations are highly susceptible to groupthink illusions of invulnerability and self-righteousness.

Inside the Park

In chapter 3, in the context of the discussion about the influence of Park's elitist culture, I noted that in the spring of 1984, the FDIC presented Park Bank's board with its 1983 examination report. The report was tough — hard on us. The FDIC concluded Park's loan portfolio was in an unacceptable condition, a product of fast growth and too much real estate lending. The Park Bank board was shocked, but Park's chairman called a special board meeting and informed the board that there was nothing serious to worry about, our plight was brought about by unsophisticated FDIC personnel unable to examine us accurately. "Regulation hasn't caught up with us yet," the chairman said. "The regulators don't understand us."

He reminded us that we had always been different, we had always been mavericks of a sort. If we were going to continue our leadership we had to select our own course, set our own pace. Ultimately, the FDIC would "recognize" the nature of deregulated banking and "catch up" to us.

No one on the board stood up to, questioned, or refuted, his evaluation!

Did the pressures of groupthink operating within Park Bank's boardroom to the up-beat of its elitist-charismatic culture influence otherwise successful businessmen to overlook and discount early warning signs that Park Bank was being sucked over the rim of the Black Hole?

An 18th-century German poet, Schiller, said, "Anyone taken as an individual is tolerably sensible and reasonable. As a member of a crowd, he at once becomes a blockhead."

Would Schiller reach the same conclusion about boards of directors?

The Last to Know

It should now be clear that when signs of potential crisis appear dimly on the horizon, whether or not a business will crash or turn its course depends upon the interpretations selected and the meanings assigned to the clues available.

It should also be clear from our discussions that the CEO has primary responsibility for determining his company's destiny. The CEO delivers the corporate gospel, interprets business reality, and, through his interpretations, architects his company's future. He encourages or discourages openness and mobility in communications that are so vital for crisis detection.

When a CEO embodies personality characteristics that permit him to deny or ignore business reality, his company is headed for the rim unless the board of directors is prepared, able, and willing to act in time. Unfortunately, the board's wisdom usually comes too late. Historically, boards have been the last to know about crisis.

Part III

The Crisis Environment

The Place Where Hell Bubbles Up
Trapper's Diary describing Yellowstone

Chapter 6

The Rim People

At the narrow pass there is no brother and there is no friend.

Indian Proverb

,

What is it like on the rim of a Black Hole?

In his book *When it Hits the Fan*, Gerald C. Meyers, former chairman of American Motors, was direct about the effect of the rim's chaos: "An unmanaged crisis is a horror. . . . It is awful."

Lee Iacocca was less direct. In *Iacocca*, his description of Chrysler's crisis concentrates on the "Hail Mary" passes thrown to pull Chrysler out during the final seconds of its fourth quarter. In retrospect, however, he reflected that if he had known what Chrysler's crisis was going to be like, he never would have taken it on. He wrote: "For a variety of reasons, Chrysler turned out to be a hell of a lot more than I bargained for. But once I was in, once I had decided what I wanted to do, I never thought seriously of leaving. Of course, that's not always the best policy. People sometimes die with that attitude. They get swamped and overtaken by events, and they're still holding on as the waters rise above them. . . . I couldn't imagine that anything . . . could be *that* bad. I was wrong. In retrospect, I have to admit there were several times at Chrysler when I came close to drowning."

The Place Where Hell Bubbles Up

In the early 19th century, fur trappers, returning from the Yellowstone region of the Rocky Mountains, described their trek through "thunderous geysers and craters of scalding mud" and called the geyser region *"the place where hell bubbles up."*

That is what the rim of the Black Hole is — the place where hell bubbles up. In this and the next two chapters I describe the tensions emanating from the rim country environment:

- The rim people who attack the collapsing business with a shark-like frenzy (this chapter);

- The legal volcanos that erupt on the rim of a Black Hole (chapter 7);

- The adverse publicity — the volcanic ash — that blankets the rim's landscape (chapter 8); and

- The blocks that thwart positive action within the company itself (chapter 9).

The Rim People

Something happens on the rim. Not everybody is affected; but I was surprised by who and by the numbers of people the rim country affected.

Sometimes Park's rim country was like a frenzy. Normally docile customers, suppliers, creditors, and stockholders struck viciously at our troubled company when they felt threatened. They often reverted to destructive, primitive forms of behavior. They wanted theirs — now. They became the *rim people.*

Inside the Park

We had had a tough weekend of bad publicity after we announced our 1985 third quarter losses. TV cameramen and reporters stationed themselves outside Park's northside Pinellas Park branch where they expected a chaotic run on the bank.

There were several people, mostly retired, in the lobby. They were concerned about the safety of their deposits, and the carefully informed tellers were doing a good job of explaining how FDIC insurance made depositor money safe.

Customer lines were long, our tellers tense, exhausted from their efforts to calm the retired customers haunted by memories of the Depression, which had occurred before most of our young staff were born. There was a minor deposit runoff, but no disaster.

Then, somebody's grandmother, close to 70, maybe 75, well-dressed, not over five feet tall came into the Pinellas Park branch lobby and made it clear that she knew about Park Bank's problems.

She screamed out that Park Bank "needed her business," that Park Bank was going to have to make concessions to keep her a customer — free checking, high interest — or else! She pounded on the teller counter with her cane. She berated the 20-year old teller as if the teller herself had piloted Park Bank to the rim. The teller, shaken and in tears, had to be led from the lobby. The elderly woman stood there, glowering with bitter satisfaction, milking the moment for vindication, and stalked out. It took the branch manager several hours to calm our teller down. She almost quit.

Rim people focus on their targeted end without any apparent understanding that their end is a product of their means. If means are wrong or unethical, ends will be wrong or unethical too. But rim people are not bogged down by ethical dilemmas. They proceed with a cavalier, Machiavellian disregard for the rights of others. Their actions can only be justified through a distorted view that the people whose rights are being disregarded have, at that moment, no rights.

Dr. Douglas LaBier captured the rim-people mentality in his book *Modern Madness,*when he described the remarks of an unidentified TV reporter: "Even when you feel you are displaying insensitivity to the point of being inhuman, you have to hang tough. Even when you feel you are doing something disgusting, or merely in bad taste, you have to follow through. Like sticking a mike under the nose of an old woman whose grandson has been stabbed to death. If I fail to do it, and a competing station did, my boss would ask me, 'Where were you when the other channel was getting the good stuff?' "

I had an experience at Park Bank that was close to that encounter.

Inside the Park

Newspaper publicity had been particularly negative. Rumors that we were on the verge of failure were rampant. TV cameras visited our branches with regularity to be ready to film the anticipated long lines of depositors withdrawing funds as we crashed. But we had kept our calm, and customers, though concerned, hadn't panicked. The TV stations started playing brief stories during their local newscasts about our plight: flashing pictures of the bank, interviewing customers, asking unanswerable questions.

I was constantly being called for interviews. Finally, I felt I had to respond to one of the local TV stations; I felt that not speaking would do more harm than dealing with the station directly. So I talked to the TV reporter first, "off the record." I explained my concern that sensational news-making could lead to panic and a run on the bank. I urged him to be cautious in his approach. He outlined his questions and what was involved. The whole interview, when aired, would be brief, two or three minutes at the most. The reporter's proposed questions sounded responsible and appropriate. I hoped the interview would lead to some community understanding. It progressed well — until the end.

Suddenly, the reporter leaned forward and the camera zeroed in.

"Park's troubles . . . tell me, Mr. Jacobs, has there been any 'hanky-panky'?"

Fortunately, when I had become CEO of Park Bank, one of the first things I did was to have Park's internal auditors, under the supervision of independent legal counsel, examine the bank for possible illegal transactions. Nothing illegal was discovered.

I was able to answer, "No."

But the implication of the question, together with prior publicity, was enough to erode customer confidence. There was a minor run on deposits the next day. (A later investigation by Park Bank's counsel Mike Klein turned up some evidence that certain loan officers had been involved in a financing scheme akin to Wall Street's Achilles heel, parking stock. A report was prepared for the FDIC. After the bank's collapse, four loan officers were indicted and three convicted. The incident is discussed in a later chapter.)

From MyLai to the Rim

In *People of the Lie*, Psychiatrist F. Scott Peck describes group evil as the "MyLai syndrome." In 1968, a group of American soldiers were on a search and destroy mission, searching out Vietcong soldiers in the Quang Ngai province of South Vietnam. In the course of their search, the first platoon of C Company, commanded by Lieutenant William L. Calley, Jr., herded frightened Vietnamese villagers together and gunned them down. By the time the massacre was over, C Company had killed six hundred unarmed women, children, and aged villagers. The massacre was witnessed by hundreds of Americans; but only one soldier tried to stop it. His efforts ignored, he quit. Dr. Peck asked: "How is it that approximately five hundred men, the majority of whom were undoubtedly not evil as individuals, could all have participated in an act as monstrously evil as that at MyLai?"

For the most part, rim people act individually. Thus, the rim experience may seem a far distance from MyLai. But there is some invisible cord — perhaps tied together by the adverse publicity that occurs so frequently on the rim — linking rim people together, causing their reactions to feed off each other. The result is a silent, surging, seemingly conspiratorial, force pressing against the troubled business, driving it even further toward the edge of the Black Hole.

Psychologists have discovered that groups have a style and a personality of their own — primitive and emotional. Dr. Peck wrote, "The behavior of groups is strikingly immature. . . . They are, from a psychological standpoint, less than the sum of their parts. . . . "

I am reminded of an experience my wife and I had when we trekked across Africa in 1982. Early one morning in the Ngorngoro Crater near the Serengetti, we came upon two cheetah shortly after they had taken a Thomson gazelle. As the cheetah finished eating, a pack of jackals moved in, gingerly at first, but then boldly. Soon they were engaged in a mad feeding frenzy on the remains of the gazelle, fighting among themselves for the spoils.

That feeling exists on the rim of the Black Hole. Rim people seem to become infected with madness.

Dr. Peck says one of the reasons for the primitive behavior in the context of a crisis environment is over-specialization. Specialization results in fractional responsibility and in fragmentation of conscience. When responsibility is fractionalized, no one accepts responsibility for, nor seemingly grasps the whole.

For example, people who engaged in atomic research were far-removed from the ultimate decision to deploy and the ultimate effect of the atomic bomb. Those who raise tobacco do not take responsibility for smoke-related deaths or relate to the hypocrisy of a government that subsidizes tobacco crops while spending millions on cancer and pollution research.

When responsibility is fragmented, participants escape the ultimate decision burden. Fragmentation is the ultimate form of buck-passing. Fragmentation gives those of us who are buck-passers the excuse to separate ourselves from ultimate responsibility, saying that whatever decision is made is not "mine" and has no effect on "my conscience." After all, "It wasn't my job!"

Inside the Park

A group of stockholders brought a lawsuit after Park's collapse. The suit was brought against the directors (including myself), several officers, accountants, my former law firm, another law firm, and others. It alleged that the collapse of our bank was related to a RICO-type fraud scheme carried on by the directors and the other defendants. (A RICO lawsuit is brought under a federal law aimed at racketeers. It is discussed in the next chapter.) The lawyers filing the suit called a press conference to announce their "discovery" of a Park Bank massive fraud conspiracy and their litigation plans. They then moved for quick court action to steamroll their way to victory; however, the defendants organized in time, and the court dismissed the complaint on legal grounds before the plaintiffs' tactics could be carried further.

The plaintiffs then sought additional parties to join them in a revised suit, presumably to share litigation costs and to increase pressure on the defendants and their insurance carriers. I received a call from a person I had known for years, apologizing for joining in the litigation. He said he meant none of us any harm — he just wanted to recover from our insurance. He pointed out to me that the lawyers bringing the lawsuit told him this was how to do it, and a lot of others seemed to agree.

I slumped in my chair, bewildered. Does he know that his lawyers and his lawsuit are publicly accusing us of fraud and racketeering? Does he know insurance doesn't pay for fraud or racketeering claims? Does he know how humiliating it is to suffer through that kind of publicity? Does he have any empathy for the families of the people sued?

A doctor who was a Park Bank stockholder and a client of my former law firm, joined in the lawsuit. Afterward, he called one of the firm's lawyers and asked that he defend him against a malpractice claim. The lawyer was astounded. He said, "Doctor, you just joined in a lawsuit suing me and my partners for defrauding you! How can I possibly represent you?"

The doctor replied, "I don't see what you're concerned about; we're just after the insurance. I get sued all the time for something. I'd be disappointed if I have to go to court without you."

If everybody is joining in, if other plaintiffs are only after insurance, if no harm is meant to the people sued, if the lawyers say it's okay, why not?

Rim people build their own form of groupthink, and solidarity is cemented by enemy-creation. When a group of people join in litigation, their common defendants are branded as the enemy, the legal process assumes the dimensions of all-out war, and the plaintiff-group becomes cemented and united.

Inside the Park

A person who had worked in the trust department of Park Bank and then went into private practice as a financial planner heard some shocking gossip about me from a client of his, who was one of the plaintiffs in the lawsuit filed against us.

His client had been to a meeting of the plaintiffs and their lawyers. Someone had verbally attacked me and claimed that, just as the bank was collapsing, I had approved a large loan to an insider, contrary to bank regulations.

When the financial planner asked me about what he had heard, I said, "Don't you remember that the FDIC was in our bank during the last weeks of Park's existence? Even if I had wanted to be so stupid, I could never have done such a thing; we consulted with the regulators about every major transaction and I met with them frequently for that purpose."

He apologized and said, "Boy, those lawyers sure have those plaintiffs worked up!"

Stress Takes Its Toll

Stress is a major factor shaping the conduct of rim people. People suffering prolonged periods of stress regress into primitive forms of behavior. Psychologist Abraham Maslow constructed a hierarchy of needs humans strive to satisfy. At the base are primitive physiological needs; at the high end are self-actualization needs. When people find themselves in difficulty, Maslow found that they retreat rapidly from activity at the apex and concentrate on activity to ensure that their primitive, basic needs are secured.

Maslow's findings are consistent with my Park Bank Black Hole experiences. People having problems repaying their loans, in particular, view financial loss as personality destruction and can react aggressively, sometimes violently, to a bank's efforts to collect their delinquent loans.

Inside the Park

His real estate loans were delinquent; the real estate market had gone soft, and to make matters worse, his project had suffered hurricane damage. He was no longer up to dealing with his project. He wanted out. We had had "ours," he said — interest payments; now he wanted "his" — freedom from debt. We "owed him." He wanted to take back the personal assets he had used as collateral for his project loan so he could start over. He wanted his antique cars, house, and a piece of raw land released. I knew Park Bank couldn't afford the write-off charge to our capital if we acquiesced, and I told him we could not in good conscience grant his wishes.

I suggested alternatives, which he rejected. Instead he threatened to sue Park Bank for causing his losses; his projects were standing unsold, the result of an overbuilt condo market on our gulf beaches and hurricane Elena damage.

He reasoned that he could show the court we interfered with his management of the troubled project; thus, responsibility for his losses were ours. He needed testimony to support his plan and approached a key person in his organization, "refreshing his memory" about how Park Bank had interfered in his affairs. Fortunately for us, the key person refused to cooperate, recognized what the troubled borrower was attempting, and called us. I was able to confront the borrower and his attorney and dissuade him from suing.

Douglas LaBier wrote in *Modern Madness*: "Stress is the test for goodness. The truly good are they who in time of stress do not desert their integrity, their maturity, their sensitivity. Nobility might be defined as the capacity not to regress in response to degradation, not to be blunted in the face of pain, to tolerate the agonizing and remain in tact."

Bait for the Bengal Tiger

Tourists from all over the world come to the Nepalese jungles of Chitwan on the India border to search for the rare, beautiful Bengal tiger. But the tiger is nocturnal, rarely visible during daylight hours. The tiger hunts by surprise, using stealth, under cover of darkness. Tourists have a problem finding the tiger. However, Tiger Tops, a lodge on the edge of the Chitwan jungle, has attracted a worldwide clientele because it brings the rare tiger to its not-so-rare tourists, who pay hundreds of dollars for an experience of a lifetime.

To improve people's viewing chances, a carefully organized program of baiting is carried out at Tiger Tops. A buffalo calf is staked out on the edge of the jungle. In a blind, not 50 yards away, Nepalese *shikaris* wait. The moment the tiger nears the buffalo, the *shikaris* dash back to the Tiger Tops lodge for the tourists.

The Tiger Tops brochure describes the experience: "Nobody who has approached one of the tiger blinds in the dark will forget the experience of walking silently up the path, with green fireflies gliding among the treetops overhead and the jungle absolutely still except for the zing of insects."

Everybody loves the experience, everybody except the buffalo calf.

Soon the buffalo's nostrils widen, moist and red, snorting blood. Its eyes bulge with terror. It smells the tiger. It tries to escape, but its chain tightens and becomes taut. The tiger fells the calf and gorges itself. Tourists watch the kill, done as God never intended. The arena is even lit, permitting the kill to be documented on color film. (I might note that, though I have been fortunate enough to search for Bengal tiger photographic opportunities in the wilds of Chitwan, I also have been fortunate enough to avoid Tiger Tops.)

In Nepal, a buffalo calf is used as bait; and a horrible, heartless experience takes place so that lodges can be filled with tourists, and the tourists' passions for once-in-a-lifetime photographic opportunities can be satisfied.

Is it possible that on the rim of the Black Hole the legal system uses people as bait — with a similar lack of feelings for the terror and horror?

As I was organizing this material, I paused for coffee and read over clippings from three months of newspaper articles. I was astounded by the pattern portrayed by events!

The March 14, 1987 *St. Petersburg Times* reported that Joseph Green Brown, whose death warrant was stayed in 1983, fifteen hours before his scheduled execution, was freed by a Federal Appeals Court because his conviction had been based on the false testimony of the state's witness. Reversing the conviction, the court ruled that the assistant State's Attorney in Tampa, Florida, had "knowingly used false testimony."

"There are those who criticize an adversary system that drives lawyers more toward winning than to realizing justice," said an August 1, 1987, follow-up story in the *St. Petersburg Times*.

When former Labor Secretary Raymond J. Donovan was prosecuted and found not guilty, a May 27, 1987, editorial in the *St. Petersburg Times* entitled "Unjust prosecution" criticized the prosecution saying that ". . . there are lessons in this pitiful case for everyone, especially over-zealous prosecutors." On the same day, an equally critical *Wall Street Journal* editorial questioned: "Who polices the prosecutors?"

Donovan's legal fees for his two-year defense of the case exceeded $13 million. After seven months of trial, the jury decided after one vote that Donovan was not guilty. The foreman of the jury said, " 'The indictment should never have been brought.' "

A June 11, 1987, *St. Petersburg Times* article entitled "Panel would include suspects in computer file," reported on a federal government proposal to increase national law enforcement computer data-bank files by including information about people suspected of crimes. Thus, people could be scarred for life though they may well be innocent of wrongdoing.   .

On June 15, 1987, *The National Law Journal* reported on the State of California's prosecution of movie director John Landis for deaths resulting from a helicopter crash in the filming of the "Twilight Zone." After 90 witnesses and 100 days of trial, the jury quickly found Landis not guilty. After reading the jury's verdict, the foreperson of the jury said, "You don't prosecute people for unforeseeable accidents." Mr. Landis, emotionally hurt and nearly broke, was outraged at a "terribly and completely dishonest prosecution."

A 1987 study by bank regulators, reported that fraud and misconduct of "epidemic proportions" was behind the failure of California thrifts. A June 18, 1987, *Wall Street Journal* article noted that the study's findings conflicted with the thrift industry's position that most of the industry's problems were attributable to the economic downturn. (In 1990, *Wall Street Journal* reporters Paulette Thomas and Thomas E. Ricks concluded that the principal S&L losses were not fraud-related. By 1990, the thrift problem, its genesis complex and diverse, had revealed more of its roots and had become a full-blown nationwide disaster rather than a localized sunbelt complication.)

On June 17, 1987, the *New York Times* reported on Justice Department criticism of the office of special prosecutor. A spokesperson for the department described "egregious abuses of power" by lawyers for whom "nothing is too trivial" because, "no independent counsel makes a reputation by deciding not to prosecute. . . ."

These stories are examples of people, and perhaps entire industries, used as bait — of governmental tyranny that, two centuries ago, led to the founding of our country and our revolt against England. In a contemporaneously written editorial, the editors of the *Wall Street Journal* concluded after describing abuses within our justice system, that "James Madison must be spinning in his grave." George Orwell's *1984* may well have been reincarnated.

Some of America's greatest business leaders have found themselves similarly used as bait. Thomas Watson was prosecuted for alleged violations of anti-trust laws before he founded IBM. After two years of appeals, his conviction was reversed; the charges were dismissed. Friends said that the experience never left Watson, affecting him deeply the rest of his life.

Armand Hammer was falsely charged with a crime early in his business career. He wrote in his autobiography how he set out, successfully, to clear his name: "Guilt and innocence are more than legal terms. . . . The innocent man cannot be free until the world acknowledges his innocence."

Walking Wounded

As difficult as it is to deal with the conduct of customers, suppliers, and others on the rim who have assumed primitive behavior, nothing terrifies more than the conduct of those sworn to uphold and defend the law who have become rim people. The crisis environment is filled with litigation and investigation. The volcanic atmosphere is ripe for abuse by those furthering their own interests or who chose to use the circumstances to scapegoat on others.

Some lawyers approach civil litigation, the kind most frequent on the rim, with callousness and disregard for the rights of others. Pursuing the "let's sue everybody on every theory we can think of and let the court straighten it out" philosophy — using the law as a legal dragnet — is not an uncommon approach for rim people who are members of the bar; in fact, these suits occur so frequently, that they are rarely viewed as wrong.

Abuses by lawyers bringing suits under the federal RICO Act in civil litigation, forcing settlements because defendants fear the risks of treble damages and of being accused of racketeering within their own communities, has been widely criticized. Legislative amendments to the Act have been proposed, but to date any action directed toward modifying the sledge-hammer effects of RICO has been thwarted by pressure groups and lack of Congressional interest.

Inside the Park

After Park Bank's collapse, my wife and I took a month off to rest and regroup, trekking through India and Nepal. I had turned the bank over to the FDIC, satisfied that what could have been done, was done. Park's officers had gone so far as to prepare a briefing book for the FDIC and Chase Bank (who won the FDIC bid for Park's corpse) to smooth out the transition.

A spokesman for the FDIC told a St. Petersburg Times *reporter, "Mr. Jacobs appears to have done a very good job of making sure everything was in order, so he could make it easier for us." Park's team had surrendered with dignity. Depositors had survived without a loss, their deposits assumed by Chase Bank. Park's staff was hired by Chase, so jobs were secure. Chase was so pleased with the way things were when they walked in that they asked that I consult with them for six months to ease the transition, a rare request under the circumstances.*

A premium of $63 million had been paid by Chase to the FDIC as its price for Park Bank. At the time, I believed the premium would provide enough money to cover Park's potential loan losses and, perhaps, leave something left over for its senior debt holders and stockholders. (Later, events proved my estimate wrong; losses exceeded the FDIC premium.) So, when I left for India, I felt sad that we had failed, but good that we had been able to hold the bank together and preserve as much as we did.

When I returned from India, however, I was met by the sheriff who served me with the vicious stockholder lawsuit, described earlier in this chapter. Over 20 persons, including bank officers and directors, investment bankers, lawyers, and accountants, were sued, accused of participating in an alleged Park Bank conspiracy aimed at defrauding stockholders.

Several Park Bank officers who were sued were relatively new employees at Park Bank, brought in to be part of Park's solution. Any minimal amount of research by the plaintiff's attorneys would have revealed the dates these people started their employments and their actual duties at Park Bank. Research would have shown that it was impossible for them to have been involved in Park's troubles, as alleged in the lawsuit.

Our community was continually reminded in the press of the alleged RICO scheme in which we all supposedly participated. Those reminders were a constant source of humiliation. Officers who left the employ of Chase during the litigation said that the allegations followed them as they sought new jobs. Marriages were strained by the pressures involved.

Each of those officers had performed responsibly through to the end, smoothing out what could have been a very costly crash landing for our community. Yet they found themselves in a position like the unappreciated, shell-shocked troops returning from Viet Nam, shot at by the stockholders who should have applauded their efforts and courage.

Means and Ends

The proposition that laudable ends aren't laudable if not pursued by laudable means can escape intense advocates of any cause, influencing them to use bait. In November 1990, a *Wall Street Journal* editorial criticized consumer advocate Ralph Nader for releasing a knowingly false report entitled "Insurance: The Next Industry in Crisis? A Report on the Financial Solvency of America's Top 20 Property and Casualty Insurers." The *Journal* said that despite knowing the report was inaccurate, Nader's organization issued it anyway "because it would serve its own long-term interests." The *Journal* concludes:

The worst part of this flawed report was not the defamation of some of the country's best-run insurers. The worst part of this flawed report is disinformation to consumers by a group that claims to speak for consumers.

Inside the Park

A year after Park Bank's collapse, I was in New York on business. My cab driver, who spoke with a heavy Greek accent, was a frustrated would-be lawyer. He had wanted to go to law school, but couldn't figure out how to afford it. On our drive to Manhattan from Kennedy airport, we engaged in an animated conversation about lawyers — in particular, about prosecutors.

Talking excitedly as he drove, he discussed central Florida's United States Attorney whose persecutory activities were at the time frequently in the news. He said, "That federal prosecutor in Florida is a beaut! He puts the crooks away!"

I replied, "He sure does; but he's been known to be political, do things for show — prosecute innocent people along the way while he's making a name for himself. The papers have been criticizing him for it."

"Wel-l-l-l," the cab driver answered, philosophically, "that may be true; but it's just a price we pay. A few innocent people have to suffer. It's like war. That's the way life is!"

Obviously, he had never been asked to play the role of the buffalo calf in Chitwan.

Chapter 7

Volcanoes of Litigation

*America's love affair with lawsuits has escalated
. . . to suits against corporate directors and officers.
Meanwhile, megatort awards have also multiplied.
The sharp rise in lawyers may simply be feeding the
frenzy.*

Edwin A. Finn, Jr.

The rim environment is explosive with litigation, lots of it. It's time-consuming, expensive, and robs an already distressed company of liquidity and energy at the very time when both are in short supply.

The litigation explosion is an attempt by litigants to right themselves in the face of an insecure world, to gain advantage at the expense of the rim-trapped company and its personnel, and to sort out unclear, competing interests and damages resulting from the business's crash.

Risk Shifting and the Litigation Lottery

When people suffer loss of control, they frequently seek a way to explain chaos in terms that avoid ego destruction. So they shift blame to others.

Dr. Anne Wilson Schaef has called the use of scapegoats a societal addiction. She said it reflects an uncompromising unwillingness on the part of people, overwhelmed by society, to take responsibility for their lives. For those inflicted, litigation has become the favorite forum, an opportunity for the inflicted to vindicate their lives and affirm their validity.

The source of the phenomenon is rooted in the feelings of people that life has gone beyond individual control; that people are victimized by events that are incomprehensible and that cannot be influenced in any sane manner. When people feel themselves out of control, they retreat to primitive forms of behavior to regain a sense of self-control. They also search for things they can control, such as material possessions and money, things that can be touched, felt, and possessed.

Of course, some rim litigation is required to straighten out adverse contentions and determine legitimate rights. Litigation cannot be avoided during business crises; indeed, litigation must be expected by anyone who undertakes to lead an enterprise from its Black Hole. Litigation is simply a part of rim life.

However, much of the rim's litigation has become a lottery. Not only is it the opportunity to point blame at someone else for the losses suffered, but it is also an opportunity to convert the rim's adversity into a big-hit opportunity. The litigation process can take on the trappings of a feeding frenzy unequaled outside the Serengetti.

And why not? When a business entrusted to its leaders crashes on the rim, leadership has failed. Like Job's friends accusing Job of wrong-doing, the constituents of the failed business conclude that the business leadership abused its trust, was greedy or was conveniently blinded to the abuses of others, whether or not the facts justify those perceptions. Any other conclusion might require the constituents to place themselves in a less than "I'm okay" posture, and they would be required to assume at least contributing responsibility for their losses. Assumption of personal responsibility would deny them an opportunity to participate in today's favorite lottery, the lawsuit.

Losses, grievances, questions of judgment, suspicions, and disappointments all feed the rim's litigation eruptions and madness. When I took charge at Park Bank, I expected litigation and investigations, whether or not my efforts were successful. I thought I was prepared; I thought the after-effects would be minimal. But the intensity and viciousness of the publicity that accompanies lawsuits and investigations exceeded anything I could have imagined. I grossly underestimated the litigious hazards of the rim country and the effects, both internal and external, of its aftermath.

Posturing For Settlement

Like chess players setting up pawns and bishops, lawyers posture lawsuits to achieve an early legal checkmate. Plaintiffs move quickly to assure a recovery with as little investment, and as much aura surrounding the validity of their contentions, as possible. Defendants want to settle equally as fast because the direct and indirect costs of litigation are debilitating, and there is always the risk of an overwhelming adverse judgment.

Litigation settlement costs, even for frivolous lawsuits, are now viewed as a painful, expected expense of doing business. It is safer to settle for a known loss than follow through to the end of a trial when the outcome and cost are uncertain. Certain costs can be assimilated; uncertain jury awards, as Texaco painfully discovered in its Penzoil litigation, can result in bankruptcy.

The English court system awards the winner his litigation costs. The American system does not, except for minor court costs or special circumstances rarely present in crisis litigation. Thus, a company defending itself has no opportunity to recover its legal fees or investment of executive and staff time, even when it prevails. The costs and time involved in defending litigation become major concerns, particularly on the rim where resources and resolve are scarce commodities.

Inside the Park

I remember a lawsuit filed by a developer seeking several millions of dollars in damages because Park Bank had refused to lend him money. His loan request came near the end of Park's life, at a time when Park's capital was stretched thin; his proposal simply did not fit Park's requirements or lending abilities.

Undoubtedly aware of Park's turmoil and the effect of adverse publicity, he sued, claiming damages for lost opportunities arising out of a purported oral agreement between himself and a Park Bank loan officer concerning his desired loan.

The local newspaper headlined, ". . . developer sues Park Bank officials in fraud case."

After a year and a half of pre-trial litigation proceedings, the developer's lawyer offered to settle for a nominal sum, fractions of pennies compared to the original claim.

I objected to any settlement. I expected vindication.

Our lawyers quickly determined the cost of legal vindication: Park-related legal fees for proceeding through depositions and document production would be several times the amount for which the matter could be settled. In addition, the executive time required for the proceedings would divert attention from other critical matters.

Reluctantly, I agreed that the suit should be settled for its nuisance value.

Settlement is the prime objective, and the most frequent result, of business litigation. According to *Industry Week,* ninety percent of business litigation cases are settled before trial. Cases against corporate directors and officers are also, for the most part, settled. Of all corporate directors sued, less than one percent go through trial. The high settlement rate does not mean that directors get off, it means that they, and their insurers, pay out measured losses rather than risk the unknown.

Litigation Trends

Near the end of the decade of the 1980s, Rand Corporation completed a study of civil verdicts in California and Cook County, Illinois. The study found that in the 1960s approximately one-fourth of products liability and malpractice claims resulted in plaintiff's verdicts; the percentage grew to one-third in the 1970s; and to one-half in the 1980s. Over the same time period, the amount of damage awards also increased. Several verdicts exceeded one million dollars. Of ten litigation categories studied, every category exhibited a similar trend: larger verdicts and an increasing percentage of wins for plaintiffs bringing suits.

Employees' Suits

A troubled company reducing payroll costs can expect employee litigation. Occasionally, employee litigation will assume the massive proportions that bankrupt Eastern Airlines faced in 1989. It found itself sued by unions seeking to block management from shrinking Eastern's work force. More often, however, employees will be faced on a more singular level.

Soon after Iacocca took over Chrysler, its work force was reduced by 15,000, including 7,000 white-collar workers. Iacocca took it upon himself to discharge the senior staff members. Maynard M. Gordon, writing about Iacocca's experience, observed that, though Iacocca thought his ouster by Henry Ford II had prepared him to handle the trauma associated with discharging people, it had not. Though he talked to his executives personally to ease their pain, the experience was disconcerting. Many dischargees cried, argued, threatened to sue, and begged him to recant.

Although we were lucky at Park Bank not to be burdened by employee suits, the risk and cost of discharging employees can be a painful part of a business workout, particularly when discharges are individualized, as they should be. One of the first tasks any crisis management team must perform is to determine which employees can be rim-performers, vital for recovery and turn-around, and which are nonperformers, excess baggage too costly to carry through the rim experiences. That process requires individual analysis, and often, the evaluation is the first in-depth employee analysis made. When times are good, it is not uncommon for management to perform perfunctory evaluations of people, overlooking marginal characteristics that become difficulties under the rim's pressurized stresses.

The discharged employees' reactions are shock and nonacceptance. They view themselves as management's scapegoats, regardless of the reasons given. Thus, employee litigation, asserting claims for wrongful discharge, can become part of the rim experience. Gregory Stricharchuk reported in the *Wall Street Journal* that employees have turned their firing into an opportunity to sue their company for libel and slander. In fact, one-third of all defamation suits are suits by discharged employees against their former companies.

Juries, the *Journal* noted, have little sympathy for corporations putting people out of work. The *Journal* reported that, in 1982, the average employee wrongful discharge award exceeded $100,000. In a September 7, 1989, follow-up *Journal* article, Milo Geyelin observed that the numbers of employee wrongful discharge cases doubled between 1982 and 1987 and that the average award had ballooned to $646,855.

Behind wrongful discharge claims is an emerging trend: society's categorization of job rights as property rights. Peter Drucker described the emerging property right attributed to jobs in his 1986 speech before the Academy of Management. He said, "Above all, the West, with the United States in the lead, is rapidly converting the individual employee's job into a new property right. . . . The vehicle for this transformation in the United States is not the union contract or laws mandating severance pay, as it is in many European countries. The vehicle for this transformation . . . is the lawsuit."

Drucker said that the trend relates to employees' demands for economic independence, substitutes for the independence provided in earlier times through land ownership.

In addition to employee discharge litigation suits are employee claims for damages from stress-related job injuries. In states where state law permits employees' suits against employers for work-related stress, employees have brought actions under workers' compensation laws, alleging illness brought about by business crisis. Michael J. McCarthy reported in the *Wall Street Journal* that during 1988, stress accounted for 14 percent of all worker's compensation claims in the United States. The chaos inherent in the rim experience will likely impact company stress claims and the resultant increased insurance costs.

Stockholder Suits

The number of shareholder suits filed against corporations and their managements quadrupled in the decade of the 1980s. The threat of stockholder suits has been a principal impetus for corporate leadership's myopic management, overriding long-term business considerations. Impatience on the part of American stockholders, demanding up-front results, is one of the reasons for America's loss of ninety percent of the computer memory-chip business to the more patient Japanese during the 1980s.

An effect of stockholder litigation against directors has been the increased reluctance on the part of skilled men and women to serve as corporate directors, resulting in a boardroom brain-drain. William A. Sahlman advised in a poignant 1990 *Harvard Business Review* article, aptly entitled "Why Sane People Shouldn't Serve on Public Boards," that he had become unwilling to serve as a director of a public company; the emotional and financial loss associated with constant director litigation, much of it unjustified and groundless, had become too high. He concluded that "if enough talented men and women engage in the same thought process and reach the same conclusion, U.S. industry could be in trouble."

Customers' Suits

In addition to employee and stockholder suits are suits by customers or suppliers aimed at avoiding contractual responsibility. For a troubled bank, such suits include suits by borrowers aimed at avoiding responsibility for repaying troubled loans. Borrower suits have increased dramatically in recent years, and claims of lender liability have been raised as an issue in virtually every troubled loan litigation.

In effect, some rim borrowers blame their bankers for lending them money that, they allege, the bankers should have known they could not repay. Others claim loan mismanagement or secret agreements with loan officers. Still others claim their bank is forcing them out of business through collection activities commenced during economically difficult times.

Not only troubled borrowers litigate with the bank trapped on the rim, but also some strong borrowers, sensing weakness in the troubled company, and acting like the primitive hunter stalking his prey, strike, taking advantage at every opportunity. Sensing the adverse effect litigation has on bank liquidity, normally placid borrowers can assume a predatory character and litigate a variety of contentions to force negotiation of discounted loan repayments.

Inside the Park

We were not immune at Park Bank to frivolous litigation brought by borrowers. In one suit, a borrower claimed that a secret arrangement with a former loan officer limited the bank's right to seek repayment of his loan. Had a secret agreement been made, it would have been illegal.

Ultimately, my deposition was taken. I testified that when the borrower claimed the secret agreement, I immediately reported it to the bank's bonding company. Suddenly, the borrower realized his plight — he had to prove the existence of an alleged agreement that, if it existed, would have been illegal. The suit was dropped.

The Weapons

Today there are many powerful legal weapons available to the rim's litigation lottery players. The biggest weapon in recent times has been RICO, the Racketeer-Influenced and Corrupt Practices Act. RICO has elevated the litigation chess game into a high stakes war game with few survivors.

In 1986, the Supreme Court of the United States decided, by a vote of 5 to 4, that the RICO Act passed by Congress in 1970 could be used as a vehicle by plaintiffs seeking damages in civil litigation. Under the RICO Act, successful plaintiffs recover treble damages. For example, if a stockholder loses $1 million on his stock investment in a collapsed company and successfully brought a RICO suit against the management, he could collect $3 million. The threat of treble damages awards have forced settlement of RICO cases by defendants even when they feel that the merits of the case are on their side. The risks of financial ruin are too great to risk a court finding against them.

Officers and directors liability insurance policies do not cover fraud claims; and RICO claims are fraud claims. Paradoxically, insurance policies require insurers to *defend* officers and directors against all claims, including fraud claims (after all, fraud claims are contentions, not facts); but insurers are not permitted, as a matter of law, to *pay* fraud claims.

Insurance companies have the duty to proceed in good faith. If a lawsuit is brought against directors alleging both negligence and RICO claims (and most suits allege both), failure by the insurance company to settle negligence claims (obtaining the dismissal of the concurrent RICO claims as consideration for settlement) may be an act of bad faith by the insurance company against its insured officers and directors.

The insurer's failure to settle the lawsuit in its entirety has the effect of forcing directors to face fraud claims on their own — financially naked, without insurance. That failure to settle can make the insurer susceptible to bad faith damage claims by directors who feel the insurer owes them a duty to settle their litigation. The threat of the bad faith litigation encourages insurance companies, vulnerable to losses not covered by their policies, to settle cases that include RICO claims.

The threat of RICO judgments has also driven directors, including those who would have preferred to vindicate themselves in trial, to demand settlement by their insurers, compromising their hopes of vindication. It is a damned if you do and damned if you don't dilemma for insurers and defendants.

The *American Banker* newspaper reported in 1985: "The civil provisions of RICO went little noticed for a decade after the law was enacted. But since 1980, aggressive lawyers frequently have used the law's extraordinarily broad language to seek treble damages from legitimate businesses. And banks number prominently among targets. Of 300 civil suits filed under the act since 1982, about a third have been aimed at financial institutions."

The article noted RICO's abuse by plaintiffs' attorneys. A partner at a "Big 8" accounting firm, one of the many who have become frequent, deep-pocket targets of RICO litigation in connection with audits done for troubled companies, was quoted in the *Wall Street Journal* as saying that, because of RICO suits against accountants, a serious reluctance on the part of major accounting firms to audit public companies is developing.

The *National Law Journal* pointed out that RICO claims in suits have become so common in civil litigation that "lawyers feel they must have a good reason not to include one." Attempts to have Congress amend the RICO statute have, so far, been unsuccessful.

It is ironic. On the one hand, RICO puts enormous pressure on business defendants to settle suits brought against them because of the financial exposure and emotional cost involved in RICO litigation. On the other hand, the plaintiff's lawyers have worked themselves into a position such that, if they elect not to file RICO claims, they expose themselves to later suits for malpractice.

In the meantime, without revision of the RICO Act, the RICO gun blasts on, used by lawyers to stir up a widening array of civil lawsuits, from corporate takeovers and breakups of partnerships through an infinite variety of commercial litigation.

The use of the RICO Act has also had a psychological effect on plaintiffs. It encourages plaintiffs to adopt their lawyers' chess-posturing that the allegations about the defendants' fraud, conspiracy, and racketeering are true. RICO accelerates the groupthink phenomenon litigants experience, described in the preceding chapter as enemy-creation.

RICO litigation attacks the fundamental integrity of those sued. Lawyers experienced in defending business executives against RICO charges say that it is a terrible emotional experience. I agree. The RICO counts were ultimately dropped from the Park Bank stockholder lawsuit, but before their dismissal, the allegations were widely publicized in our local papers. Their implications scarred those of us who had been the target of the allegations. Being publicly called a racketeer strikes at the core.

Sadly, as the 1990s rolls on, the RICO attack remains a routine part of corporate litigation roulette. At this writing, proposed 1990 amendments have, as in prior years, been set aside by Congress.

Too Many Lawyers?

The litigation frenzy has been attributed, in part, to the explosion in the numbers of lawyers in this country. In 1950, there were 220,000 lawyers; in 1987, there were 640,000 lawyers — one lawyer for every 350 people. By the year 2000, American Bar Association predictions indicate there will be 1,000,000 lawyers, or one for each 300 Americans. In contrast, in Japan, there is one lawyer for every 10,000 Japanese.

Driven by pressures from too little business to go around to too many lawyers, as well as by the 1980s short-term philosophy, many lawyers are focused on the business aspects of law, to the detriment of their professional responsibilities. *Shark Tank* author Kim Isaac Eisler summed it up in a quote from a law firm rainmaker: "Praise the adversary. He is the catalyst by which you bill your client. Damn the client. He is your true enemy."

Critical of lawyers' emphasis on practice volume and fees rather than on professional development, United States Supreme Court Chief Justice Rehnquist concluded that the pressures on lawyers to litigate ". . .

contribute to the ethical miasma." Federal Judge William Terrell Hodges, speaking to the St. Petersburg Bar Association, said, "It's almost as though lawyers are sitting in their offices looking around to see who else is chargeable."

The rim of a Black Hole is one of the territories litigation lawyers stake out as fertile hunting ground. Despite the fact that a lot of litigation is justified when businesses collapse, too many rim lawyers pursue their prey as if they, the lawyers, were rightful participants in the feeding frenzy on the business corpse. They proceed with little concern beyond the immediate kill of all the game they can get. The *American Bar Association Journal* reported in August 1987: "The thing that never comes out is the viciousness of plaintiff's lawyers."

Another thing that rarely comes out is the cost. Denise Kalette reported in *USA Today* that troubled savings and loan associations devote in excess of 25 percent of their operating costs to legal expenses. In contrast, in good times, S&L legal fees approximate 2 percent of operating costs. Park Bank's litigation costs ran as high as $500,000 a month near the end of its life.

Other Costs

Though legal costs can exceed thousands of dollars each month, even for a small company, the indirect costs are even more.

Gossip within the company about litigation and litigation-related rumors divert attention and sap energy, adding to the company's burden. The constant parade of damaging news creates both a flight response (employees are frightened, humiliated, embarrassed, and want to escape) and a heads-down mentality (employees hunker down, assuming a "non-work" posture — as if by doing so they avoid being noticed and, therefore, being damaged). The psychological effects are horrendous for people who define themselves by work. Crisis litigation usually peaks at the same time that the company's executives are already stressed to their limits, often causing capable people to leave when their contributions are essential and could be critical.

When a company is in trouble, its employees live its trouble, at work and at home. For example, Steven Fink reported that during Johnson & Johnson's Tylenol crisis, children of J&J employees were taunted at school because their parent worked for J&J, a company that "killed people." Personal feelings of worth, pride, and esteem are hit hard. Litigation and its never-ending publicity exacerbate the damage.

Inside the Park

In mid-1985, after we had made a management decision about a threatening matter, a mid-level manager from our finance department came into my office, his face drawn and his hands trembling. He didn't want to leave; he didn't want to run out, he said. He felt loyal, but he was torn. He and his wife had talked it over: they had spent too many sleepless nights; there was too much risk to their financial future at a time when their young family needed stability.

For what?" he questioned, in obvious pain. Fortunately, for us, most of our good people did not resign, but his loss was felt. There was no opportunity to recruit and train replacements at a time like that!

The threat of rim litigation stifles and demoralizes corporate leaders and managers, forcing them to shift toward running their company safely, not necessarily successfully. Management becomes defensive because of litigation focusing on failure avoidance rather than on success opportunities. Strategy is sacrificed. Bunker mentality takes over.

Public Image

The effects of crisis litigation go even further. Maintaining customers in the face of the sensationalist media coverage that surrounds litigation is difficult, often impossible.

Repeated media reports of innuendoes and allegations are soon believed by their audiences. Public distrust grows. Facts in the minds of the public become lost; perceptions, even if untrue, become reality.

When perceptions replace facts, the troubled company operates under the weight of a deteriorated public image and loss of confidence. A rim-bound company may win its lawsuits; but winning lawsuits is not enough. The company must also win its public media trial if it is to survive. Legally, a defendant never carries the burden of proving innocence within the courtroom; but, pragmatically, a troubled company and its executives carry the burden of proving to the public that they will survive with integrity intact.

Inside the Park

During the crisis Park's press was generally fair, though excessive. During Park's aftermath, however, an article quoted allegations made by certain plaintiffs as if they were fact. When that occurred, I felt I had to respond because the allegations were directed at me. I felt it was necessary to take a stand by writing a letter to the editor to counterbalance the negative affects of the publicity. So I wrote the following:

> *I have read, with interest, your two-part series on the "aftermath" of Park Bank (Nov. 30 and Dec. 1 [1986]).*
>
> *Unfortunately, because of the pending litigation, it is not possible for me to comment specifically on the series as I have on past series. However, in the interest of correctness, and perhaps in the interest of my spirit, I feel I should at least note that various events, attributed in the article as actually having occurred, seem to have their sole source in the allegations contained in the pending litigation. They certainly did not come from my real life experiences.*
>
> *It appears to me that what happened is that various "allegations" made in litigation were somehow inadvertently converted to "facts" during your long research process. Thus, contentions were not always separated from events.*
>
> *I am not trying to be critical of the investigative process. I have long favored public disclosure despite its occasional handicap to some of us. We just need to recognize its imperfections. I suppose, in the overall scheme of our community's life, it is a little thing. But, now, emotions are somewhat high about the whole affair.*
>
> *Eventually we will all settle down and develop a balanced view as to what happened at Park Bank. There is an old saying, "The only thing better than learning from your own mistakes is to learn from others." I would hope that at least some of us who crash-landed Park Bank would end up being good teachers; and, as the process unfolds, also end up as good examples.*

The media trial is never-ending; it goes on throughout the crisis and its aftermath. For Park Bank, the media trial lasted more than five years: two crisis years and over three years of aftermath. The newspaper clippings I collected fill six scrapbooks. If I were to eliminate the clippings that deal with litigation, I would have barely two scrapbooks left. If I were to keep only the positive reports that were written during the crisis, I would retain but a few pages. The good things that come out of a crisis rarely make the front page.

Chapter 8

Black Ashes of Publicity

Reality is what the public perceives to be true, and if the public grasps reality in a certain way, that is what it becomes.

Gerald C. Meyers

Adverse Publicity and Employees

Black Hole publicity, relentless and nearly always adverse spreads an ashlike blanket of trouble over the rim country.

One of the many articles published during the 1987 Wall Street Boesky-insider-trading episode was titled " 'I Am Not a Crook': Image Problem Dogs Investment Bankers." The article was about the negative "halo effect" endured on Wall Street after the insider trading schemes became public.

A Wall Streeter was quoted in the *Wall Street Journal*, "For the first time in 10 years in this business, I was ashamed to admit I'm an investment banker."

Investment bankers found themselves bearing the brunt of cruel jokes. An example: Two drunks meandered through the graveyard of a church located in New York's financial district. One of the drunks tripped over a grave marker. Through reddened, blurry eyes, he read the grave marker: "Here lies an investment banker and an honest man." The drunk called to his friend, "Hey Charlie! It's getting so crowded here they're burying two people to a grave!"

Unrelenting, adverse publicity about the company where people work, or about what people do for a living, has a negative effect on the lives and feelings of those involved. That kind of publicity is hardly a joke. Dr. Douglas LaBier has observed that much of our self-definition and our self-evaluation comes from achievements and contributions in our work. When a company is on the rim, there are no feelings of self-worth or of status. People with a company on the rim feel like losers, and it doesn't feel very good.

People *want* to feel good, but how can they when their company is failing? Are they also doomed to fail? Unsettled feelings about their troubled company color feelings about their personal lives.

Inside the Park

Our employees were stunned after we released our 1985 third quarter results showing a loss of more than $17 million, despite the fact that I had held meetings to explain what was happening at Park Bank and what employees should expect in the way of publicity and customer reaction.

Shortly after the staff meeting in which I made the announcement, a Park vice president came into my office, crying. "I want to help. I don't want to leave. I know how hard it is. But will I have my job in December? Will I be able to buy my family Christmas presents? What should I do?"

This kind of encounter is a daily occurrence during crisis. People feel absolutely helpless when their company is being sucked over the Black Hole's rim. That is how our vice-president felt: lost and helpless, her life and her future out of control. Her helplessness led to fear and depression.

For some, Black Hole feelings manifest themselves in anger. When employees find themselves on the rim, they feel betrayed and at risk, at risk of income loss, reputation loss, physical and emotional loss.

When adverse publicity hits, it exacerbates the loss-of-control feelings experienced by employees because it confirms their worst fears. The publicity not only drives home to employees that their company has become a poor provider, it also reveals that fact to their entire world.

The press is usually balanced and accurate in its reporting of news about the rim-bound company, but that accuracy does not keep the battle-weary employees from being reminded about their troubles by the publicity week after week.

Inside the Park

During the crisis, Joe O'Neill, associate editor of Tampa Bay Business, *asked me how I felt about the press and the adverse effect of constant publicity. I replied, "As a whole, I would say the press has been pretty accurate and objective. The biggest thing, I think, is the number of times we've been in [the press]. It eventually gets to the point where it wears on people. . . . There's no question that being in the press has an effect. It makes it difficult."*

Publicity Fuels Gossip

Psychologists tell us that gossip is the primary bonding tool among those in the work place who feel powerless. Frightened feelings need expression and gossip provides that expression.

Rumors dominate the conversations of employees on the rim. Coffee-break and other "down-time" conversations focus on the newest gossip. Ultimately, rumors and gossip are elevated to the status of facts and are assumed to be reality.

Negative information is given more significance than positive news, confirming inner suspicions and feelings. News in the press feeds the rumors and the gossip, building momentum. The more gossip and rumors, the less productive everyone becomes. Instead of working, employees spend their time talking about the company and what will happen.

Inside the Park

In the fall of 1985, I asked a bank consulting firm to take a look at some of the things we were doing at Park Bank in order to see if an outside perspective might offer some ideas that could help us. Prior to bringing in the consultants, Park's senior management had approved the plan and had met with junior managers, explaining the role of the consultants.

But when the five consultants arrived one Monday morning as scheduled, wearing conservative dark suits and carrying black brief cases, and dispersed themselves throughout the bank into finance, operations and the branches, many junior managers and their staffs were convinced that they had been tricked. They were certain that these people were not consultants, but take-over regulators from the FDIC, secretly infiltrating the bank. Who else but a team of regulators would come into the bank on a Monday morning so stern-faced and conservatively dressed?

The bank was rift with rumor. A physician who was in the bank when the consultants came in rushed to the doctors' lounge at the local hospital and told the medical staff that Park Bank was falling into the hands of the regulators. Six doctors immediately left the hospital, came to the bank, and withdrew their funds, one doctor shouting irrationally as he left that Park was "gone, closing." It was "time to bail out."

The consultants operated under the name FBIC, a poor name choice. The FBIC name, exhibited before Park's already tense people on the consultant's documents and business cards, confirmed employee misconceptions.

I asked the FBIC people to leave — the only way I could convince our people that these men were consultants, not regulators.

Next, I wrote each of the doctors a letter, explaining what had happened. Several returned and reopened their accounts.

Finally, I wrote a memo to the staff explaining what had happened: "One of the 'whirlpools' in a company's turnaround-recovery stream is the rumor whirlpool. . . . And we have to paddle through it. . . . The effect of rumors can be thwarted by each of us. Rumors need not be passed on or exaggerated. If at any time. . . something as adverse as the recent rumor happens, you will hear directly from me — first, not last."

Adverse Publicity, Competitors, and Customers

Competitors also pick up on the weaknesses of a company on the rim and twist adverse publicity to their own advantage. A company too troubled to focus on its customers will be easy prey for competitors. After all, how can a company in trouble deliver on time? Back up its warranties? Keep up its services? Or, in the case of a bank, be a reliable source of loans or a safe place to deposit money? Adverse publicity acts as a catalyst confirming innuendoes and helps competitors woo customers away.

Inside the Park

The newspaper had just published our third quarter earnings for 1985. We made sure the reporter had the facts showing that, despite the negative turn of events (we lost $17 million for the quarter), we were in no immediate danger of failing.

The reporter called the Division of Banking for the State of Florida, which confirmed the information and said that the state was planning no action at that time. There was a small, but not out of control, run on deposits after the news came out.

However, a local bank saw an opportunity to take advantage of our weakness. Its plan was simple: put an unheard of, ten-day local check hold on any Park Bank check presented for deposit or for cashing; then to say, "Sorry, we just don't know about Park Bank. We want to make sure it will be around when we present your check."

There is nothing like a long hold on checks to precipitate a loss of confidence among depositors, especially among Florida's retirees who grew up during the Depression.

Fortunately, I learned of the plan from our downtown branch manager before it got out of hand. I quickly confronted our competitor's president. Before any serious damage was done, the tack was stopped by the president, who with an embarrassed grin assured me it was all part of an unfortunate misunderstanding.

Some borrowers also will try to take advantage of adverse publicity. Knowing that banks in trouble are likely to have liquidity problems spawned by deposit runs and nonperforming loans, those borrowers will negotiate for substantial discounts on their loans in exchange for prompt payments that provide the institution with needed cash.

Borrowers also bring lawsuits, and countersuits, designed to forestall or offset repayment of their loans, often sensationalizing that process with media publicity. The greater the publicity, they reason, the more likely others also will sue, and the more likely that that pressure will force a settlement in their favor.

Inside the Park

Park Bank certainly received its share of publicity. Here are just some of the newspaper headlines about Park's litigation that appeared during the last half of 1985:

- *July 5, 1985 — "Park Bank hit with lawsuit contesting its use of prime rate."*

- *July 15, 1985 — "More prime-rate suits may be filed."*

- *October 25, 1985 — " 'People Against Park Bank' meets to recruit disgruntled customers."*

- *September 6, 1985 — "Developer sues Park Bank over loan agreement."*

- *December 3, 1985 — "Developer's suit charges fraud in Park Bank's loan procedures."*

Each article had an elaborate description of the plaintiffs' allegations. (The plaintiffs and their attorneys made sure the press got their version.)

For the most part, we in the bank had not seen the lawsuits at the time they were reported by the paper, because lawsuit papers are filed in court several days before they are served on defendants. In the interim, newspaper reporters pick up the records. When the paper reports cases before the suits are served on the defendants, defendants are put in an impossible position; so even the most factually reported story, by its nature, ends up looking one-sided in favor of the plaintiff.

Interspersed during that six-month period were some dozen articles about Park's troubled real estate portfolio, its annual stockholder meeting, and its quarterly losses, each article adding fuel to the rim's volcanic fires.

What happened to the lawsuits? The prime rate suit was dismissed by the court a year later because the plaintiffs took no action after it was filed, except that the lawyer tried to recruit additional plaintiffs. Ultimately, the lawyer dropped out of the case and no one replaced him. The borrowers bringing the suit against Park Bank, seeking loan off-sets, were not relieved of debt payment obligations. The developer's loan agreement suit was dismissed after a year and a half after request of the plaintiff. No damages were paid. The developer was not released from his debt payment obligations. The developer's fraud suit was withdrawn voluntarily by the plaintiff before it was served on the bank or its officers (but, unfortunately, after it was reported in the paper). No damages were paid. The developer was not released from his debt payment obligations.

Adverse Publicity and Regulatory Agencies

Adverse publicity also attracts the attention of agencies responsible for overseeing public or regulated companies. If management keeps these agencies informed, the possibility of a precipitous response is minimized. Even if the governmental agencies are fully informed, however, rumors about pending actions and inquiries of reporters add their own nervous intensity. On that point, we did a good job during the crisis of keeping the regulators informed.

Rumors and Reporters

Although I found reporters usually accurate during Park's crisis, sometimes, in their zeal to publish news, they failed to check the accuracy of the sources of their stories.

Inside the Park

In January 1986, the St. Petersburg Times *reported that the lawyer who filed the developer's loan agreement lawsuit said that the Securities Exchange Commission was investigating Park Bank's prior sales of stock. An article, entitled "SEC examining stock dealings of Park Banks," was published on January 11. I was interviewed and expressed surprise; I was unaware of any SEC investigation. The article went on to review the earlier lawsuit filed by the developer as well as a laundry list of our loan problems; the same bad news all over again.*

I immediately called our lawyers, who called the SEC. There was no SEC investigation. To this date, there has been none.

Reporters on the rim can also become overly aggressive. During Park's final days, after each announcement of bad earnings or major litigation, video camera trucks were positioned to zoom in on human reactions as TV reporters interviewed customers coming out of Park's branches: "How do you feel about banking here? Are you concerned about Park's problems? Are your deposits safe?"

Near the end of Park's life the cumulative effects of reporters aggressively seeking story material wore Park's employees down, contributing to morale problems and drove depositors away.

When the effects of aggressive news-gathering and adverse publicity all accumulate, momentum gathers, accelerating the troubled company's trip into its Black Hole. Ultimately, the company loses its ability to stop its plunge over the rim or maneuver a turn-around. Employees lose determination and give up when their fears are confirmed by what they, their families, and friends read.

Inside the Park

In January 1986, one month before the collapse of Park Bank, I was advised that the St. Petersburg Times *planned a three-part series on the Park Bank "dream derailed." I talked to the editor and asked if the article could be delayed. I was working on a sale of the bank; I was afraid that further adverse publicity, even if fairly presented, would erode the last of our employees' and customers' confidence.*

The editor said that the paper had waited long enough. The public was entitled to know the results of its investigation into Park's at-hand demise. The article was actually quite accurate and balanced, and started out,

It was the Friday before the three-day Veteran's Day — the kind of weekend bank examiners reputedly love for taking over troubled financial institutions. Three WTVT "Pulse News" reporters waited outside Park Bank of Florida headquarters, hoping to catch some live footage of a regulatory invasion. Two banks called the Park Bank executive office, hoping for a chance to purchase the remains.

Actually, nothing was happening. No federal agents, no executives even, were inside the Plaza in downtown St. Petersburg. Secretary Linda B. Melleney sat alone in the main office, waiting to get the photocopy machine fixed. Why was Channel 13 downstairs? "I don't know," she said pleasantly. "The rumors, I guess. Channel 8 was here yesterday."

But accurate, balanced reporting didn't help; and the rumors didn't stop. Deposit withdrawals accelerated, though slowly. Fortunately we were prepared. We had arranged a line of credit at the Federal Reserve, which we used for liquidity. Our people did an excellent job in dealing with our nervous public. There was no panic.

Selective Reporting or Omission of News

Fortunately, I had no experience with the impact of selective reporting or omission of news during Park Bank's crisis, but I did three years after Park Bank failed.

Inside the Park

In the late 1980s, the banking and thrift industries erupted in convulsions. The repercussions are still going on and are apt to be felt by Americans through the turn of the next century.

In 1989, Congress passed the Financial Institutions Reform, Recovery and Enforcement Act of 1989 (known as "FIRREA"), a thrift bailout bill. During the early stages of Congressional hearings about the Act, both the banking and thrift industries and their regulators, as well as their professional advisors, were heavily criticized. Remedies for the criticisms are contained in the Act. Park Bank, at that time the seventh largest bank failure in the country, found the smoldering ashes of its collapse described within the pages of a Congressional Report *(from the Committee on Governmental Operations — 77th Report). The report contained exaggerated allegations shaped, in part, from a letter to the committee sent by the counsel for the stockholders in the suit against the Park Bank directors and officers. The lawyer's letter described his litigation claims as if they were fact. The report treated the claims as true and, supported by flimsy background data, cited the letter as a basis for Congressional action.*

Picking up on the revelations contained in the Congressional Report, *a series of blistering articles about Park Bank appeared in the* St. Petersburg Times *near the end of 1988 and during the first half of 1989. The theme of the articles received additional impetus from the indictment of former Park Bank officers. During that period, four former Park Bank loan officers (who had been discharged shortly after our management changes) had been indicted on charges of engaging in an improper financing scheme involving themselves and a loan officer at another lending institution. The scheme had been partially uncovered by Mike Klein, Park's counsel, in his investigation during the last months of Park Bank's life, but the implications were inconclusive. The board, however, authorized him to prepare a report, later provided to the FDIC. After the bank's failure, the FBI was able to complete the investigation.*

The Times, *apparently unaware of the Klein investigation or the report that had been prepared, implied that those indictments indicated that the government's investigation of Park's demise was working its way up from Park Bank's "small fish" to its "big fish" — and the big fish included everyone on Park Bank's board! The articles suggested that the U.S. Attorney's office should accelerate the pace of its "hunt."*

Outraged by the implications, I wanted to strike out, at least write to the editor of the Times *and call the reporters involved to set them straight. Chuck Ruff, my attorney, said no. We were in the process of settling the final bits of Park Bank's civil litigation, including the shareholder's suit. Now was not the time to speak out. That time will come, he assured me. Internally, my rage grew. I had been back in private law practice for about a year and had finally begun to settle into what I hoped would be near normalcy; the horrible publicity was disrupting.*

Then, a few weeks after the scathing publicity and during the trial of the loan officers, the prosecuting attorney asked me and another director if we would testify on the government's behalf. The prosecuting attorney wanted our testimony because the former officers had claimed, in their defense, that they were merely following orders from myself and others. I jumped at the opportunity to testify for the government. I insisted that I do it openly — I wanted no deal. Surely, I felt, after we testified openly, the Times *would change its tack and conclude that there was no scheme perpetrated from Park's boardroom.*

We submitted ourselves to both examination and cross-examination. Our entire testimony was open, frank, and, from our and the prosecutor's viewpoints, successful.

The paper ignored the testimony. Not a word was printed.

Two days later, I went back to court as a rebuttal witness for the government. One of the defendants, Park's former senior lender, while testifying in his own defense, had claimed that I was the mastermind behind the financing scheme, that I had said it was legal, that I had on several occasions met with him and the people involved. To add credibility, he referred to a diary of dates about the alleged meetings.

As the evidence proved, not only was I unaware of his plan or the meetings, but his allegations were factually impossible! I had been out of the country during the entire period and was not present when the loan was approved by the board. I testified with documents in hand: my trip itinerary, passport, dated photographs, and a copy of the speech I had given while I was gone. His defense was destroyed.

The case presented by the prosecuting attorney demonstrated that the loan officers had acted on their own, hiding the matter from the board and myself. During his closing argument, the prosecuting attorney made it clear that the loan offier and the others had deceived their superiors.

Following my testimony and the prosecuting attorney's closing argument, I rushed for a copy of the local paper, assured, in my mind, of vindication. There was none. The paper again was silent, not a word about my rebuttal testimony.

The reporters ignored Park's history, which was available from their own paper's data banks. They ignored the course of the trial, the role of Park's directors in the trial, the evidence about the board's lack of knowledge about the alleged scheme, and the theory of the prosecuting attorney on which three of the loan officers were ultimately convicted (one of the loan officers was released).

Instead, the Times *final article pressed on about those so far unscathed, the "bigger game" still out there for the government to catch! The article ran two days before my fifty-eighth birthday. I was fifty-four when Park Bank failed. The aftermath from Park's collapse was still not over.*

A year later, I had an opportunity to discuss this incident with Andy Barnes, the editor of the *St. Petersburg Times*. He was obviously taken back and disturbed, unaware of the important incidents omitted from the articles written by his reporters.

As Andy and I talked, I thought back to a 1987 editorial he had written about President Reagan being unaware of Oliver North's role in the Iran-Contra affair. Barnes' editorial concluded that if Reagan didn't know what North had been doing, "he damned well should have." I didn't have the heart to bring the editorial up. It would have been too Jobian.

Now, I can joke about it.

Chapter 9

The Crew's Rim Experience

*Here is a test to find whether your mission on earth
is finished; if you're alive it is not.*

Richard Bach

What is happening inside a company on the rim? For a time, at least, employees' efforts, bonded by corporate culture and traditions, can be channeled by strong, motivating corporate leadership. Ultimately, however, there is individual stress-overload; employees are no longer able to cope with the effects of stress and reach their break-point. Individual stress-overloads convert into company overload when virtually all of the key people within the rim-bound organization are beyond their individual crisis break points.

Deferring the time when the company will most likely experience its crisis break-point is a primary goal for corporate crisis leadership. If the company's crisis break-point occurs early during the rim experience, it is impossible to turn away from the Black Hole course. How quickly that break-point comes will depend upon:

- the individual value systems of the employees within the company;

- the collective value systems of the company, as reflected in its culture and traditions;

- the ability of the company's leadership to find meaning in the rim experience; and

- the crisis-overload within the company.

The principal objective of this chapter is to describe the internal corporate environment after the company experiences crisis-overload. However, first examining the factors that affect individual, and company, crisis-tolerance capacity should be helpful.

Individual Value Systems

The capacity among members of any group of people to function under crisis conditions of ambiguity, transition, and turmoil vary dramatically. The rim is rife with problems that exhibit no clear-cut choices or readily perceptible solutions. Many people lack the flexibility needed for effective responses to the rim's unpredictability. Many can't operate effectively in a crisis situation because they cannot deal with the risk of failure.

Especially vulnerable are people sensitive to peer pressures, to how others think about them and react to them. They can become immobilized in situations where they might be criticized. Intimidated by their own fears that they will not measure up to what they believe are peer expectations, these sensitive people often become the first casualties of rim pressures.

The person who seems to survive better in the rim's atmosphere of criticism and chaos is the person who is not thwarted by the negative reactions of other people. He responds to crisis like Abraham Lincoln who during a Civil War criticism said, "If I were to read, much less answer, all the attacks on me, this shop might as well be closed for any other business."

Paradoxically, the overly committed person is often not the best equipped for the harsh realities of rim life. People who define themselves by their work can be driven by unyielding loyalty and corporate dedication, and can become overly committed. When the company finds itself trapped on the rim, the overly committed will support the company to the end, but unfortunately, their support may help bring about the end if it is not directed toward positive, solution-oriented results.

Overly committed employees view rim-like problems as threats to their company and, by extension, since they define themselves through the health of their company, to themselves. They tend to defend existing corporate policies and programs as if there were no alternatives and therefore may support outmoded operational methods, resisting change in the face of clear evidence that change is necessary. They sometimes become so overly committed that they suspend judgment and commit crimes to support their company. They thus sap vitality from their companies when it is most needed.

The overly committed are like Jeb Magruder, one of the Watergate conspirators, or Colonel Oliver North, willing to lie to Congress and deceive the President to support a cause.

Pressures on the CEO

When companies do exceptionally well, their CEOs receive too much credit; when things go exceptionally badly, their CEOs receive too much blame. Corporate failure is mostly viewed by employees, suppliers, customers, and stockholders as the personal failure of the company's leadership. Consequently, executives, particularly CEOs, can suffer severe pressure and pain of life on the rim. They find their feelings of self-esteem, as well as the respect accorded them by customers, employees, and others, damaged by the taint of crisis innuendoes, increasing guilt feelings and hampering their efficiency in meeting problems.

Customers and suppliers overtly or subtly back away from the company and its executives, even those with whom long-standing relationships have existed. Customers bargain. Suppliers require COD. Business friends back away. The executive feels more and more guilty for the situation his company is in and more and more isolated and lonely.

Never-ending rumors and adverse publicity focus on the competence of corporate leadership, diminishing executive stature. Soon it affects his ability to steer the company away from the Black Hole.

Finally, pressures related to company troubles become felt by executive families. Families find themselves shunned in social settings; children find themselves criticized in school and on the playground.

The cumulative effect on an executive accelerates his arrival at his crisis break-point, until he too is likely to become a rim casualty.

The Company's Value Systems

Just as a company's culture and traditions can affect the ability of its executives and employees to spot an approaching crisis, corporate culture and tradition can shape crisis responses and the break-points of people trapped on the rim.

Corporate culture and traditions provide shared values — accepted and comforting frames of reference through which people interpret situations, shape judgments, and formulate responses. Culture and tradition have a bonding effect on employees, providing a sense of community and internal stability. During a crisis, values and traditions will sometimes help provide employees with clear direction and guidance, by defining and clarifying the ethical boundaries of acceptable action within the organization.

Corporate culture, normally positive, unfortunately can also be negative. Reporter Rick Wartzman has observed that "even the most upright people can become dishonest and unmindful of their civic responsibilities when placed in the typical corporate environment." A national survey by a Boston University professor (reported on by Selwyn Feinstein in the *Wall Street Journal*) found that, nationwide, 41 percent of American workers believed that people act out of idealism; however, 43 percent of the workers believed that putting up a false front, doing whatever it takes to make money, and lying are basic parts of human nature.

A corporate environment dominated by such cynicism tends to be nonproductive and fraught with mistrust and miscommunication possibilities, especially toward its leadership. Upward communication is nonexistent.

Corporate cultures that demand unquestioned loyalty can produce the overly committed employees discussed previously. They are likely to have tunnel vision, inflexibility, and unquestioning trust, or to use quick fixes that don't last. Their loyalty can blind them to alternatives, causing them to suspend judgment at the very times their companies require their critical thinking.

Boss-Watchers

Tom Peters wrote that employees are "boss-watchers," particularly when the influence of outside factors on their company are unclear and the direction of their company is vague or ambiguous.

Inside the Park

The meaning of Peters's observation became evident to me early on. I had an "open door." People walking by my office knew that if I were there, they could come in and talk with me about anything. One day, my door was closed all day. I had been holding a series of meetings with potential investors. Normally, I held extended confidential meetings in the conference room next to my office; however, for some reason, that day I used my office for the all-day meeting.

After the meetings one of the senior vice presidents rushed up to me and said, "You scared everybody; your door has been closed all day; what's going on?"

From then on, I went back to my tradition — an open-door office; long, confidential meetings would be held in the conference room.

In part because people are boss-watchers, the influence of the crisis leader is great. If the crisis leader leads by positive deeds and example, by rolling up his sleeves and not shirking tough tasks, his efforts will be emulated by employees and his example will provide them strength and security and act as a lifeline for the entire organization.

Advance Warnings

One of the most important jobs for the crisis leader is to provide communication to employees about the actual state of the company's affairs. In that regard, he should be forthright and accurate. Otherwise, his communication will create a crisis of its own.

Ironically, as if corporate America doubted the wisdom of the prior statement, a national debate resulting in federal legislation calling for communications about plant closings was adopted in 1989. Research surrounding the law that requires companies to provide employees with not less than 60 days advance notice about planned closing of facilities indicates that employees are more likely not to slack off when they are promptly informed about pending crisis events. In fact, employee productivity may actually increase. Some increase their efforts to hold on to their jobs or get recommendations for the future; others respond to the challenge and excitement. For all employees, advance communication helps them work through their grief and ease their transition through the hurt and disappointment.

When Crisis Systems Finally Overload

Unless a rim-bound company's CEO can successfully lead the company on a new course, the systems of the company's employees and other constituents will ultimately overload. When that occurs, "momentum effect" will take over, and the momentum of the crisis's own force will so overwhelm the company that recovery is impossible.

At that time, the impact of the rim's environment on the behavior of otherwise calm, predictable people can be devastating. The weight of the factors becomes intolerable, and sometimes out-of-character, even bizarre, behavior may occur. When the cumulative stress-causing factors overwhelm the rim-bound company's officers and employees, that company has experienced crisis-overload; it has crossed its crisis break-point.

At that time, the CEO cannot ignore that the sheer weight of crisis-caused stress can affect the conduct of people in unpredictable ways, regardless of their corporate position or his leadership. They adopt behavior that provides them with greater opportunities for personal survival, regardless of the cost to their company.

The research of Cameron, Whetten, and Kim, appearing in their article, "Organizational Dysfunctions of Decline," indicates that the behavior of a person who has reached his crisis break-point tends to become rigid, antagonistic, and secretive; he looks for scapegoats, hunkers down, adopts a bunker mentality, and engages in a variety of other ego-protective measures. When crisis break points are reached in those upon whom corporate survival depends, the end may be near. The will of employees to continue is lost and productive activity screeches to a halt.

The collective effects of dysfunctional behavior on corporate systems, as described by Cameron, Whetten, and Kim, and other researchers, blended with the Park Bank experience, are described in the next section.

Effect on Corporate Systems

When crisis-stressed systems within the business begin to overload, corporate decision making centralizes within executive management, and instead of delegation and task assignment, retrenchment occurs. This compounds problems because executive managers, now charged with running everything, tend to jump from issue to issue without enough time to prioritize and develop solutions.

Scapegoats are sought; others or circumstances outside the company are blamed for the crisis. This further centralizes power; for executives view themselves as righteous protectors against outside intruders. The wrong issues are thus addressed, and the wrong problems are solved, adding immeasurably to the woes of the company.

Centralization of decisional control tells junior managers and other employees that the executive management has little confidence in their abilities. Executive management's diminished expectations become self-fulfilling prophecies, and employees withdraw, saying in effect, "Let them do it if they're so smart." As a result, the upward flow of information, so vital for problem identification and solving, further evaporates.

Even when given the opportunity, lower-level employees often back away from decision making with a "Here, you take the monkey" attitude. Few are willing to take on responsibilities for decisions that could be wrong and cause their company further trouble, or that could adversely reflect upon them, increasing their job insecurity.

Thus, the executives at the top of the rim-bound company act; the rest stand by and watch.

As a company's fortunes decline, pressures also arise to cut back and restrict the uses of its now scarce resources. Conflicts and power struggles erupt, diverting efforts and focus away from the company's critical problems. Often, instead of cutting back step-by-step on a priority basis, in order to minimize infighting and turf-protecting, cuts are made across the board. Ultimately, non-prioritizing leads to more scarcity, more conflicts, and more infighting.

As human and material resources diminish, the company loses its flexibility to cope with new events. Projects, training schools, and corporate backup systems are the first to be eliminated. Uncommitted resources are diverted to operating expenses. There is loss of flexibility and competing demands for funds by various divisions or departments.

When flexibility in allocation of resources is lost, turf protection increases, which leads to infighting and resistance to change. This resistance is related to the belief that any change could mean that people whose turf is eroded will lose their jobs or have their skills devalued.

Conflicts increase the fragmentation of the organization into various cliques and interest groups. Where once people were able to function with management, now, suffering crisis-overload, they withdraw to either isolated, small, trusted-member group activities or work alone, every person doing for himself.

There is gossip, rumor, and poor morale company-wide. Lack of believable information reduces feelings of security and trust. Employee dissatisfaction increases because employees no longer find opportunities for meaningful achievement in their work.

As the stressed-out people disengage, they direct their efforts toward survival. They may withdraw from company activities; or they may become disoriented and confused or angry and hostile.

Soon employees take out their anger and frustrations on executive management, which loses its credibility.

Personnel who, in the past, saw corporate leadership as providing them with security and stability, now see executive management as not succeeding in turning the business around nor in protecting employees from loss of jobs.

Credibility also suffers if management sends conflicting messages to employees; for example, if lower-level salaries rather than executive salaries are cut. (General Motors's management was highly criticized by employees and others a few years ago when they negotiated a tough union contract based upon "shared sacrifices" and then followed that action with a new formula providing overly generous executive bonuses.)

Sooner or later, discussions about selling the troubled business come up. If the CEO has been viewed as a father figure by his people, selling is equated to his abandoning them, further reducing trust and confidence.

As trouble increases, losses of key people accelerate. Departures of the key managers both weaken the troubled company and make its competition, who then employs them, stronger.

Because the demand for survival-directed action dominates, there is no long-range planning. Ultimately, competitors position themselves to take advantage of the situation. Since there is no effective research and development, the company's ability to meet evolving competition diminishes each day.

Researcher Richard A. D'Aveni has pointed out that one of the reasons troubled companies fall behind in innovation is that legal and financial people play major roles in turn-arounds. They create managerial imbalance by focusing on risk avoidance, controls, and financial issues rather than on necessary, but more unpredictable, marketing and business development themes. People, even those brought into turn-arounds, often focus on what they know how to do best, not always on what is required.

Finally, the company's culture and traditions are questioned. Now doubted, they no longer provide core value support.

Identifying Crisis Systems Overload

Identifying when people have crossed their crisis break-points and when the company suffers crisis-overload becomes one of the great management challenges.

Inside the Park

I knew early in 1986 that the people at Park Bank were at the brink of overload. Our plans to raise capital had been blocked, and our efforts to sell the bank were unsuccessful; only one suitor remained. Our capital was negative. Borrowers increasingly resisted our efforts to collect loans. Depositors were nervous; withdrawals and closed accounts occurred with increasing frequency. Employee morale was slipping as people lost hope of any future.

Finally, during the first week of February 1986, our lawyers and I met with the Division of Banking and agreed to surrender the bank voluntarily on Valentine's Day if our only remaining possibility for a sale fell through. We implemented a plan to operate to the end, as if we would survive, while at the same time preparing the bank and our people if we did not.

I wrote my final message to the staff and reluctantly concluded it by quoting Lincoln, who said, "When you have a running elephant by the hind legs, there comes a time when you have to let go." I added, "And now it is time for us at Park to let go. We have fought the great fight. We have done all that is humanly possible. . . . Always remember the value of what you have given. Contributing is truly the mark of the ultimate winners in life."

The cost of continuing was impossible and would only have increased the damage to everyone involved.

The Rim Country Challenge

You have now seen the environment of the corporate Black Hole. You have met its rim people. You have seen how the rim burns from the volcanic eruptions of litigation and the smothering ashes of adverse publicity. You have gone inside the company and observed how the company's people react to their pressures and stress, and what happens when the company's personnel experience crisis-overload.

Being on the rim is truly hell.

And there is also a challenge. A company cannot always be saved from its Black Hole, but those involved can prevent their own destruction by facing the crash with head high, maintaining dignity and class to the end.

It has been said that what man fears most is not extinction, but extinction without significance. Having an impact in the rim country and surviving it forges significance; it is the difference between crashing and crash landing.

Inside the Park

Although the people at Park Bank suffered, sometimes miserably, from their crisis-overloads, we were able to stick together and minimize the damage of Park's collapse.

After Park's sale to Chase Bank, I was interviewed by the Southern Banker, *and the reporter noted: "Looking back over his efforts, he [Jacobs] says that he had two major fears: 1) that there would be a run on the bank, and 2) that his employees would desert him. Although his efforts [to save the bank] terminated in stark failure, there never was a run on the bank and employees remained faithful to the end."*

In no way can I take any singular credit for those who stuck together until the end, or for our avoiding a damaging run on deposits that could have robbed us of all liquidity, causing us to close Park's doors prematurely at tremendous loss to everyone. That entire effort was a team effort by very dedicated people who extended themselves to the utmost.

Robert B. Reich said it well: "The old myth of the entrepreneurial hero remains powerful. Many Americans would prefer to think that Lee Iacocca single-handedly saved Chrysler from bankruptcy than to accept the real story: a large team of people with diverse backgrounds and interests joined together to rescue the ailing company."

At Park Bank, Park's team was the hero, not for saving Park, because by the time the needed changes were completed, saving Park was impossible, but for their effort in the face of almost certain disaster and for preserving what could be saved with as little selfishness as I can imagine.

Part IV

Through the Rain

"If we should fail?
We fail?
But screw your courage to the sticking place,
And we'll not fail."

Shakespeare

Chapter 10

The Costumes of Man

On the stage he was natural, simple, affecting.
'Twas only when he was off he was acting.
Oliver Goldsmith

In a troubled moment, Beth, one of the leads in Sam Shepard's play, *A Lie of the Mind*, holds her man's shirt out saying: "Look how big a man is. So big. He scares himself. His shirt scares him. He puts his scary shirt on so it won't scare himself. He can't see it when it's on him. Now he thinks it's him. . . ."

That is where we start. We start with man the playwright, on his stage, acting out the role he has created, wearing the costume he has chosen. Understanding the playwright in each of us is essential if we are to learn how to make it through the rim country's rain.

Impression Management Revisited

In Chapter 4, we were critical of impression management, IM, and what a person does to manage the impression others have of him. Executives use IM when they project planned images of themselves and their companies to influence other people, both within and outside their organizations. Our prior discussion focused on IM's abuses.

Properly used, however, IM becomes an important executive tool, particularly on the rim, where a CEO must communicate his commitment and belief that, with supreme effort, the course of the troubled company can be turned. To this end, a CEO's use of charismatic, inspirational, and motivational forms of symbolic communication become all-important.

Executives use a variety of IM techniques to present themselves. Researchers William L. Gardner and Mark J. Martinko have organized IM presentations into six categories: self-descriptions (what managers tell others about themselves), accounts (explanations of predicaments), apologies (explanations that what happened is not a fair portrayal of the manager), entitlements (maximizing identification of the manager's responsibility for something good), enhancements (favorable explanations about what happened), flattery (complimenting others for its reciprocal effect), and favors (doing nice things to be liked).

The CEO of a rim-bound company, like an embattled general in the midst of war, must create the belief that saving the company is a goal worth fighting for. Communication of that message requires him to commit himself, for without his own commitment he cannot communicate commitment.

It is through IM that the CEO conveys to his employees that he has committed himself without reservation. He projects that he is caught up in his cause and demonstrates his confidence and beliefs by serving as example and mentor, motivating and encouraging those who follow him.

Professor Bernard M. Bass has written: "History is replete with examples of how a combination of confidence in one's capabilities, and the belief in the correctness of one's cause produced extraordinary effort and success."

Like Beth's man on the *People of the Lie* stage, the CEO in the rim country puts on his costume and plays out the role he has, perhaps consciously, or, most likely, instinctively, written for himself. That is what IM is all about.

As important as that whole process is, acting out IM exacts a toll. The CEO's problem can come about in two ways. First, IM encourages the executive who hides behind his "work-costume" to define his worth by what he *does*, rather than by who he *is*. Second, IM encourages the executive who hides behind his "manhood-costume" to disguise his vulnerabilities, to conceal his innermost feelings from both himself and others.

When Work Defines Us

When a CEO who defines himself only by what he does discovers that what he does is destroyed, his identity is also destroyed. He becomes like the actor whose real-life has become indistinguishable from the stage character he portrays. He lives for the applause that comes from his business performance. When disaster occurs, when his business fails, his theater closes. His role is over and his self-image obliterated.

In contrast, people who have many areas of interest and identification usually can step back more easily from disappointment and failure, appraise their situation, and form new insights. For people with multifaceted interests, involved in several aspects of life at the same time, damage to one aspect is not as traumatic. For example, a person whose "I am a banker man" aspect is damaged but whose "I am a family man" and whose "I am a photographer man" identities are not affected, suffers less from stress or crisis defeat because his other aspects of self-identification continue.

Private Men

Corporate environments, in good times, are dominated by affairs of the intellect, not of the heart. But on the rim, the executive's intellect alone will not guide him through his emotional experiences of humiliation, anger, guilt, helplessness, estrangement, or anxiety. Unfortunately, for the most part, a businessman, raised and trained to rely on the use of his rational mind, doesn't know how to react to emotional perils as threatening and deep as those felt on the rim.

The reason has partly to do with the ways in which most males are raised to control emotions, to admit few doubts, to show no fears. From childhood on, men are molded to be solid as rocks, the providers, the protectors, the dependable ones. Early on, a boy learns to wear the costume of a man.

How is a strong man supposed to react to adversity? A psychiatrist, interviewed by researchers Steven Naifeh and Gregory W. Smith, said, "Men learn to fake it. They have to fake confidence when they are in a panic, knowledge when they are at a loss, interest when they are indifferent. . . ."

The forces that create the symbols of manhood (parental indoctrination, images of the trappings of manhood, and fears of dependence) keep most men private, self-contained, and closed. They usually learn to guard their feelings, keeping themselves emotionally distanced from others and themselves as well. Most men do not reveal themselves to others, indeed, rarely to themselves.

Yet, the pressures experienced on the rim require that the CEO confront and deal with the emotions that go on inside himself; if he does not, he runs the risk of self-destruction. He needs to shed his costume of invincibility.

Inside the Park

In July 1985, I met with our attorneys in Washington. Park Bank was moving closer to the edge of its Black Hole. The SEC continued to delay approval of our last, now desperate, plan to raise capital. The first of a series of RICO law suits had been filed. Negative publicity was mounting. Borrowers were becoming antagonistic as we were forced to call their loans. Our staff strained under the pressures.

At dinner, Charles Ruff, my personal legal counsel, said, "Dick, be sure you have a friend. There will be more lawsuits, investigations, and a lot of bad publicity. It will tell on you. You need a friend to talk to."

Going It Alone

Is it easy for the CEO on the rim to entrust a friend with a revelation of himself and his vulnerabilities?

Hardly.

Less than one man in twenty has a person with whom he will discuss his feelings, wrote Letty C. Pogrebin in *Among Friends*. Men don't make friends; they have buddies: golf or tennis buddies, fishing or hunting buddies, card-playing buddies, buddies at work. Lacking depth, these superficial relationships preserve each participant's privacy, revealing little about the inner person. Some aspect of his public self may be revealed to one or more of the buddies, but no one is permitted to know the whole of the man.

Conversations among men tend toward the topical: sports, the market, work, women, wars. Talking about feelings — fears, anxieties, burn-out, cowardice, failure, falling short — with other men is rare. Feeling-talk is contrary to man's image about men.

So how does a man confront the fears and anxieties tearing at him when he is on the rim?

The rim partly provides its own solution. On the edge of a Black Hole, as in war, men's relationships with others in the crisis deepen; in a sense, a cult is born among those struggling together. Comaraderie, born under fire, provides support, particularly for those working close together as a team. They become foxhole buddies.

Outside the Huddle

But the CEO is the quarterback. He stands alone, outside the huddle. Those in the huddle depend on him, his strength, and his judgment. That dependency may stretch his capacity, but it can also compound his internal pressures. Some CEOs thrive on the trauma of crises. But even CEOs who thrive on the rim's chaos stand alone. At times, terribly alone.

Timothy D. Schellhardt reported in the *Wall Street Journal* that a survey of 1,000 corporate executives indicated that when it comes to deciding ethical business issues, issues that are integral parts of almost every rim decision, 44 percent of the executives consulted with no one but themselves.

Standing alone makes for good stories when a crisis is successfully resolved. But for every Grant there is a Lee. The effects of isolation when facing defeat can be disastrous. When every effort to escape from the rim is destroyed by failure's compounding momentum, the Black Hole's shock waves build relentlessly. The CEO trapped on the rim, faced with the possibility of being crushed by the weight of the Black Hole's overwhelming difficulties, soon understands there are limits to his capacity to grit his teeth. When the CEO approaches his own crisis break-point, further withdrawal risks physical and emotional breakdown.

Even the CEO programmed to draw on his inner strength during crisis must share his fears and vulnerabilities if he is to minimize his damage from psychological pressures. Whether he will admit it or not, the rim-trapped CEO needs a friend. With a true friend, he may be able to feel safe enough to expose his vulnerabilities and risk destruction of his carefully composed masculinity. Executives who find someone with whom they are willing to share their feelings make their way through the rim country with the least damage to themselves and, perhaps, make the best decisions for their companies.

Finding the Friend

Where does the CEO find the friend with whom he will share his inner feelings? Psychologists tell us that men are more likely to divulge their feelings to women than to men. Women are generally emotionally open and able to speak and think in terms of feelings. In *Why Can't Men Open Up?* Steven Naifeh and Gregory W. Smith reported research indicating that the only persons most married men completely trust are their wives; wives are their only truly close friends.

The survey on business ethics showed that 29 percent of the 1,000 executive respondents said they talked ethical business issues over with their wives. Marriages in which the partners are trusting and nurturing, wherein husbands and wives communicate innermost feelings and consult openly with each other, can provide the deep emotional support required to traverse the rim country.

Unfortunately, some men are unable to relate to women. Those men, more private and closed than others, have greater difficulty sharing their lives with anyone, even their wives. Their marriage relationships may have chosen to permit them to continue their private, uncommunicative styles; in fact, they may harbor conflicting hates of women.

Workaholics especially have difficulty opening themselves because they are driven by fear, often using work to cover up unresolved personal problems. Workaholics are likely to seek the counsel of no one. In fact, a workaholic obsessed with work is likely to smother his wife's feelings, squelching her ability to relate to him as a friend.

When Crisis Crushes In

If the CEO is the type who denies the possibility of failure, seeing the rim as simply another challenge or a nonexistent problem, any advice will be ignored. Only the crush of the crisis itself will stop him. He only stops when his internal system has been so shocked by the crisis experience that he literally drops in his tracks and, if he is still alive, is forced to reevaluate his life. Such a man is stripped of all of his vanity, as Master of the Universe Sherman McCoy was in Tom Wolfe's *The Bonfire of the Vanities*. When McCoy's wealth was destroyed, when he was indicted for a crime he didn't commit, when he was abandoned by his friends and supporters, he finally stood naked before his desperate situation, and before himself. And, stripped of his pretenses, he accepted himself. No longer was he shaped by outside events and opinions of others. His internal systems finally gave him strength.

The romantic lore of business is that CEOs, masters of life's events who are immune to bad luck, do not share the vulnerabilities of ordinary men. Trying to live up to that belief can mean broken health, a broken marriage, or a broken spirit, tributes rendered needlessly to the mythical and jealous gods of manhood.

Inside the Park

I was not good at dealing with my fears and vulnerabilities during the aftermath of our collapse. What I have written, I have had to learn by painful experience.

The difficult struggle to gain control of Park Bank and, after we knew we were too late, our all-consuming efforts in preparing for the inevitable crash landing produced adrenaline, an instant source of energy.

Everyone involved felt a sense of urgency, of comradeship and purpose. We were on a mission, a mission with a high community purpose, and we were on it together. A strong emotional bond developed among the Park Bank family as we worked closely with each other, providing each person with a source of support and strength. Personally, I benefited tremendously from the group.

When the bank collapsed, the St. Petersburg Independent, *in an editorial appearing on February 18, 1986, wrote, "Depositors are protected.*

Consumers have been kept fully informed by Park's chief officer, Richard Jacobs, who, like a pilot of a failed aircraft, has guided the bank to the safest possible crash landing." I felt I had reason to feel good about the process we had been through.

During the first few weeks following the crash, I received a number of letters and calls from local business persons, customers, and stockholders, all complimentary.

That's when my wife and I went to India and Nepal to trek and relax.

On our return, I found out about the lawsuit filed by several stockholders, alleging board and management racketeering and fraud.

I was shocked. I felt anger, feelings of betrayal and unfairness, and powerless to control my life. The feelings were heightened by publicity surrounding the lawsuit. I was overcome with humiliation, embarrassed to go to places I had always gone: to the country club, even to our businessmen's lunch club.

The close community of Park's people, which had been so supportive during the crash landing, was missing. I was no longer involved with the bank or with those who had been my support group during the crash landing. There was a void in my life; I was in transition to whatever was to become my next reality.

My prior business life had been in law, and lawyers don't bring home client problems. When it came to my own troubles, I had never learned to use emotional outlets. I did not know how to share my feelings with my family or how to seek their support. My early attempts at family conferences were disasters. No one, including me, knew what to say when we started. We had never done it before. "Dad" had never shown any vulnerability.

Finally, I have learned — no, I *am* learning — to acknowledge and to deal with my inner feelings.

Privileged Communications

The importance of good intra-family communications became increasingly clear to me as Park's litigation grew in intensity during the more than three years following Park's crash. Lawyers will advise you, as did mine, regardless of right or wrong, fault or no fault, not to talk about the substance of any lawsuit with anyone who could be subpoenaed to testify. Stray communications muddy the issues and increase the probability of miscommunication or misunderstanding. Doing that, however, increases the tensions and stress. A significant part of your life is sealed off: you are unable to reveal it to anyone. Constant bombardment by the press drives the pain deeper since you can't respond. Someone in that position must learn to take it, or learn to talk to someone with whom revelations are privileged.

Fortunately, communications between husband and wife are legally protected. Husbands and wives can talk to each other without fear that their very private communications will be discovered by anyone. In addition, communications with doctors, psychiatrists and psychologists, and lawyers are privileged. However, privileged communications do not include communications with other family members, friends or lovers. So, when litigation pressures bear down, relief from stress can best come from private conversations about litigation matters with your lawyer, your doctor, or your spouse.

Beyond Heroic Male Courage

Heroic courage is part of the "John Wayne myth" we identify with rugged male individualism. But heroic male courage — the willingness to stand alone against overwhelming odds — has some serious limitations in real life, including the resultant physical and emotional self-destruction of the heroic myth-holder and the distortion of his interpretations of crisis events and their causes.

Beyond heroic courage, the CEO who finds himself on the edge of a Black Hole needs courage to confront his fears and to reveal his vulner-abilities. He must have the strength to deal with what psychiatrist Frederich Flach calls the "reality of emotional pain."

Heroic myths and positive thinking, though immensely useful on the rim, will not provide sufficient strength or staying power. Professor Warren Bennis wrote in *On Becoming a Leader:* " 'Letting the self emerge' is the essential task for leaders." The first step in that essential task is for the self to emerge to the self. The CEO will succeed in that mission when he learns to shed his costumes, the mythical, and perhaps mystical, shackles from his past.

Chapter 11

Strong at the Broken Places

*The world breaks everyone and afterward many are
strong at the broken places.*

Ernest Hemingway

Though crisis behavior patterns among groups collectively follow
predictable patterns, each person works through those stressful situations
in ways that are personal. People vary, not only in abilities, but also in
passions and sensitivities, and in the programmed responses their personal
histories have imprinted upon their sensory systems. And, of course, crisis
situations vary in their characteristics.

We improve our ability to survive on the rim, regardless of its
unpredictabilities, by developing understanding of our peculiar crisis-
handling propensities and reactions. If we anticipate our own probable
reactions and stress points, we can use our strengths where they are
needed. Likewise, if we understand employees' likely crisis responses, we
can better guide them through the rim's eruptions.

What kind of personal information is useful in preparing for crisis? It
is important to know your:

- outside stress pressures;
- health status and health requirements;
- strengths, weaknesses, and blind spots; and
- self-mastery and support systems.

Outside Stress Pressures

Stress Overload

Psychologists tell us that a stressed-out person goes through three stages: alarm, resistance and exhaustion. When exhaustion is reached, burnout results. Burnout is the crisis break-point. Stress overloads the energy available to resist crisis, accelerating the beginning of exhaustion. When an executive's break-point is reached, his health is imperiled. Estimates are that some 70 percent of illnesses prevalent in Western society is stress-related.

Executive stress-overload occurs most frequently when the executive is unwilling to accept his limitations, driving himself beyond exhaustion to protect his image of personal infallibility. A classic example of this kind of exhaustion was that experienced by Englishman T. E. Lawrence, *Lawrence of Arabia,* during World War I as he led Arab troops in desert attacks against the German allies, the Turks. His biographer, Anthony Nutting, wrote how Lawrence constantly drove himself beyond exhaustion, to the point of total breakdown, to avoid losing face among his Arab tribe followers. Describing one of Lawrence's desert treks of over 125 miles, Nutting wrote: "For a fit man this six-day camel ride would have been a severe enough test. But Lawrence was ill with fever and dysentery when he set out and was only kept going by the extraordinary determination never to give way to physical suffering. . . ."

An executive's ability to come back from stress-overload is related to the amount of *adaption energy* he has. Hans Selye's research, reported by Dr. Peter Hanson in *The Joy of Stress,* discussed the ability of people to recover, to snap back, after periods of intense stress. He concluded that every individual has a finite amount of adaption energy and that once adaption energy is spent, it does not replace itself. When adaption energy is used up by a person, that person's ability to rebound from his crisis is lost.

Intense, total concentration, blocking out every interference, works well when dealing with short-term, episodic forms of crisis, for example, a plant explosion or an earthquake. Positive stress, called *eustress*, prepares the body with bundles of energy needed to operate when quick bursts are needed. However, when the crisis environment continues day after day and month after month, as it does during the reorganization and turn-around of a troubled company, eustress is inadequate. Most business crises build from shortcomings that have accumulated for years. A long time in building, they are also a long time in solving. Exhaustion occurs before the crisis is over. Pushing beyond the point of exhaustion increases the probability of psychological and physical damage.

Self-Testing Questions

Ask yourself the following questions to test your own stress load:

- *"What is happening in my personal life?"*

The stress in each part of one's life influences the reservoir of inner strengths available for combating the rim's crisis environment. Pushing beyond the point of exhaustion, beyond one's available adaption energy, increases the probability of an individual's permanent psychological damage. Behavioral researchers have shown that one's private life — family and marriage difficulties, financial problems, substance abuse, deaths, injuries and health considerations, and, simply, the fast pace of everyday life — add to business-related burdens. Lack of personal satisfaction, that is, lack of love, pleasure, or joy in personal or family relationships, also produces stress and weighs a person down at the time he needs all his energies.

- *"What else is going on in the business ?"*

Changes in the work environment as well as work pressures are also stress producers. The organization's policies, working conditions, systems, and relationships, even in relatively good times, can create anxiety. Newness on the job or with the company — or participating as a member of an untried management group — add anxiety.

- *"Is the company's philosophy compatible with mine?"*

One's personal value system must be consistent with the company's mission, value system, and culture. If they are inconsistent, if either are so entrenched as to be unchangeable, the situation will prove impossibly burdensome.

- *"Can I financially afford the risk required?"*

The answer to that question depends upon available financial strength and one's ability to recover if a risky venture fails. Recovery difficulty is also influenced by age. Older may be wiser, but not easier when it comes to recovery.

Inside the Park

I underestimated the effect of the crisis aftermath on rebuilding my career. I had naively assumed that, if Park's failure occurred, my all-out effort and my business reputation would be sufficient for me to rebuild my career in any manner I chose. That assumption was one reason I was willing to throw myself completely into the effort to save the bank.

I underestimated the potentiality of damage to myself from Park's failure. I measured myself by my effort to do the best possible under the circumstances. I mistakenly thought that that effort would be enough, regardless of the outcome. I was, as Grantland Rice suggested, relying on how I played the game.

I was fortunate to survive Park's crash landing with liquid assets, and I was exceedingly fortunate to have good friends in both the business and legal world who helped me begin rebuilding my career. But many opportunities I would have liked to explore, whether or not they were right for me, were blocked until the aftermath subsided; and I was less than effective for months, even years, as I worked through my residual feelings.

How Stress Factors Add Up

Researchers T. H. Holmes and R. H. Rahe have developed a measuring system for scoring the cumulative effect of various stresses. Add up your score for the stresses experienced within the past twenty-four months from the chart they developed.

Life change	Relative weight
Death of spouse	100
Divorce	73
Marital separation	65
Jail term	63
Death of a close family member	63
Personal injury or illness	53
Marriage	50
Fired at work	47
Marital reconciliation	45
Retirement	45
Change in health of family member	44
Pregnancy	40
Sex difficulties	39
Gain of new family member	39
Business adjustment	39
Change in financial state	38
Death of close friend	37
Change to a different line of work	36
Change in number of arguments with spouse	35
Mortgage over one year's salary	31
Foreclosure of mortgage loan	30
Change in responsibilities of work	29
Son or daughter leaving home	29
Trouble with in-laws	29
Outstanding personal achievement	28
Spouse begins or stops work	26
Begins or ends school	26
Change in living conditions	25
Revision of personal habits	24
Trouble with boss	23
Change in work hours or conditions	20
Change in residence	20
Change in schools	20
Change in recreation	19
Change in church activities	19

Change in social activities	18
Mortgage or loan less than one year's salary	17
Change in sleeping habits	16
Change in the number of family get-togethers	15
Change in eating habits	15
Vacation	13
Christmas	12
Minor law violations	11

A score of 300 points indicates that you are experiencing enough stress to damage your health.

Anyone serious about stress management must find a way to deal with life's changes and interferences. The efficacy of counseling by psychologists or physicians specializing in stress management should not be overlooked. Several Park Bank executives consulted regularly with psychologists during our rim encounter. I am convinced those consultations helped.

The State of Your Health

The impact of stress on health can show up in a variety of ways: back pains, headaches, heart disease, ulcers, substance abuse, overeating, anxiety, withdrawal.

Dr. James M. Rippe, author of *Dr. James M. Rippe's Fit for Success: Proven Strategies for Executive Health,* wrote that many executives, when faced with a high prospect of failure, commit what he calls "achiever suicide." When faced with failure, these executives engage in self-destructive conduct; they abuse their health, overeat, drink excessively, have affairs. The prospect of failure is more than their egos can stand.

In contrast, Dr. Rippe found that those executives who balanced business and personal priorities, worked out regularly, were careful about their diet, rarely smoked, and controlled their drinking were generally able to manage stress better. Their fitness increased their energy, stamina, self-confidence, and mental activity, and gave them extra strength to cope with their stress.

The state of our health can influence how well we handle stress; but allowing enough time for self-care practices is difficult when business problems take every minute. Time-consuming rim pressures weigh heavy, sapping all available energy. Yet, every executive on the rim must take care of his health. Rim judgment distorted by fatigue and stress when health is not at its peak increases the risk of crash.

Inside the Park

Shortly after Park Bank collapsed, I was asked to consult with the CEO of a troubled company. When we met, his face was flushed from high blood pressure. He had put on a lot of weight, 30 to 40 pounds, since I had seen him last. He smoked incessantly. His concentration and dedication to his company and its problems, which were not of his own making, had been enormous. Now he was unsure of himself. It took no trip to the doctor's to determine that he had suffered stress-overload. However, he rejected my advice to develop self-care practices to improve his now fragile health. He continued to devote tremendous time and effort toward saving his company, abusing himself in the process.

But his company could not be saved. Similar to my experience at Park Bank, he was sucked into a Black Hole by unrelenting momentum effect. His business collapsed. So did he, but his crash was several months earlier, in the hospital, exhausted, damaged by the stress-overload he carried and refused to face.

Diet and Exercise

A quality diet is essential to maintain good health under stress. That means plenty of salads, fruits, vegetables, and fiber-rich cereals. Consumption of salt, sugar, cholesterol and saturated fats should be minimized. Weight must be controlled. Smoking should be curtailed, and drinking moderated. A daily vitamin-mineral supplement, especially a stress formula with good supplies of B and C vitamins is worth considering.

Exercise is essential. Many studies have confirmed that exercise is one of the best ways to alleviate stress. Exercise improves circulation and respiration, dissipates tension, relaxes the mind, and generates natural mood elevators called endorphins.

Your physician can advise you about specific things you might do that pertain to your particular health status.

Keeping up your health will also set an example for others, improving their opportunity to maintain clear heads and perform productive work.

Mind Care

Care of the mind is as essential as care of the body. Constant mental turmoil can impede clear thinking, prevent good sleep, and even damage the body's natural immune system.

It is sometimes helpful to use relaxation techniques or forms of meditation to provide at least momentary flight from the rim's chaos. The techniques are learned best through professional instruction. Most communities have stress management clinics and there are a number of excellent self-help books and audio-tapes on the subject.

Even shifting gears can rest the mind from the rim's stresses. Playing tennis, going for a swim, working in the yard are all forms of shifting gears. Long walks are especially good. Walking also improves creativity and vigor through its aerobic mind effect. Aristotle, Jefferson, Thoreau, and Einstein were all long walkers. Philosopher and mathematician Bertrand Russell, also a walker, said: "Unhappy businessmen, I am convinced, would increase their happiness more by walking six miles every day than by any conceivable philosophy."

A bonus from shifting gears is that, while the conscious mind diverts itself and rests, the subconscious continues to sort out the rim's chaotic problems. Unblocked thoughts work to the surface, and on the surface, the refueled conscious mind can judge them with refreshed perspective.

Inside the Park

Throughout our crash landing, and during the aftermath, I used many of these techniques to maintain my health. I lifted weights and jogged. I abstained from smoking, ate health foods, was careful about my diet and drink. I watched my sleep. Fortunately, I did not develop ulcers or high blood pressure, but I could not escape all physical stress symptoms. Pain settled in my back, my weak spot. My lower back knotted up and my

hamstring muscles grew taut whenever the rim's environment closed in.
My wife, Joan, suggested I consult a muscle therapist. I took the sugges-
tion, and thereafter, weekly massage treatments provided the physical
relief I needed.

Although I did not meditate, I found that jogging, walking, reading
and diversions — my interest in photography — helped immensely. I also
took time to study the difficult situations and life examples provided by
other people, whose problems and challenges far exceeded mine at Park
Bank. From reading about their philosophies, my perspective was con-
stantly revitalized.

Stepping aside occasionally from Park's problems, diverting myself,
and letting my subconscious mind work on its own, helped me develop
intuitive solutions to problems as well as counteract the effects of stress.

David M. Ogilvy wrote in *The Creative Organization* that if one wants
to develop creative ideas — equally as essential in times of crisis as in the
daily world of advertising — one must set aside time to permit one's brain
to be inactive: "While thus employed in doing nothing, I receive a constant
stream of telegrams from my unconscious, and these become the raw
material for my creative work."

CEOs Who Must Control

Instead of pacing, prioritizing, and delegating, some executives try to
do everything about everything, all at once, everywhere. Trying to control
the uncontrollable is unworkable and is a primary cause of executive
health damage. Tight control might work when crises are episodic and of
short duration, but otherwise it can be destructive to both personal and
company health.

A CEO's efforts to dominate the external world become impossible
during severe crisis. His efforts paralyze his movements. Driven by stress,
fatigue, and fear that he must keep active, the CEO may engage in
thoughtless activity that requires little energy while ignoring important
issues.

One answer is consciously to select priorities. In the Pacific during
World War II, General MacArthur picked his battlegrounds and his battle

times to conserve resources. He island-hopped. All Pacific islands were not of equal importance. He targeted islands to invade and passed up others according to priority selection.

Inside the Park

When Mike Klein, Park Bank's lead counsel, and I sat down to examine some "what if" possibilities facing Park Bank, it became obvious that there was too much to do. We had to prioritize.

As my first responsibility, I chose to provide symbolic leadership. That kind of leadership would help give purpose, strength, and stability to Park's people so that they could continue to work in the unsettling rim environment.

The next objective was to continue to seek capital, and then, when the SEC finally blocked that alternative, to negotiate with potential buyers for the sale of Park Bank.

The third priority was to keep regulators constantly informed and also to seek their advice on various workout problems where legal answers were not clear.

The fourth priority was to communicate, openly and frequently, our position to the press, our customers, employees, and stockholders. It was important that we prevent panic. We could not afford an uncontrolled run on the bank's deposits. Also important was interacting with a nervous, concerned board of directors, management personnel, defaulting borrowers, frightened depositors, concerned suppliers, and cautious banks with whom we had relationships.

Then, there was litigation to be dealt with; and, of course, I felt it necessary to just "walk around," to learn the prevailing feelings and events happening throughout the branches.

Attempting to deal with those issues, and controlling whatever else went on at Park Bank at any one time, was simply overwhelming.

Mike Klein suggested a simple, if perhaps crude, way of organizing priorities. He called it the waste basket approach. *"Dick, when problems come in, write them up, throw each of them in one of the baskets by your desk. Label the baskets. You take care of the ones in yours. Give me the ones in mine, the managers the ones in theirs, and so on."*

Mike listed the burdens he would assume, including time-consuming supervision of Park's internal audit investigation and investigation of complaints made by troubled borrowers, and we set primary assignments for senior managers. When we still were spread too thin, we brought in outside help to advise us.

Problems were categorized and assigned as they arose, according to priorities that reduced both fatigue and oversight risk. It worked. An otherwise overwhelming job became manageable when broken into parts.

Mastery of the rim is achieved when one is willing to let go of environmental control. To do so you accept the fact that, at least for now, you are trapped on the rim's uncertain terrain, among its eruptions and smothering ashes. Only after the environment is accepted can you make the most of it.

Flexibility is important. Gerald C. Meyers wrote in *When it Hits the Fan*, "The rare executives who are the best at dealing with crisis are those who have a high tolerance for the unstructured and can hold several conflicting views simultaneously until a resolution is found."

Toward a Positive Self-Image

A CEO who survives a crisis also needs the inner strength that comes from a strong, well-developed self-image. That image can provide the inner strength necessary to allow risking of the self at times when every prediction proves wrong, when nothing works, and when solutions must be tried without clear (or any) indication of the outcome.

The CEO with inner strength is able to take what The Reverend Paul Tillich has called a leap of faith, from the known to the unknown. He understands intellectually, and accepts emotionally, that risk, even measured risk-taking, always involves the possibility of failure. The failure may be painful, but because of his inner strength, it will not destroy him.

The CEO lacking self-esteem is usually paralyzed when faced with decisional choices that could reveal what he fears most: his potential incompetence. The company suffers when those fears and unsure feelings about himself, rather than business considerations, underlie his decision making.

Dr. David Viscott wrote in *Risking:* "When a businessman ignores a real need to risk, the day when he will be in deeper trouble will come to him on its own. . . . When personal issues become the main factors in making a business decision, a safe outcome is unlikely."

At the same time, as James Campbell Quick, Debra L. Nelson, and Jonathan D. Quick wrote, the CEO needs to differentiate between being independent and being self-reliant. He seeks self-reliance. He accepts that he is not independent. Those with him on the rim are vital to his cause. He needs to rely comfortably on other people when the demands of the situation warrant reliance.

Self-Control and Support Systems

Two Kinds of Disasters

Two kinds of disasters confront mankind: disasters of nature's making and disasters of man's making. Nature's disasters are easier psychologically for people to accept. There is no one to blame.

Man-caused calamities are different. When that which man controls goes wrong, people assume, like Job's friends, that someone is to blame; it is hard to rationalize that calamity occurs because man cannot always pilot his course.

Even in man-caused disasters, there are some things that can be done to help.

Minimizing Disaster's Stress

Andrew Baum concluded in "Disasters, Natural or Otherwise" that individuals suffer less from disaster if they:

- control their emotions,
- do not scapegoat, and
- establish support networks.

Controlling emotions and avoiding scapegoating do not, however, mean burying emotions inside where they smolder without control. Instead, those trapped on the rim must first accept and then deal openly both with the rim, and their own anxiety.

Doing so requires both discipline and courage. Being afraid is okay.

Accept Responsibility and Clear the Mind.

I was in New York on business after Park Bank's crash. The hotel I stayed at had an atrium off its lobby. When I arrived in mid-morning, I noticed that in the corner of the atrium behind some potted trees, a large man, about aged 50, sat quietly smoking a cigar. When I returned that night, he was still there, slumped over, sleeping in his chair. The next morning, when I came down for breakfast, he was there again — in the same chair. For each of the seven days I spent in the hotel, he sat in the same chair, sometimes smoking a cigar, sometimes sleeping, sometimes talking to himself. But never communicating with anyone else.

On my last day in the hotel, while at lunch I asked my waiter who the man was and what he was doing. The waiter shrugged his shoulders and said, "It's hard to explain. He's here every day when I start work. He stays until we close the bar. He's not a guest. He just sits there and sleeps and mumbles to himself. I hear that he was the president of a bank. It failed."

It's important after a failure to empty your mind or, like a computer disk burdened with too much trash, your system can overload.

It is particularly difficult not to experience mental overload during the crisis aftermath when the requirements of litigation compete for every minute. Sara C. Charles, M.D., wrote that when she was sued for medical malpractice, the litigation "swallowed my life completely, demanded constant attention and study, multiplied tension and strain, generated a pattern of broken sleep and anxiety because I felt my integrity as a person. . . had been damaged and might be permanently lost."

Crisis thoughts dominate your entire world until your mind can be cleared. Clearing in the sense used here does not mean escaping from thoughts. Clearing means restoring inner quietness by defining the subject of thoughts and reducing their monsterlike proportions.

It helps put the contradictions and ambivalences into perspective if you transfer them to paper. Kierkegaard said that, though life can only be lived forwards, it "can only be understood backwards."

Keeping notes, a scrapbook, or a diary during crisis, or even writing it up afterward, helps cleanse negative thoughts from the mind and places events in perspective, allowing confrontation and reduction to more nearly actual size. You can also get control of disordered thoughts by assigning specific times to deal with them so that they do not overwhelm every moment. Set aside a specific time of day; then, at that time, sort out your fears and anxieties and deal with them consciously. Assign each one an appropriate action, making brief notes to aid the process. Then act on them on an appropriate schedule.

In Zen, disruptive negative thoughts are called *mind weeds*. "Pulling the weeds gives nourishment to the plant."

Having a cleared mind does not mean that one does not fear; rather, it means that one no longer fears to fear. It means facing the fear, accepting it, and then letting it go.

Accepting Responsibility and Facing Others — Openly.

Many of the most trying Black Hole situations do not come from strangers but from within the rim-bound company itself. Primitive forms of behavior erupt, and in a company crisis, the CEO will be a target.

If the company is to continue on course, if the CEO is going to maintain the respect and devotion of his people, he will be required to force issues and deal with persons who scapegoat. The CEO cannot be timid or avoid confrontation.

Inside the Park

We had confrontations during the final months of Park Bank's life. Newspaper articles revealing the documentary exhibits that were included in lawsuits provided a glimpse of what the Tampa Tribune *called the "confrontations between embattled executives and directors" that occurred during the final months of Park Bank's life. After Park's management changes, which included the resignations of three directors, I set out to force those former directors to repay loans that were either delinquent or at a level too high for the amount of capital we then had. (Our capital had been reduced by losses. Loans to any one borrower of a Florida state-chartered bank cannot exceed 25 percent of the bank's capital. Losses that reduced capital reduced our legal lending limits.)*

When I asked the board for support in enforcing the collection of former directors' troubled loans, the board refused to act, immobilized in bewilderment about our circumstances, unwilling to deal with the problem. I had written one former director, a life-long friend, saying, ". . . debts of you and [names of two other directors] cannot be tolerated. These loans must be eliminated."

Because the directors were frozen into inaction, I arranged with Mike Klein, the bank's attorney, to negotiate with the former directors. When asked why, I told Mike in frustration that "the board was not up to it."

Not only will some officers and directors be a challenge to your perseverance and internal strength, but stockholders who have been friends and whose support you seek will disappoint you. I was flying to Denver about a year after Park's crash. Sitting next to me was an executive whose father-in-law had taken over three small Midwestern troubled banks a few years ago. He managed to save two of them and lost the third. As the traveler described the emotional experiences his father-in-law and his family had gone through, I recognized a great similarity to those of my own.

"You know," my fellow passenger said, "my father-in-law's greatest disappointment was in the reactions of business friends, men he had known for years — some more than twenty years. They turned on him. Emotionally, it nearly destroyed him. The suits went on and on. Nothing was a bigger shock to him."

It is a shock when people you've known for years join in lawsuits, deserved or undeserved. Consoling comments such as "Don't worry, we aren't after you, only the insurance"; "It's nothing personal"; "I know you'll come out okay in the end, and it's really the *other* guys we're after"; do not appease.

Inside the Park

A ten-year business acquaintance in his late sixties, was a close personal friend of one of the attorneys representing the plaintiffs. He joined in the lawsuit filed against us as a plaintiff during the third revised filing of the complaint, about a year after the initial filing of the litigation. It hurt when he joined in; I thought he knew the other board members and myself well enough not to consider such a thing. But I recognized his relationship with the attorney; and I knew the original plaintiffs had been soliciting people to join them.

Through a friend, I learned that he was joining in the lawsuit "just for the insurance" and "meant no personal harm." He had lost money on his Park stock, and his business wasn't doing as well as it had in past years. Money and taking care of his family were on his mind.

I decided I would face him. I went to see him and said, "I've known you for a long time and I have always respected you. I am sure you have your reasons for joining in the suit — and I don't want to know them. I just want you to know, when this is all over, you will not be disappointed in me. I don't want to burn any bridges. So I'm not going to let myself act on my disappointment; life is going to go on. We'll still be talking in the end."

Was it the right thing to do? I felt better. For me, perhaps even for him, I think it was the right thing to do. Do not assume that I intended to acquiesce to the plaintiffs' demands in their lawsuits. Standing up aggressively against the plaintiffs and their attorneys is an issue easily differentiated from burning bridges. Each decision was centered in the same kind of consideration: validating oneself by doing what seemed right.

Confronting circumstances as they are is an absolute requirement for rim survival and any chance of success.

Networks

In addition to having a key friend to talk to, networks — supportive connections with empathetic, understanding people acting individually or as groups — can help avoid the worst ravages of stress. Wide-scale networks can be important support systems, if they are not what psychologist Herbert J. Freudenberger has identified as *networks of busy-ness.* Networks of busy-ness occur when networks become ends in themselves, serving as a form of crisis problem avoidance. In contrast, solid networks provide advice and act as safety nets.

Psychologist Richard P. Borough, who established a support group for executives known as Master Mind, has concluded from his experience (reporter Jeanne Saddler writes) that people need connections to succeed and to survive stress. Network feedback enhances perspective, provides alternative analyses of issues, makes available public and private perceptions about one's company and its business, and provides a sounding board for new approaches.

Strong at the Broken Places

Moving through the rim country is difficult. Self-discipline and self-understanding are required to make it through. But the Black Hole experience, even if it destroys the business, does not have to be the end of the story.

The Black Hole experience can become a positive turning point in life. As you grow through it, you get in touch with yourself. The rim experience can lead you to a reappraisal of priorities as you center and shift to inner-directed values. In a sense, rim-type experiences make the leader.

Abraham Zaleznik said:

Leaders grow through mastering painful conflict. . . . Leaders are "twice born" individuals who endure major events that lead to a sense of separateness, or perhaps estrangement, from their environments. As a result, they turn inward in order to reemerge with a created rather than an inherited sense of identity."

Afterward, as Hemingway so aptly described, "many are strong at the broken places."

Chapter 12

Bracing Against the Sirens

First comes the belly.
Bertolt Brecht

Every leader on the rim faces crossroads that require him to select among difficult, unclear, seemingly impossible alternatives. Ethical considerations are usually involved. Whether the rim-bound CEO exhibits the moral strength and integrity required or cracks under the Black Hole pressures is critical to his company, to those who depend upon him, and to his own well-being.

The Black Hole experience produces a paradox of people: heroic, inspiring leaders and followers who perform beyond expectations; and those, the rim people, who succumb to the pressures of the moment, reverting to primitive forms of self-interested, often destructive, behavior. It is important that the CEO be the role model.

The CEO as Model

People trapped on the rim are hungry for inspirational, transforming leadership. When a company is in crisis, its people want an exemplar. The CEO fulfills that need when he becomes the role model for his employees.

To set fire to their spirits, the CEO must communicate his character and his conduct, his strength and his integrity. Character, Peter Drucker has said, is the one qualification that every manager must bring with him. It cannot be acquired on the job.

For the ethical health of a rim-bound company, its people need a CEO who will encourage critical thinking and questioning and who will set off appropriate boundaries for human behavior.

Whether or not a CEO will be the kind of role model his company requires has a lot to do with his self-esteem, inner strength, and integrity. In the face of pressures demanding that he do what is expedient, popular, or profitable, he must be able to do what is right.

If the CEO's personality characteristics are sufficiently strong to enable him to resist crisis-induced temptations that could compromise his moral code, his display of ethical behavior will provide the inspirational, transforming leadership his company requires and its people seek.

But even a CEO bent on setting the best example may find himself pressed to his limit in the rim environment. How does he prepare himself to cope with pressures that could overwhelm him?

In the last chapter we examined the importance of self-understanding as well as understanding the outside pressures a CEO is likely to face. In this chapter I go a step further and examine the results of behavioral research and researchers' conclusions about human reactions to a crisis environment.

Behavioral Research

The work of researchers Maslow and Milgram is quoted extensively in both stress and crisis literature; however, their conclusions are rarely applied to the actions of leaders involved in crisis management.

The Work of Maslow

Abraham Maslow's most famous contribution in the field of human motivation was a paper published in 1943. He concluded in his study that human motivations can be arranged in a hierarchy of needs that man seeks to satisfy.

- First — *physiological needs.* Basic needs: thirst, hunger, sex, and sleep. They provide motivation for a person until they are satisfied, then he or she will seek to satisfy higher levels of needs.

- Second — *safety needs.* Physical and emotional security.

- Third — *love needs.* Belonging, friendship and affection.

- Fourth — *esteem needs.* Self-esteem and admiration from others. They relate to status, achievement and power.

- Fifth — *self-actualization needs.* Fulfilling human potential.

Transforming leaders operate at the fifth level and, if successful, through motivation can help lift their followers to this stage.

Later work by Maslow revealed that human behavior does not always mature through the hierarchy of needs in step-order; lower levels of needs are not always satisfied before a person reaches for higher levels. Behavior is multimotivated and multidetermined.

Milgram's Findings

Dr. Stanley Milgram studied the influence of events and authority on one thousand adults. The subjects were told that they were participating in an experiment about the effects of punishment on memory. A person was strapped in an "electric chair" in a room visible to the subject through a glass window. The subject was told that whenever the occupant of the chair made a mistake, the subject was to pull a lever, sending ever-increasing amounts of electrical shock waves to the person strapped in the chair.

As increasing amounts of current were applied, cries of desperation and horror from the person strapped in the chair grew louder. Whenever a subject wanted to quit applying additional amounts of electric current, the experimenter ordered him to go on, saying, "You have no choice; you must go on." Finally, the subject was ordered to apply the maximum voltage — an amount sufficient to cause severe injury. More than two-thirds of the subjects followed directions and applied the voltage.

The subjects were never advised that they, not the person in the chair, were the targets of the experiment, that the electric shock was illusory and that the person in the chair was an actor. Disturbed by his findings, Milgram reported, "With numbing regularity good people were seen to knuckle under the demands of authority and perform actions which were callous and severe. Men who are in everyday life responsible and decent were seduced by the trappings of authority, by control of their perceptions, and by the uncritical acceptance of the situation, into performing harsh acts."

Milgram's findings have been used to explain the atrocities that occurred in World War II and at MyLai. They also explain much that happens on the rim.

Maslow and Milgram at the Rim

Milgram's findings and Maslow's work provide enlightenment about the conduct of persons who succumb to unacceptable behavior under very difficult circumstances, such as those encountered on the rim.

Milgram shows that situational pressures can be sufficiently strong to make a person's behavioral patterns inconsistent with, and unpredictable from, his known personality traits. Maslow's work indicates that when a person's basic physiological or safety needs are threatened, that person will adopt behavior that satisfies those fundamental, primitive requirements. He abandons his higher purposes until his sense of security and balance is restored.

As Bertolt Brecht put it in the *Three Penny Opera*, "First comes the belly, then morality."

However, that conclusion is not without exception. Man's needs are overlapping and interdependent. Professor Bernard M. Bass observed that, though people customarily do not focus on higher levels of human behavior until their basic needs are met, transformational leadership can intervene, lifting people's aspirations and performances.

Thus, the CEO has a dual task on the rim: maintaining his self-control so that he does not resort to primitive forms of behavior that could be unethical or illegal, destroying not only his company but himself in the process; and conducting himself so that his transforming qualities, which empower him to motivate his people to perform under circumstances in which they would rather do otherwise, will be effective.

When the CEO's Behavior Becomes Primitive

What happens when the CEO slips into primordial conduct? Let us consider some possibilities.

One Noble Lie

Deceptive conduct designed to shield a threatened interest is rarely viewed as inappropriate by the perpetrator. He rationalizes his actions as those needed for saving his company or a key program from disaster.

Is deceptive conduct ever justified? Should the rim-bound CEO lie or destroy adverse information to protect his troubled company?

After all, it was Martin Luther who suggested that "a good strong lie" for the benefit of God could be appropriate; and it was Plato who advocated the use of *"one noble lie"* to aid Athens.

But the CEO who philosophizes that *one noble lie* is all right overlooks that, however noble *one noble lie* seems, it blocks the value of revelation to the company's communities of responsibility. When reality is obscured, people working in the troubled company, and those with whom it engages in transactions, are lulled into a false sense of security. Crisis signs are missed; corrective action is not taken. Unsuspecting, unconsenting people and companies are exposed to danger and needless damage.

An understanding of the kind of tragedy that can occur when data is confused intentionally can be gained from considering what happened in 1986 when the spacecraft *Challenger* exploded and its crew died. Evidence about the infeasibility of the *Challenger*'s launch was withheld from top-level NASA officials. Their decision to launch was made without a clear understanding of the risks involved. Mitroff, Shrirastawa, and Uduadia, writing in the *Academy of Management Executive* that NASA "could have prevented the disaster. . . . The evidence shows an organization impervious to bad news. Instead of deliberately designing monitoring systems to pick up danger signals, NASA designed, in effect, a management system that would intentionally tune out danger signals or downgrade their seriousness."

NASA investigations instigated after the crash revealed that the *Challenger*'s cover-up problems were not uncommon. *Wall Street Journal* reporter, Jonathan Kwitny, wrote that NASA's contract administration people frequently developed close relationships with space-project contractors; when a contractor blundered a cover-up was common. Vital information was blocked, distorted, not communicated in a meaningful way to decision-makers.

There is a difference between lying and being lied to.

However tempted a CEO on the rim may be to follow Plato's advice, his decision to save his company with *one noble lie* can drive both him and his company over the edge of the Black Hole. It can also take a number of unsuspecting, undeserving, people with them.

Inside the Park

A troubled bank must face the potential effects on its customers and others if the expended efforts do not avoid its crash. One effect of bank failure is that customer deposits in excess of $100,000, unprotected by FDIC insurance, can be wiped out. That kind of loss, particularly to retirees in a community like St. Petersburg, Florida, is disastrous.

A troubled bank, like Park, has a responsibility to work with its large depositors so that their uninsured deposit exposure is eliminated. The bank has conflicting interests. Those large deposits are essential for liquidity, and without liquidity, a bank's survival becomes impossible.

Does a troubled bank have the right to lull large depositors into maintaining uninsured deposits because those deposits enhance the bank's opportunity for survival?

Absolutely not. The bank's risk of destruction cannot be shifted to unsuspecting people who have absolutely no idea that they bear the bank's risk of obliteration.

We reviewed our large depositor base early on and assured ourselves that, should Park's recovery efforts fail, no person would unknowingly bear the risk of uninsured deposits.

Excessive CEO Loyalty

A rim-bound CEO may be overly committed to his cause, trying to save his company at any cost. He believes no sacrifice could be too great, no action improper, that, indeed, the end justifies his means. Since his objectives are good, he is likely to think that any means he decides to use must be good.

Let us consider an example that is common in crisis.

A rim-bound CEO demands of his staff that the course of their company be turned at any cost: "Get the job done!"

In the pressure-filled rim environment, the person charged with carrying out the task interprets the CEO's message as an absolute, a final edict for results. When an overly committed employee hears the message, he feels minimal or no responsibility for the message's ethical implications. For him, the order "Get the job done!" carries the subliminal message, "I don't care how!"

What should be done? Quick fixes? Shortcuts?

How employees cope with those kinds of dilemmas is influenced by the messages they perceive they have received from the company through its culture and from its leaders. Does an "I-don't-care-how" culture and rewards system seemingly condone unethical conduct? Faced with the dilemma, employees will be torn between taking no action, a form of paralysis, and selecting courses of action that are at odds with their personal codes of conduct.

What do they do?

If they are overly committed, they may well attempt to solve the problem through unethical or illegal tactics; something they would never do except for the force of the moment and their desire to please authority, which has been accepted with unquestioning loyalty.

Inside the Park

I had an experience during the last months at Park Bank that, in retrospect, painfully illustrates the point. It occurred during November 1985. It seemed at that time that each day brought one more stressful event after the other; and I was in the middle of them all.

Since we reported a quarterly loss of $17 million on September 30, we had to prepare SEC and press statements that needed great care and accuracy.

Trips to the regulators were required to update them about our troubled progress, losses, and the precautionary measures that were designed to minimize panic.

Meetings with staff had to be held to keep them on track; the huge loss had a devastating effect on morale since it dashed our hope for recovery as an independent bank. We told the staff that our only hope for survival now was with a sale. The stress induced by contemplation of a sale to an unknown, unidentified institution (which might cut employment) added to the already heavy stress-load people carried, all just before Christmas.

Meetings with the press, customers, and stockholders had to be held in an effort to keep the situation as calm as possible so that there would not be a run on the bank's deposits.

Arrangements had to be made to solidify alternative lines of liquidity with the Federal Reserve, just in case we experienced a deposit run.

Plans needed to be completed to assure that deposits in excess of $100,000 were moved to other institutions or reorganized in ways that would protect deposits against loss of FDIC insurance.

We had to deal with false rumors that the SEC was planning an investigation.

Two directors, experiencing personal loan problems, resigned at the request of the board. Their resignations added to our publicity.

We continued negotiations with various groups of potential buyers; and that required additional meetings at the bank and trips to New York and elsewhere.

And personally upsetting, I met with an impasse over a decision with my law firm involving Park Bank, and I resigned from the law firm that had carried my name for over 15 years. The resignation arose out of the outstanding loan discussed earlier that Park Bank had granted to a developer who then suffered a heart attack. The real estate project funded by Park's nearly $10 million loan was incomplete, and more funds were needed to complete it. Park Bank could not advance the funds because its legal lending limits, which were a percentage of capital, had been reduced through losses.

We struggled to find a solution. We finally found a qualified buyer who was willing to acquire the project. However, Park Bank had to suffer a loss, about $2 million, to make the sale. The decision to suffer a loss at that time was difficult to make, but Park Bank could not take the project over; Park Bank had no further funding ability. The developer could not go on because of his health and loss of resolve.

If the project was left to sit in its present condition, Park Bank would have had a non-earning asset of $10 million, costing over $1 million each year in lost interest, plus the expense of securing and maintaining the property encumbered by our loan. The developer was willing to cooperate with our sale arrangement, but he wanted to be released from personal liability for the deficiency the bank would experience. Since his life's assets were tied up in the project, that kind of a release was practical; in substance, we were giving up nothing. However, he also wanted the return of the municipal bonds, worth about $300,000, that we held as additional collateral so that he and his wife would have something to live on while they started over.

After considering the alternatives, I felt that returning the bonds was appropriate under the circumstances. In part, the loss of the bonds would be made up from other real estate added into the workout; the time value of money would make up the difference. If Park Bank could complete the sale of the property now, even with the loss, it could get assets back on an earning basis immediately. If Park Bank sued the developer, and he went into bankruptcy, months or years would go by before Park Bank could convert the project to an earning asset. In the meantime, Park Bank would have incurred substantial legal costs and the costs of maintaining the collateral, the sale would have been lost, and Park Bank could well have become a notation lost in local history.

It seemed like the right course to follow. And, as I had told Park's lawyers earlier, if there was any doubt about what to do in any situation, I would always select the course of action that seemed most likely to preserve the bank.

My law firm, still the bank's general counsel, had represented the bank on the original transaction and had been asked to close the workout sale for the bank. Instead of responding positively, they refused; they resigned from legal representation of the bank.

I was shocked. I felt that I had raised many of the lawyers in the practice, had helped them develop their skills and their client bases. Now they were abandoning me when I needed them most.

Angered and hurt, I met for several hours with the law firm, struggling to comprehend their position. All I could get out of them was that they were concerned. The members at the meeting were hesitant to speak out.

"About what?" I demanded.

"About you!" shot back the reply.

I was taken aback.

A spokesman for the firm, a lawyer with whom I had practiced for years, said that they knew how much pressure I was under. They knew how important it was to me to save Park Bank. They knew that I had not, and would not, ever intentionally do anything wrong, but that this loan workout had gone too far. I should not have recommended the release of the bonds. It wasted bank assets. They also feared that the regulators might think that the workout was structured illegally and that, if the law firm closed the loan, the FDIC would insist that they assume financial responsibility.

I was shocked. How dare my partners — no matter how tough the times — imply that I would place them, or myself, in that position! I accused them of abandonment and a few other things. But, they insisted that they cease representing the bank.

I melodramatically resigned, demanding that my name be removed from the firm's title, painfully ending 15 years of my life.

Park Bank employed new counsel experienced with banking and completed the transaction as planned — after, I might add, consultation with the regulators.

Although the law firm confrontation was handled with anything but tact on either my part or on the part of the law firm, the incident illustrates a key point. Somehow, members of the firm felt that I was stressed to the point that I would do anything to save the bank; and to those lawyers, that meant, literally, *anything.*

The thought had never crossed my mind, but perhaps my intensity communicated that impression.

To the law firm's credit, the lawyers did not cross ethical boundaries or acquiesce to handle a closing merely because I wanted the closing. Though I never thought about doing anything unethical or illegal to save the bank, after that event I consulted regularly with counsel and the bank examiners about every major workout.

Communicating Integrity

The CEO's integrity is involved in the kind of dilemma I experienced. How do employees interpret a demanding statement or attitude that says, regardless of the words used, *"Get the job done!"*? What has the CEO indicated by his demeanor, attitude, and example? Does he want results regardless of shortcuts or illegal or deceptive methods?

Or, has the CEO set standards that create a caring, tolerant, give-and-take atmosphere among his staff, permitting each person who acts upon his instructions the opportunity to clear up doubt about the meaning of his assignments? Does the CEO's conduct clearly indicate that, under no circumstances, are his staff members to promote *one noble lie* for the benefit of their troubled company?

Conflicting messages can be communicated subtly. Companies do not always reward the behaviors they claim to cherish, and the behaviors companies reward are most likely the behaviors they get. The rim-bound CEO must project carefully, anticipating how his messages will be interpreted. There should be no doubt about his fundamental, underlying objectives, about his insistence that no one deviate from ethical conduct.

Inside the Park

During the first quarter of 1985, shortly after assuming the position of CEO at Park Bank, I made a major effort to walk the right talk and improve what had become bad internal and external communications.

- *Energies were directed toward improving Park's faltering press relations. I met with the press and explained factually and openly where we were and what we felt was ahead for us. Previously, the press had been treated as enemies. Without a press dialogue, we never knew what to expect and were always off guard. Not knowing when or where the press would dig up information, we were unable to prepare our employees, stockholders, regulators or other con-stituencies for the disclosure, and every time Park was in the media, the bank rippled with shock waves. The* St. Petersburg Times *responded positively after the first meeting with a story entitled "Putting its house in order." The article talked about us rolling up our sleeves and sorting out the challenges brought on by too rapid growth. It helped settle people within the bank and outside.*

- *In a speech entitled "Our Tough Decisions of 1984," I advised Park's employees, all 350 of them, about the board's decisions to increase 1984 loan loss reserves and our anticipated 1985 losses. The talk closed with my favorite oriental proverb, "We are continually faced by great opportunities brilliantly disguised as insoluble problems," and a thank you: "Thanks to all of you, I'm glad we can all be a part of our opportunity and future." The speech was reprinted in* Inside the Park *as a tone-setting reinforcement and as a message for employees' homes. From then on, we had a series of company-wide information meetings throughout the crisis. We timed meetings to the release of information to the press, stockholders, regulators, and SEC.*

- *A communications committee was established within executive management. I advised management that their opinions and views were important, that each manager should, at all times, feel free to discuss and question anything with me. Written minutes of communications meetings were circulated for those who could not attend. We called our relationship a "go to hell" relationship; we wanted total communication freedom.*

- *I met with the FDIC, the Federal Reserve, and Florida's Division of Banking in the first of many open and frank updating sessions.*

- *We held quarterly "stockholders' information meetings" at multiple locations convenient to the majority of our 1,000 stockholders. Occasionally the meetings were far from pleasant, but they minimized potential hostility, at least until the end.*

Even during a stress-filled crisis, business considerations and proper conduct need not exist in opposition to each other; in fact, they should be inextricably entwined. One of the leadership objectives of the CEO is to prove that point.

The CEO must never forget that he is the role model, the standard-bearer; what he does and says speaks to employees about business morality. Thomas R. Horton, CEO of the American Management Association, summed it up: "The moral tone of any organization is set by its chief. If, in the executive office, a corner is cut here, a decision is shaded there — no matter how high-flown the company's written code of ethics may be — questionable conduct will soon develop at all levels."

When the CEO's Stress Loads Press Too Hard

During periods of severe crisis stress, there can be a reversion to primitive, survival modes of conduct because the stress-overload blocks a CEO's ability to see the situation clearly. The person simply cannot admit to himself what he is experiencing. He ignores alternatives, and he fails to appreciate the outcome of his conduct.

For example, a common occurrence in closely-held businesses experiencing a cash flow crisis is to fail to pay federal payroll withholding taxes. Failure to pay withholding taxes to the government is absolutely illegal. If those taxes are not remitted to the IRS but are used by the employer in its business, the business is spending its employees' funds, and cheating the government. Yet, this tactic remains a common occurrence in the life of a troubled business with cash flow problems.

I dealt with several payroll tax cases during my practice as a tax lawyer. Rarely were employee's payroll funds used for the CEO's personal benefit. Usually, the funds were used to "insure survival" (often to make employee payroll) of the troubled company. Typically, the company had receivables believed sufficient to cover the delinquent taxes. If the CEO paid the payroll taxes and couldn't meet payroll, employees would quit and the business would collapse.

The CEO's dilemma, then, is in choosing between survival (pay employees, not taxes) or disaster (pay taxes, not employees). Not unexpectedly, many CEOs opt for survival. A late tax return means a penalty for the CEO; but a penalty is better than not surviving.

But suppose the receivables are not collected? The tax is never paid. The act meant to save the company turns out to be a crime. It is not hard to imagine how a CEO, bent on survival, could feel that his decision was both ethical and essential. And it is not hard to imagine how his employees, scared, yet willing to struggle with him through the crisis, could praise him for his decision; after all, their families were able to eat that week.

Inside the Park

In the crisis environment, you will come to understand that your company's situation needs decisive action, yet what constitutes proper, decisive action on your part under the circumstances will rarely be clear.

During the crash landing at Park Bank, decision making was always tough; there was rarely a clear answer, and any potential decision was subject to conflicting ethical interpretations. One example: Park Bank had financed several real estate projects that were partially completed when, during our crisis, the projects' loans matured. At that time, we were experiencing a liquidity crunch and Park's capital had been reduced from cumulative losses, limiting the legal amount that we could lend developers to carry their projects forward. What should we do? We knew it was almost impossible for developers to refinance projects in midstream.

State statutes were unclear about our authority to advance funds to "preserve" our position in such a project. We asked the regulators what the proper thing to do was. They didn't know.

If we advanced funds, the FDIC or Florida's Division of Banking could claim we violated the law by lending amounts in excess of our legal lending limits; if we didn't lend the money required, the developer could claim we injured his project by not following through with our original plan and, worst of all, the collateral for our loan might well deteriorate while nothing was being done to preserve it.

What was the right answer?

Another example: How much interest should our branches pay to depositors to keep their deposits? Park Bank needed deposits to fund its outstanding loans and maintain its liquidity; yet, paying the high interest rates required to keep skittish depositors increased Park's operating costs, further reducing its capital and the legal amount it could lend. How could a reasonable balance between liquidity and interest rates be maintained?

High interest rates also attracted investor money—uninsured $100,000 plus deposits. To avoid exposing depositors to uninsured loss, we would *have to limit the size of deposits. When we turned excess funds of depositors away, we risked loss of all of their funds and bad publicity in the process.*

Which interest rate decision was the right one to make?

Deciding the Impossible

How does one decide nearly impossible questions in the volcanic environment of the rim? How does one make decisions when there are no clear answers, especially when any choice selected, in the light of hindsight, might be viewed as unethical, or illegal?

The CEO will be torn by his dilemmas. But he will have to come to grips with his plight. Psychiatrist M. Scott Peck wrote: "Life is difficult. . . . Once we truly know that life is difficult — once we truly understand and accept it — then life is no longer difficult. Because once it is accepted, the fact that life is no longer difficult no longer matters. . . . Life is a series of problems. Do we want to moan about them or solve them?"

Questions to Ask

The rim requires a realistic assessment of the effect of any course of action. In *Workable Ethics,* Gerald Nierenberg details a series of questions Professor Laura L. Nash developed to measure the efficacy of business decisions:

1. Have you defined the problem accurately?
2. How would you define the problem if you stood on the other side of the fence?
3. How did this situation occur in the first place?
4. To whom and to what do you give your loyalty as a person and as a member of the corporation?
5. What is your intention in making this decision?
6. How does this decision compare with the probable results?
7. Whom could your decision or action injure?
8. Can you discuss the problem with the affected parties before you make your decision?

9. Are you confident that your position will be as valid over a long period of time as it seems now?
10. Could you disclose without qualm your decision to your boss, your CEO, the board of directors, your family, society as a whole?
11. What is the symbolic potential of your action if understood? If misunderstood?
12. Under what conditions would you allow exceptions to your stand?

Sobered by Reality

I have a psychologist friend who specializes in counseling cancer patients. Most patients are going to die soon. I have had long discussions with him about the way cancer patients react when they are told they are terminal. After his explanation, I realized that cancer patients react the same way a rim-bound CEO reacts when he knows his business is about to crash.

The first thing a cancer patient usually does is deny the reality of his plight. The patient refuses to accept his condition. Then he may retreat into isolation, trying for more time, or become angry — "Why me?"

Later, fear, panic, despair, feelings of hopelessness set in. Finally, slowly and laboriously, the patient arrives at acceptance, admitting that life is not always fair. As realism takes over, a rekindling of the spirit usually occurs.

Abandonment of optimism is not necessary in the face of crisis. A positive success-bias is healthy and helps maintain self-esteem, but optimism not grounded in realism can become a self-destructive force.

Cancer patients who learn to handle their plight successfully do not hide from reality; they make the best of it. They recognize that during their allotted time they can continue to influence the lives of themselves and others.

In March 1987, Billy Carter, the late brother of President Jimmy Carter, was diagnosed as having incurable cancer. His doctors gave him less than two years to live. His attitude? Acceptance. He made the most of his days. He lectured about the dangers of alcoholism, the root-cause of his problem.

Once locked into the unyielding momentum effect of a business Black Hole, you, too, must have acceptance. You must come to the realization that crisis will be your life until it is over. Whether you chose to or not, you will deal constantly with reporters, investigators, regulators, lawsuits, over-stressed employees, intolerant creditors, uncompromising suppliers, and opportunistic competitors who seek advantage from each weakness.

Inside the Park

In late 1985, I met with Mike Klein, Park's lead counsel. I expressed my frustration with the rapid onslaught of traumatic events occurring in Park Bank's life. I said, with a dramatic sweep of my arms, "If we only had more time I could do it, I could turn Park around."

Mike looked at me and smiled, "That's what everybody says. But there is never enough time." The minute he spoke, I knew that Mike was right. Mike jolted me into reality. We switched from playing the pointless game "if we only," to the game of "what if."

We worked out two "what-if" plans: one plan for continuing action should we succeed in our capital-raising and bank-saving attempts, and another plan for use should we fail and have to crash land.

From that moment on, we operated the two plans on parallel courses.

The CEO and His Blind Spots

If the CEO's pressures threaten his self-esteem, he will be increasingly susceptible to Milgram's "press of the moment" and is likely to resort to survival behavior. If his overriding objective becomes personal survival, he may not be strong enough to resolve the ethical dilemmas posed by the business decisions he must make. And he may end up choosing ethically questionable courses of action.

A CEO who measures his success by the trappings and possessions of his life especially has trouble exercising solid judgment on the rim, particularly if his possessions are highly leveraged and a business crash could wipe him out. He views destruction of his possessions as an obliteration of his personality and all that his life stands for.

Inside the Park

Park's board was not steeped in an understanding of either Maslow or Milgram — or of the concept of leveraging leaders.

At the time the bank was acquired, Harold Kelley, its first president, was financially leveraged through involvement in a number of real estate projects. John Kearney replaced him as CEO after Park's board finally recognized that Kelley's outside pressures not only were taking too much of his time away from the bank, but also were coloring his judgment by placing him under tremendous amounts of stress, to the point where his health was visibly affected. At the time he replaced Kelley, Kearney was also building an empire on the basis of real estate leverage. Published documents indicated that the total debt of his companies approached $80 million. When his real estate fortunes sagged, the St. Petersburg Times *reported, ". . . personal financial problems dragged Kearney away from his bank responsibilities. Meanwhile he and Jacobs clashed over the seriousness of Park's problems and how to deal with them."*

Those two events, Kearney's leveraged real estate problems and our clash about what was going on at Park Bank, were closely related.

Following Kelley's and Kearney's strategy, Park Bank ended up lending money to others who sought to build their wealth as they did, through leverage. Kearney, Kelley, and Park Bank all crashed when interest rates skyrocketed and Florida's West Coast real estate market collapsed, each burdened with the same problem, over-leverage.

Kearney and Kelley each exhibited what turned out to be massive blind spots. Neither would admit that Park's real estate lending strategy was wrong. In retrospect, it seems clear that for them to admit to themselves, or to Park's board, that extensive leverage was a wrong strategy would have been to admit that they had erred in their personal philosophies; that, philosophically, leverage, the underpinning of their own real estate empires, was flawed.

During the early stages of Park's crisis, the board's struggle to come to grips with Park's problems was thwarted by Kearney's assertions that Park Bank had no problem, that the FDIC lacked an understanding of what Park Bank was all about. Outwardly, Kearney was talking about Park's lending policies. But, psychologically, was he not advocating his personal philosophy? Was not a defect in one the blind spot of the other?

The Times *reported: "Shortly after Jacobs tightened his grip, the goblins he feared might be haunting Park Bank began to come out into the open. The risky loans began falling apart. The tepid real estate market froze. President Reagan's tax revision plan created uncertainty in the condominium market, and the 1985 hurricane damage along the Gulf beaches further irritated the financial wounds of many borrowers."*

Yes, outside factors had an affect on Park's real estate loan portfolio, but those factors were of secondary import. Park's initial lending strategy was flawed. That flaw became Park Bank's crisis turning point, the product of the defective observation of Park's executives and board of directors.

George Anders and Constance Mitchell reported in the November 20, 1990, *Wall Street Journal*, in an article entitled "Junk King's Legacy," about a related leveraging leader strategy of the 1980s, one that has bankrupted many of America's corporations and torn apart its financial institutions. That strategy, the birth-child of Michael Milken, operated from the mindset that high amounts of corporate debt leverage company profits in a positive way, and that junk bonds used to finance that leverage are solid investments. Billions of dollars of defaults and insolvent companies and lenders now prove Milken's strategy flawed. His legacy has almost singularly guaranteed that the 1990s will be America's workout decade!

Bracing against the Sirens

The story of Homer's Odysseus and his ten-year journey home to Ithaca after the Trojan Wars may be a myth, but it is also a story about human behavior during crisis. Odysseus's journey home was treacherous. He was shipwrecked. He was marooned. He was diverted to Hades. He lost his possessions. His men died. He was tested by distractions. The goddess Calypso, for example, appealed to him to stay on her island forever, promising him that if he did, he would never grow old. He resisted her temptation. His journey passed through the lands of the Sirens who, he learned, "enchant all who come near them."

The enchantress Circe cautioned Odysseus that anyone who listened to the songs of the Sirens would never go home for the Sirens would seductively "warble him to death." She advised Odysseus to fill his and his men's ears with wax so that they would not be distracted by the melodies and songs. However, Circe continued, if Odysseus insisted on listening to the Sirens, he should have his men bind him to the mast of his ship. When the Sirens' songs became so strong that Odysseus would want his men to unloose him, Circe cautioned, "they must bind you faster." When Odysseus' ship approached the Sirens, he filled the ears of his men with wax, and they bound him tightly to the mast of his ship. "Come." the Sirens sang, "No one ever sailed past us without staying to hear the enchanting sweetness of our song."

Odysseus fought against his bonds, calling to his men to free him; but, prepared, they bound him tighter to the mast and rowed on, "out of hearing of the Sirens' voices."

The music one hears on the rim is not melodious like that of the Sirens, but, like Odysseus's journey, the rim will present dilemmas that will have to be overcome by consciously selected behavior, disciplined to the test of the moment.

The Sirens were Odysseus's weakness, but not his blind spot. He plugged his men's ears and ordered them to bind him to the ship's mast. Consciously, he embarked upon a course of behavior that carried him through his danger.

The rim-bound CEO would do well to understand the weaknesses and vulnerabilities that could tear at him, and then, like Odysseus, brace himself against them.

On Self-Determination

Outside factors and certain psychological principles are important, but humans, including CEOs, are not helpless victims driven uncontrollably by external forces. And the CEO on the rim should not use such forces as a scapegoat.

After experiencing imprisonment in a concentration camp during World War II, Psychiatrist Victor E. Frankl wrote about people's ability to select their behavioral responses under very difficult circumstances.

He concluded (the potential implications of Milgram and Maslow notwithstanding) that man does have a choice, even under the most difficult of times. The choice is "the last of the human freedoms — to choose one's attitude in any given set of circumstances, to choose one's own way. . . . Some of our comrades behaved like swine while others behaved like saints. Man has both potentialities within himself; which one is actualized depends on decisions but not on conditions."

Each board member, each CEO, each person involved in crisis, must make his own way — choose the decisions, the responses, and the actions for the environment in which he finds himself. No other reality is available to him. Despite the pressure of outside factors, the blinding effects of his own stress, or the welling up of primitive urges within himself, he has the ultimate responsibility for himself and his choices.

Part V

Transforming the Board

Among the most concerned and potentially the most effective group is the board of directors. In itself, it can act as a crisis management team that takes hold of the company — preferably with the chief executive, but without him if necessary — and searches for alternatives to oblivion. . . ."

Gerald C. Meyers

Chapter 13

The CEO As Catalyst

Executives are, essentially, powerless until the time comes when followers grant their leaders the authority to lead.

C. Barnard

In chapter 5, we examined the difficulty boards have in recognizing the approach of business Black Holes. The directors' difficulty must be overcome, not only because boards bear ultimate legal liability for their companies' destinies, but also because their help is needed, though that need may not be recognized by the CEO and the executive officers of the crisis-bound company.

Effective directorship is not easy to come by. As pointed out previously, this is partly because directors often lack in-depth knowledge about the businesses on whose boards they serve, they perform in roles that are part time, and they are subjected to psychological group pressures.

The Dual Role of the CEO; Boardroom Balance of Power

Another, less obvious reason makes effective board service difficult: typically, the boardroom leader occupies a dual role. He serves as board chairman, charged with the responsibility of guiding directors, and as CEO, reporting to the board, supplying and interpreting information, and implementing policies adopted as the board's response to that information.

If, for example, the CEO's vision, as he reports to the board wearing his CEO hat, is blinded to potential visible or invisible crisis signs, it will be equally blinded when, as chairman, he leads the board through possible interpretations he and his executives have supplied — or not supplied because they thought it not relevant or potentially embarrassing or damaging. The duality places the CEO/chairman in a powerful position and in the typical boardroom gives him the clear balance of power.

Inside the Park

The significance of the power that accompanies the duality of a person's roles as chairman of the board and as CEO became apparent to me when I tried to convince fellow Park Bank board members that we had missed our own crisis warning signs and that the interpretation of Park's reality, as expressed to us by our CEO/chairman, was wrong. I found it impossible to challenge the chairman in a board meeting, the seat of his power and authority.

During a frustrating moment, I warned the board about the awesome power of the combined office, "Nobody says no to the CEO." Only after heavy jaw-boning outside the boardroom was a challenge successful.

Few directors are willing to stand up to the CEO's interpretation of the situation; Park's board was certainly not among them. The mindset of directors to conform and be supportive, and the comfort inherent in avoiding boardroom conflict, are factors that, for most board members, override whatever urge any individual director may have to seriously challenge the CEO.

The CEO may report to the board; but as its chairman, he is clearly their leader, and in a position to challenge any board member who seeks to alter the corporation's course he has set.

When a person serves in the dual role of chairman and CEO, he is, for all practical purposes, his own check and balance. Whether or not he will use his power for the good of the company or for his own selfish purposes, even if he is sensitive to the difference, is a basic question that sets the course for the business.

The dual role of chairman of the board and CEO frequently has been criticized. Geneen, who occupied both positions at ITT, said, "If the board of directors is really there to represent the stockholders, what is the chief executive doing on the board? Doesn't *he* have a conflict of interest? He cannot represent the shareholders and impartially sit in judgment on himself."

Geneen's sentiments were echoed in a *Harvard Business Review* article by Arch Patton and John C. Baker appropriately titled, "Why won't directors rock the boat?" The authors wrote: ". . . Board practices work against director's effectiveness. . . . We're opposed to the same person being both chief executive and chairman of the board."

In his book, *Pawns or Potentates,* Professor Jay W. Lorsch states that "it's no exaggeration to say that, in most instances, directors understand the company through the CEO's eyes." He recommends that the power of the CEO/chairman be diminished by separating the two positions.

Critics of the dual role argue that the hero effect resident in the duality, coupled with boardroom pressures and protocols, tempers or eliminates constructive executive criticism and makes it difficult to ferret out crisis signs, evaluate business alternatives (such as measuring the worth of a takeover bid in the face of management's proposed leveraged buyout), sort out conflicts, set executive compensation, and question inside directors about activities and corporate policy.

Yet, for many of today's corporations, the CEO is also chairman of the board. Is the dual role wrong? My experience and the criticism I have described to the contrary, I believe that for most companies duality is appropriate. Despite the clear potential for abuse, the concept should not — and in most cases cannot effectively — be discarded. Leadership in contrast to management is difficult, if not impossible, to bifurcate in any successful way.

Crisis periods in particular are times in which corporations clearly benefit from consolidating the voice of leadership in one person. Crisis leadership is best seated in one person if it is to engender organizational empowerment. A crisis leader's relationship with his followers must *link* and become interactive. The interactive relationship between crisis leader and followers is the subject of Section VI.

If balance of power in the boardroom is essential, consideration about *what* balance of power means and *how* balance should be achieved are critical. Reducing the power of the CEO/chairman reduces the leadership ability of the most knowledgeable person in the company. Professor Lorsch points out that the CEO/chairman's knowledge about the company is his primary source of power. Appointing another, less knowledgeable person as chairman certainly does not seem to me to be in the best interests of the corporation.

What is needed is not a reduction in CEO/chairman power; what is needed is a positive increase in board member power. How that increase can be accomplished is the subject of this and the next two chapters.

The relationship between the CEO/chairman and the board should be strong, positive, and interactive; the board simply cannot be subordinate in a passive, never questioning, always accepting way. That means that the director's role must be reexamined and redesigned if boards are to provide the kind of give-and-take leadership and support required.

Reducing the strength of the most knowledgeable person is a form of boardroom "Atlas Shrugged." A few years ago Ayn Rand wrote *Atlas Shrugged,* a novel (in actuality, a treatise) about the havoc that occurs when leaders withdraw — shrug, as Rand dramatically describes it. The motors of their enterprises stop. I cannot help but believe that some motor-stopping happens in corporations that split up their leadership, particularly during crisis times.

Increasing the knowledge and the skills of the board members, matching as near as possible the CEO/chairman's knowledge and skills, is positive, and that is what will give the boardroom vitality and meaning.

Defining the Role of the Board

As we stated, the director's role, a difficult job in the best of times, and a brutal one on the rim, must be reexamined and redesigned if boards are to provide the kind of leadership and support required, particularly during crisis. Unfortunately there is confusion about the correct role for directors.

Consider the matter of corporate strategy and policy, a primary director responsibility under classic corporate organizational and legal doctrine. Research has shown that whether or not the CEO is the chairman of his board, he is, for all practical purposes, the principal architect of corporate strategy and policy.

Realistically, who should have primary responsibility for designing business strategy in today's competitive environment — the CEO and staff who spend their full time on corporate matters, or part-time directors from other professions and industries (who, on the average, spend fourteen days a year on boardroom activities)? The question answers itself.

There is another factor: the evolution of, and conflicts within, the laws of corporate governance. Because of the recent increase in lawsuits against directors, corporations have experienced difficulty attracting competent people to serve as directors. Recent changes in corporate laws have attempted to redefine the role of directors to make the position less liability-prone, and, therefore, more attractive. However, the statutes come up short of their objective. For example, the laws do not limit director liability under federal securities laws, and, in the case of banks, do not limit director liability in FDIC suits. Furthermore, the laws require that directors act in good faith, "with the care an ordinary prudent person in a like position would exercise under the circumstances." The laws provide sparse guidance concerning the *how* of ordinary care; and second-guessing the *how* is what director litigation is all about!

During the next several years, the courts will clarify these definitional matters, and flush out the evolving legal boardroom duties; however, a return to what some hope will be risk-free corporate board membership (the kind politicians and celebrities who serve on prestigious boards like) is unlikely.

But, regardless of efforts to limit director liabilities, two fundamental questions must be asked and answered for each corporation defining director responsibilities:

- What do the corporation and its constituencies — its stockholders, customers, suppliers, regulators, public and employees — need and have a right to expect from the board of directors?

- What kind of help does the CEO (and his executive officers) need and have a right to expect from the board of directors?

The answers to those questions, and the implementation of those answers, must take into consideration that outside board membership is not a full-time occupation even though, legally, it is a full-time responsibility; that most board members have other business interests that take a higher priority; and that most board members do not have in-depth knowledge about the businesses they direct or about the environment, people, and appropriate strategies for their companies.

How does an effective board define its role for times of crisis, as well as for good times? I suggest that the board, cognizant of its responsibilities, must:

- recognize that the CEO has the primary role in creating an effective and transforming board of directors;

- develop the board's ability to identify, and deal with, visible and invisible signs of potential business crisis while there are still viable "alternatives to oblivion;"

- audit corporate activities and results;

- determine whether the CEO can deal successfully with the Black Hole environment, and, if he cannot, replace him;

- facilitate the CEO's ability to deal with crisis by consulting with him and by insisting that communications be open and interactive; and

- insist that the corporation develop strategies and plans to deal with the potentialities of Black Holes.

These considerations will be discussed in some depth in this and the following two chapters. They can serve as a guide for any board that seeks to define its crisis management mission and role as "active." Gerald C. Meyers pointed out in *When It Hits the Fan:* A board that remains passive and uninvolved will miss signs of an approaching Black Hole, will not understand what brought their company to the rim, and will not know how to deal with crisis once it appears. Solutions conceived in panic and born of frustration are frequently ineffective.

Transforming the Boardroom

In the preface to the *Harvard Business Review* study, *Boards of Directors: Part II,* Kenneth R. Andrews wrote: "Thus the dignified, well-meaning, competent, but largely inactive board of the past, relaxed in its support of the chief executive who brought it together, is being asked to cast off its old skin. It is now expected to show itself as the active, informed, and objective guardian of the shareholders' and the public's interest."

That preface was written in 1977. Has today's boardroom changed — or changed enough?

- John Crudele wrote in *New York* magazine in 1988 that present company management is looking for board members among "big name businessmen or former politicians" who will be "loyal to the management."

- In a study of the causes of bank failures occurring between 1979 and 1987, the Comptroller of the Currency concluded that 89 percent of bank failures related to poor management, and of the most significant management causes, a passive, uninformed or inexperienced board of directors was present 60 percent of the time.

- In a 1987 study made by Risk Management Corporation regarding the attitudes and understandings of outside directors to its members, the report showed that most directors had an extremely low awareness about their exposure to risk and liability as a board member. The study stated: "Most outside directors said they trusted that others had adequately investigated and evaluated those issues for them." The study also pointed out that outside directors also perceived themselves as being better qualified than inside directors, viewing themselves "as having a better overview of problems, and possessing skills and contacts inside directors lack." The study noted that this view was prevalent despite admissions by outside directors that their biggest obstacle was "obtaining sufficient information necessary to make good independent decisions for their boards."

• In 1989, Professor Lorsch wrote that despite the trends toward increased director independence, board members, "as did their predecessors of a decade ago," feel constrained by a variety of factors that diminish their ability to be effective, including inadequate time, deficient knowledge, and lack of clarity as to their mission.

Clearly today's directors are not "merely the parsley on the fish," as directors were once described by the late Irving Olds, then chairman of U.S. Steel; however, boards have changed little in most of corporate America.

The Catalyst for an Effective Board

What is required to make the boardroom as effective as it might have to be in crisis and pre-crisis times?

In my view, the initial step is for the board to: *Recognize that the CEO has the primary role in creating an effective and transforming board of directors.*

In his article, "Corporate responsibility and the competent board," Victor H. Palmieri was emphatic: "Any given board of directors, notwithstanding the competence of individual members, will tend to be inactive or ineffective unless forced by circumstances or strong leadership to be otherwise."

Despite Palmieri's logic, there are unsettling indications that boards of directors are not popular with CEOs. Management consultants Patton and Baker have stated categorically that, in their experience, strong CEOs don't want strong boards.

CEOs who oppose strong boards of directors are missing, or misusing, what could be one of the most valuable resources their corporations have: active, strong, independent thinkers who have insights and guidance from various experiences. A strong, independent, functioning board complements, and does not divide, the CEO's power, if the CEO has the ears to hear and the eyes to see.

Let's review what is involved.

CEOs Need Coalitions of Power to Govern.

Abraham Zaleznik has written that no organization can function unless power is consolidated in "the relationship of a central figure with his select group." Absent a coalition, Zaleznik says, decision-making paralysis and in-fighting result. This is particularly true during times of crisis when all relationships within the organization are strained, and the transforming leader must, by will-power, courage, emotion, and intellect, pull everyone and everything away from the rim's edge.

Should the board be part of the CEOs select group?

Some would say no. For example, Patton and Baker position the board in an adversarial role with executive management. Is that where the board belongs, outside the company's select group, as the auditor of management on behalf of the stockholders? I don't think so.

The opposite, a non-adversarial relationship between board and the CEO, exists when the CEO has handpicked a supportive, friendly board from among his company's advisors, suppliers, customers, or from among the community's prestigious leaders. That kind of board does little more than bolster the self-esteem of the CEO. It offers him minimal balance, and no opportunity to counter his blind spots.

Zaleznik pointed out that the most brilliant of CEOs frequently fail to understand that their driving power and focused strength causes them to operate with massive blind spots that limit their vision and their ability to maneuver in the face of rim-like problems. Those CEOs fail to recognize the utility of support coalitions against the negative effects of blind spots. Zaleznik concludes: "The need to control and dominate in a person is perhaps the most serious of all possible blind spots which can affect a chief executive, because he makes it difficult for people to help him, while creating grievances which sooner or later lead to attacks on him."

The CEO must create coalitions, not only with his officers and employees, but also within his board. Strong coalitions provide him with honest input, provide balance, and maintain perspective. Conflict is utilized in a positive way. True leaders, James MacGregor Burns observed in *Leadership*, embrace rather than shun conflict.

The process of building solid boardroom coalitions is transforming. The CEO consents to the board's leadership — as chief executive officer he is the board's follower, and the board consents to his leadership. As chairman, he is the board's leader. It sounds circuitous, it's paradoxical, but it is energizing.

Transforming Leadership and Follower Consent are Needed.

Lao Tsu said centuries ago, "To lead, one must follow."

Transforming corporate leadership begins with followership. The transforming leader obtains his strength because his people want to follow him. They consent to his leadership because they believe their needs will be met by doing so. When they view the leader as being attuned to their objectives, they will want him to lead. Because the followers expect to reach their goals through his leadership, they entrust their CEO with leadership power, energizing him to lead in a transforming way.

What may not have been widely recognized is that the same follower-leader rationale describes the effective CEO-board relationship.

In his article,"On an Effective Board," L. W. Cabot commented: "Directors function well only when management gives board effectiveness a high priority."

Thus, the CEO has to want an effective board in order for a corporation to have an effective board.

Ironically, the board of directors is, by law, granted the legal authority to manage the business of the corporation. But, when it comes to effective leadership, the grant of legal authority to the board only adds to the myth that surrounds boardroom activities. Not until the CEO calls the board into active leadership can the board's legal responsibility merge into a meaningful reality.

As chairman of the board, the CEO brings out the board's leadership character. He does this by empowering the board to participate in the substance of corporate activity in a well-thought-out role.

George M. Prince, in the *Harvard Business Review*, faulted the traditional role of a board chairman, that of directing discussions, forcing conformity to agendas, making snap judgments, forcing meetings along in non-think fashion. Prince, writing in 1969 (long before the concept of empowerment was widely recognized), criticized any chairman who powered his way through board meetings. He saw the chairman as being a servant to the group, creating an open atmosphere where no one had to defend himself, where energy was kept at a high level, where discussions were open, provocative, and healthy, where the chairman listened to what was said and was sensitive to what was implied, where he kept members informed, and where he sought the contribution of every person in the group. It is the synergy that develops between a potent board and a dynamic leader that becomes motivating and revolutionizing.

The powerful role of the CEO is evident even in those boards that have separated the positions of chairman and CEO. It is not the chairman, it is the CEO, who leads. University of Georgia Professor William R. Boulton concluded from his research: "Having a board chairman separate from the chief executive was not sufficient to provide for board development. In fact, while the majority of boards involved in our research had separated the job of chairman from that of CEO, it was usually the CEO who was the key in the development of the board."

The CEO will provide his board with transforming leadership when he accepts and believes in the contribution a vital, independent board can make. The board, in turn, responds to the CEO's acceptance with fresh, occasionally controversial, ideas in a positive, supportive, yet challenging way.

Harvard Professor John P. Kotter has stated that leadership is the management of complex interdependencies among diverse groups of people. Within corporations, a healthy maintenance of the inevitable conflict between various stakeholders leads to creative solutions and minimizes waste of resources.

Inside the Park

The board at Park Bank saw itself as active, particularly in the early years; however, Park's first CEO viewed the directors' efforts as an interference with the prerogatives of management. I am convinced that the CEO's initial attitude, which led to executives keeping information to themselves, contributed to the difficulty Park's directors had in recognizing early warning signs of trouble.

In reflection, however, the board's approach to executive management contributed to management's idea that the board was interfering. The board and the CEO never sat down together to draw up a "bill of rights" that would clarify what was expected from each other.

The Effective Board

Effective boards start with corporate leadership, with a CEO willing to manage complex interdependencies within the corporation, including his board relationships. It is the CEO who must perform the role as transformer of the board of directors. The board becomes effective, and becomes alive, when the CEO empowers it with its appropriate leadership role. That role validates the board, converting it into a transforming agent within corporate life. No board of directors will be effective unless it is empowered. The CEO is its catalyst.

Chapter 14

The Ingredients of the Director's Job

The traditional definitions of the board's responsi-
bilities limiting it to "setting policy" or "monitoring
management performance" are useless if not dan-
gerous in today's world.

Victor H. Palmieri

Early signs of trouble are rarely visible to top management, and never to the board. When things go wrong, they start a long way from the plush, isolated, ivory tower where the boardroom is located.

A crisis looks like an isolated event at first; as such, it is easily explained away by identifying external causes. Upward communication of information that would provide early signs rarely occurs. Impressions of those closely involved, employees or line managers, are most likely to be that any trouble signs are job-threatening (something to protect against by not involving superiors), not company-threatening.

The board, of course, like Pentagon generals operating far from the war, obtains its information from reports passed between layers of managers, distilled, summarized, and rationalized at each step along the way. Directors have little or no contact with the people on the line. When the board does finally receive adverse information, its own set of recognition problems, influenced by groupthink pressures and distilled by the CEO's interpretations, hampers it, further delaying reaction.

I have pointed out the struggle Park Bank's board had in agreeing that the negative signs presented by the FDIC were as significant as they turned out to be. Apparently, our board was not alone. Former FDIC Chairman William Isaac, speaking at a Washington, D.C. conference on Failed Financial Institutions in 1987, said that the signs of trouble in financial institutions are virtually ignored until they are beyond solution. He concluded, "People don't get to the problem soon enough. They spend their time fighting the regulators instead of working on solutions."

A company's norm in crises is usually to delay recognition of and then to respond inappropriately to early warning indicators. It is the responsibility of the board to alter that norm.

Recognizing Warning Signs

Thus, our second admonition to the board: *The board must develop its ability to identify, and deal with, signs of potential business Black Holes while there are still available "alternatives to oblivion."*

The board can sharpen its members' sensors, tuning up their abilities to recognize impending disaster. How? By insisting that:

- board members become educated about their company,

- information-providing systems give the board the right information;

- information-gathering systems deliver information from the bottom to the top in time;

- board members understand board decision-making processes and not operate by consensus; and

- board membership be adjusted to admit periodically new and independent persons.

Learning About the Company

Each director must want, and must agree, to be educated in the important specifics about the company and its industry; and the CEO must insist on directors' education.

As difficult as the director's interpretive job is without specific experience, it is impossible without knowledge. Everyone, even the most intuitive of directors, must do his homework. Lack of industry and company know-how handicaps directors in discerning trends, strategies, and conclusions from the information furnished by executives who have already applied their own personal interpretations. Unless he has done sufficient homework, and has the ability to discern the material involved, the board member has little choice but to adopt whatever version of reality is presented to him.

A board member must come to grips with the fundamental fact that it is impossible to understand the operations of a company, and, therefore, to be an effective director, merely through attendance at regularly called board meetings. To develop specific knowledge about the company and how it operates, the board should meet with executives in charge of various functions or divisions.

The process involves more than executive briefing; it involves "directorship by walking around" to obtain first-hand observation of facilities, systems, and people. Board members should be exposed to multiple levels of operations and locations, not just to executive management and executive quarters. The board must understand competition, technology, and obsolescence.

Executive management has the responsibility to arrange the board's education. The board should take the time to listen, to observe, and to question openly, without embarrassment. Open questioning by board members is always difficult. People in executive or professional positions (and most board members come from those positions) are reluctant to risk embarrassment by asking about unfamiliar things, so the process requires leadership. The CEO leads by participating in the inquiry process.

The boardroom is not the best place for observation. The board should observe managers and others at work; they should assess employee dedication and on the job competence, as well as company effectiveness in communicating information upward. However, extensive time spent by directors in managers' work places can be interpreted as interference with management, a sensitive issue, so care in planning the board's education is required.

Retreats (attended by managers and board members) and committee work (done with assistance from middle and junior managers) give the board opportunities to judge the people who provide any information about early crisis signs. Typically, board committees are audit and finance related. Patton and Baker suggest that committee activity of boards be expanded to include other facets of the business, such as marketing and manufacturing.

Inside the Park

Park's board gets mixed grades on the education issue. There were periodic visits by directors to various departments and with different managers, but there really were no in-depth discussions between board members and lower-level managers. Some board members got occasional feedback from customers. Information about industry trends and happenings within the bank were mailed to the board on a regular basis. But most of the significant information was presented to the board in structured board meetings.

The board attempted to get outside itself by having quarterly, unstructured "think tank" meetings away from the bank. However, attendance was limited to board members and one or two executive officers. Thus, a broad overview about what was really going on at the bank was never attained.

Instead, board think tank meetings had the opposite effect; they became an ethnocentric forum that promoted unjustified, but comfortable, feelings that everything was all right in the bank because of "the way we do business." The board became overly dependent upon executive management for information.

Board members became increasingly isolated from the bank by using the think tank meetings to keep themselves current. Each think tank meeting provided reaffirmation of the board's original interpretation of reality, despite growing criticism from regulators and in the press.

Interestingly, one early expression of the board's version of reality was a marketing piece entitled:

The Gospel
According to
Frank,
Peter,
Gary,
Richard,
John,
Harold,
Phil,
Vern
and
Bill.

These are the first names of Park's original directors. The Gospel assured bank customers: "Being businessmen themselves, they [the board members] understand your problems. . . . Since they own the bank they can afford to be flexible with none of the bureaucracy and red tape associated with large banking chains."

Was there reason to reconsider that philosophy when, five years later, the bank's assets and deposits were one hundred times larger than they were when Park Bank was purchased? When board members no longer personally knew most of the bank's customers? When banking complexities and competition increased through deregulation? And when there were one thousand new stockholders who had bought shares of stock in the bank and the board no longer owned the bank by themselves? Of course.

But the mind-set of the board did not change fast enough. Fundamentally, directors' education, needed to interpret Park's visible and invisible crisis signs and respond to its rim events, was lacking. Coupled with groupthink pressures, it was too much.

John Nash, President of the National Association of Corporate Directors, a pioneer organization in director training, has been quoted in the *Wall Street Journal* as saying that each director of a public company should be required to pass an examination to determine the level of his knowledge about the business on whose board he sits.

I would not go that far; however, I do believe that any board member who is not committed to educating himself about the business of his board should resign. Otherwise, he will find Machiavelli to be painfully right when he wrote in *The Prince*, "The man who does not recognize ills at their inception does not have true wisdom. . . ."

When directors develop meaningful knowledge about their businesses and their operations they have the background to understand the information being presented to them and have the confidence to express their views openly, making full use of their varying analytical and intuitive interpretive skills in non threatening ways. The boardroom environment no longer suffers from the discomfort of director insecurity that comes from inadequate knowledge.

Becoming an informed board member is not an overnight experience. Research has verified that it takes from three to five years for a director to gain the experience and knowledge required for in-depth understanding of a company. But when directors become truly informed, the balance of power lacking in today's boardrooms is righted in a positive way.

Information-Gathering Systems

Boards operate on the information presented to them by the CEO and his staff. Both the board and the CEO must insist that directors obtain the kinds of information they need. To accomplish this objective, certain general principles apply.

The board should:

- receive board material in sufficient time before each meeting to study it carefully;

- obtain the pros and cons on each issue;

- be provided data and information in forms that do not bury important points;

- take enough time on each issue;

- allow, and encourage, full boardroom discussion; and,

- arrange for board executive committees to deal with routine corporate matters.

More, however, is required for boards to develop their abilities to smell out Geneen's "real facts." University of Georgia Professor William R. Boulton has suggested organizing the board's roles into legitimizing, auditing, and directing functions. He suggests what kinds of information are required for each category of involvement, from basic legal requirements through financial reviews, objective setting, and policy determinations. The board needs information about the corporation's past and present for its legal and audit functions, and about its future for its directive functions.

Professor Boulton's message is clear: Directors must do more than accept information and react in a passive way. Boards, with managements' input, should custom-design information systems tailored to provide the data and interpretations required. Professor Myles L. Mace supports Boulton's conclusions: "Management information systems for directors need to be tailored to accommodate the particular and unique requirements of each company. For each company, there are critical factors. . . ."

I would add that any board information system should also recognize and consider the following:

- Crisis management requires quick feedback. Information systems must be responsive and anticipatory.

- Facts from paper are not the same as facts from people. Seeing a person's eyes and reactions are important for forming perceptive judgments about the person's information and assumptions. So the board's information systems should provide for frequent personal interchanges with others up and down the management hierarchy.

- Special studies by consultants may be indicated when the board senses early warning signs of crisis. "How did things get into such a mess?" is a tough question to answer when the only information utilized by the board is management's self-evaluation.

- Each fact should be treated as what Robert H. Waterman, Jr., calls a "friendly fact." Everyone, at all levels, must demonstrate that information is important and wanted, whether it is negative or positive, because it provides guidance about the actual state of affairs. Executive management and the board must want facts, must seek facts out, and must encourage factual development and factual communication.

Directors do not in fact manage their company; but they cannot escape responsibility for how the company is managed. Good information systems help the board fulfill that responsibility. Too frequently, directors are surprised by events because information systems have been inadequate. Writing in May 1971 about this frequent occurrence, the editors of *Business Week* wrote, "In too many cases, Penn Central for example, no one was more surprised than the directors when the management finally admitted that the company was in deep trouble." The same was true at Park Bank. In retrospect, Park's education and information systems were inadequate and did not provide its board with reliable early warning signs about what was in store.

Critical to the adequacy of the corporate information system is its quality, not its quantity, and the ability of its users to apply critical judgments to its offerings. Without the ability to comprehend in depth the information available, directors will not be able to exercise their authority in a competent way. Information systems must be integrated with director education strategies or form will have triumphed over substance.

Getting Information to the Top

Traditionally, corporate communication systems have been described as providing data from the top to the bottom of the organization. Important, however, particularly for crisis control, is the flow of information *from* all parts of the organization *to* the top. Management's primary concern should be about how information flows upward, not downward, as Peter Drucker pointed out in *People and Performance*. Management and the board must have accurate, adequate, and timely facts if they are to recognize early signs of an approaching Black Hole.

The upward flow of data and information is often interrupted, however, when lower-echelon managers fail to comprehend the significance of events at their level. They rarely pass on bits and pieces of data to other divisions or departments. We noted in chapter 3 that information has to be synthesized for its significance to be comprehended; and narrowly focused, specialized corporate units lack sufficient information to form universalized judgments. It's the old story of every unit manager seeing a different aspect of an elephant, not understanding the whole animal.

Geneen, as might be expected, was outspoken in *Management* in his criticism of managers setting their divisions up as separate territories, giving little consideration to the company as a whole. He observed, "The system works as long as every executive in the chain of command does his job well. When one of these key men fails and a crisis looms, the chief executive often does not really know enough about the situation to judge what he should do about it."

Good information systems must get all important (and the truly important includes much of the seemingly irrelevant) information to the top — and on time. Lacking that, uncontrolled disaster can ensue. It is useless to expect to detect the first signs of potential crisis by focusing on the "bottom line" of the company's financial statements. By the time crisis signs are visible on a company's financial statements, it's too late.

Inside the Park

The significance of the time-lag before signs of crisis show up on financial statements and other reports cannot be overemphasized. When the FDIC indicated its first concerns in 1983 about the potential effect of Park Bank's rapid growth, its observations were minimized, in part, because Park's "bottom line" looked good. Park's financial reports, showing that 1983 profits were $2,651,840, up from 1982 profits of $1,470,080, supported Park's chairman's conclusions that Park's business plan was solid, that the regulators were wrong. After all, Park's return on equity was "right on target." What more could the regulators demand?

But crisis spirals downward in increasing geometric proportions. By the time its financial reports confirmed the FDIC's admonitions, Park Bank was over the rim, dragged irrevocably into its Black Hole.

To minimize the problem of delayed and inaccurate upward communication, Peter Drucker has proposed flattening the organizational chart of a company, cutting out the opportunity for error, and shortening the time it takes for information to flow upwards. Drucker advocates an organizational structure that is information-based, tied to the company's maximum "span of communications." That span relates to the number of people who will accept responsibility for communications — upward, downward, and sideways communication. How much that system, or any system, will help drive information to the top where it is needed will depend upon the openness of management — *genuine* openness.

One negative characteristic of the internal crisis environment is that crisis management systems close. Senior managers withdraw into themselves. They deal with problems as if others were not qualified to help. The process leaves everyone else standing on the sidelines, angry, hurt, and distrustful. It results in the development of bunker mentalities among employees. That form of inattentive, heads-down inactivity blocks the upward flow of data. Thus, those managers who have taken it upon themselves to solve every problem lack the essential facts about the obstacles they are trying to overcome.

Upward communication systems also suffer from the normal reluctance people feel about providing data they believe to be critical of their personal achievements. Fred Luthans observed in his *Organizational Behavior* that "even when subordinates do communicate upward, the content is often meaningless because they send up only what they think the boss wants to hear or reports are distorted or manipulated so that they contain only information that makes subordinates look good."

So a flattened organization chart alone won't solve the information problem. The communication system also must be open and based upon trust. Geneen said that it took him years to establish a truly open, trusting upward communication system with his managers; but he considered it essential.

People must be convinced that they can communicate freely, that communication is a way of life and that, contrary to what has happened to messengers throughout history, the messenger will not suffer the misfortune associated with his message. The message must be received, and it is the highest responsibility of management and the board to see that information flows upward, accurately and in time.

The board has two responsibilities in this regard. Its review, or audit, of management systems should indicate that management information systems are conducive to the upward mobility of information. And the board should insist that it be the beneficiary of that information. The board must thus assure senior management that it, indeed, will not shoot its messenger.

Even Machiavelli recognized the importance of encouraging upward communication when he wrote in *The Prince:* "The wise prince gives men of his state the opportunity and the freedom to tell the truth about matters he asks. . . .He should question them about all matters, [and] listen to their opinions. . . ."

Inside the Park

During the initial stages of our workout, Park's information systems did not permit a free upward flow of information about troubled loans. We assigned each delinquent loan to the officer who made the loan because we believed that the person who was responsible for the problem could straighten out the problem. Loan officers, however, became protective. After all, they had "sold" the bank's board on making the loans in the first place, and they wanted to believe their customers could pull out of whatever trouble they were in. Thus, they tended to be overly optimistic about their long-term restructurings and their customers' ability to perform. Obviously, failure of loans for which they were responsible was also a threat to job security and to self-image.

A few years earlier, a Wall Street Journal *article describing how C&S Bank in Atlanta handled loan workouts had made that point. What was right for C&S proved to be wrong for us and, I think, for most banks.*

Board Decisional Processes

The real test of independence for a board member is in whether or not he will exercise independent judgment. Board members cannot exercise independence if they believe that their decisions must be unanimous or if controversies have no place in the boardroom.

There is real corporate benefit in constructive boardroom and management dissent, even though General Motors apparently felt otherwise when it spent some $700 million in 1987 to buy out its openly critical board member, Ross Perot. In contrast to General Motors, other corporations have appointed a member of executive management as the corporate "devil's advocate" so that all possible issues and points-of-view will be considered. It takes strong, self-confident management to allow this kind of activity without feeling threatened; however, the devil's advocate process can be a powerful tool to expose weaknesses and provide fresh alternatives.

Closely related to consensus decision-making is *decisional coasting,* which is the failure to exercise critical judgment because others on the board have apparently already made the decision. Not infrequently, a CEO will submit a proposal to a board member outside the boardroom. Pressed for time and presented with a proposition already reviewed, he thinks, by the other members of the board, a board member might easily give his tacit consent without full consideration of the issues involved. After all, a director easily rationalizes, "The other guys have reviewed the proposition; they're always careful; they must have checked it out. Therefore, I don't have to; it must be sound." A similar form of decisional coasting occurs when boards are presented with the proceedings of board committees. Rarely is there discussion of committee reports in boardrooms; approval is quick and perfunctory.

Directors must also understand the group decision making process, the problem we discussed in chapter 5. Board members should never overlook that group decisions are potentially more risky than individual decisions, particularly when the choice is perceived by the group to be a choice between losses. Group fiascoes occur most frequently when directors view their decisional choice as opting between one certain loss and one risky loss, the latter being potentially more damaging if the gamble is lost. Researcher Glen Whyte has pointed out that, when faced with that kind of decision dilemma, groups almost uniformly pick the risky choice that offers some hope.

Effective boardroom decision making starts with a clear definition of the problem and an understanding of the board's interpretive baggage, which often distorts meaning. Then follows a thoughtful design of the specifications, Drucker's boundary conditions, any boardroom answer must satisfy. Finally, the effective board will place a strong focus on the ultimate decision, engaging in a healthy discussion about choices and alternatives, and install a sound action plan, with check-points and follow up. Intelligent and effective boardroom decisions grow out of constructive disagreement, thoughtful dialogue, and careful choices, not acclamation.

Add New, Unaffiliated Board Members Systematically

It may seem strange that this suggestion is included under the subject of crisis detection, but new board members bring with them fresh points of view, new perspectives, new ideas, new questions, all vital for crisis detection.

The new outside directors should be independent in the sense that they do not run affiliates or supply or purchase the company's goods or services. Company lawyers, investment bankers, distributors and other suppliers of goods and services should be excluded from the board. Fortunately, the trend within public boards is to exclude service providers.

Inside the Park

Members of the board of directors at Park Bank included several suppliers of goods and services, including myself. Stockholder reaction, once the bank became public, was, at best, skeptical.

The St. Petersburg Times *reported on an interview with me several months after we had begun to eliminate internal conflicts, "When the bank was small," Jacobs said, "all we worried about was getting the job done and not who was doing it. But if you bring in outside people as owners, then you're as concerned about how things appear as (much as how) they are . . . We grew so darned fast we were always catching up."*

It was true. As a consequence of Park's perpetual growth and activity, Park's board never slowed down enough to step back, examine the various relationships that had developed, and straighten them out.

I don't doubt that similar problems occur in other fast-growing organizations. The real concern for any company, of course, is whether or not those close supplier relationships among board members adversely affect independent judgment. In retrospect, I agree with those who recommend that companies exclude providers of services or goods from their boards, including lawyers whose firms serve as general counsel. Board members who are beholden to the chairman for their jobs or their businesses, or who are engaged in outside business activities with him are less than independent.

The issue is not necessarily an ethical one. Research has shown that companies governed by independent boards are no more or less ethical or legal in their conduct than companies governed by inside boards. The issue is whether members have free, independent judgment, uninfluenced by personal considerations about the outcome, their personal relationships, or the loss of related business. Without freedom, their crisis-detection sensors are muted.

Director independence and freedom are influenced by the director-selection process. For most corporations the CEO handpicks the directors. The trend among public companies today is for independent director nominating committees to nominate potential board members. However, as Professor Lorsch indicates, the CEO maintains his dominant influence in director selection, recommending the majority of acceptable nominees.

What characteristics should those charged with nominating board members consider? In 1988, the international accounting firm KPMG Peat Marwick Main & Co. published a study entitled *The Audit Committee.* That study included a series of personality and experience factors worthy of consideration by those charged with selecting audit committee members. In reality, Peat Marwick's recommended factors should be considered in the selection of board members themselves. The study suggested the following factors:

- broad business experience;

- knowledge of the company, its operations, finances, auditing, and accounting;

- facility to obtain information by inquiry;

- commitment;

- time; and

- ability to develop continuity of membership.

Geneen and others suggest that officers who report to the CEO be excluded from the board, because they feel it is practically impossible for anyone in that position to be independent about policy or other important matters. Maybe; but if the board has a solid complement of outside members and if the CEO and the board have established the open communication system we advocate, that exclusion seems unnecessary.

Although research reported by Patton and Baker indicates that directors who have healthy stockholder positions are more likely to ask tough questions and provide penetrating analysis of issues, stock ownership as a criterion for board membership has its drawbacks.

Inside the Park

Each of the Park Bank directors had a significant stock position in Park Bank; in fact, the board as a whole owned about 20 percent of the company. The board's stock ownership posed a problem in that, during the last few years of Park's life, several board members either then approaching retirement or with growing outside interests were unwilling to consider changes in control of the board or in the board's composition, even though they were spending more and more of their personal time away from St. Petersburg. Because of their travels, some members attended board meetings by telephone conference calls; legal, but not as effective as face-to-face meetings.

A consultant recommended to Park's board that it develop a directors' retirement plan and phase in new, younger board members from the local business community. A plan to accomplish the objectives was designed and presented to the board, but the board never formally considered its implementation. The thought of retiring, of not being at board meetings to "protect their investments," was too traumatic to some board members; and the controversies in the bank ultimately were too great to consider change.

If Park's board composition had been changed, would it have helped us see the signs of approaching danger? In retrospect, I think that, as Park's directors neared retirement or developed additional interests that competed for their time, their minds stayed set on "the way it was" during Park's early days; "the way it was becoming" escaped them.

The Audit Function

Our third boardroom recommendation: *The board must audit corporate activities and results.*

There are those who claim that the auditing role of boards is their *central role.* They argue that a board's audit committee fulfills the board's primary responsibility for monitoring and guiding the legality and morality of the corporation by, as Ralph Nader describes it, "constraining executive management from violations of law and breaches of trust."

Few would go as far as Nader; however, no one today doubts that boards have vital roles to perform through their audit committees, measuring the adequacy of internal controls, evaluating reports provided by outside auditors, appraising information systems, and making management aware that it is being monitored and graded in regard to its performance and responsibilities.

Most of the work of audit committees at present is focused on financial and accounting matters. But, in my view, other matters should be considered for periodic, audit-type review. For example, human resource issues, such as morale, training, turnover, productivity, and communication openness should be reviewed. An audit of the company's long-term performance, as an aid in judging its ability to deal with the outside environment, should also be done. Often the committee can enlist the aid of outside consultants for these purposes.

Inside the Park

During our struggles at Park, Human Resources arranged for an "audit" to be taken of Park Bank's employees' attitudes. Although this was not done at the request of the board or any board committee, the final report was helpful both to the board and to management in dealing with the employees during troubled times.

Management might view the workings of an audit committee as adversarial. Certainly, Ralph Nader sees it that way. But, if the board's relationship with its CEO is open and honest, the CEO should welcome the work of the board's audit committee as providing him with Waterman's "friendly facts," facts that might acknowledge work well done or that might offer early indicators of trouble in time.

I have the following recommendations concerning audit committees and their processes:

- The CEO should be strong enough, and secure enough in himself, to welcome being graded on what he and his managers have done. He is looking to the board for its help; anything less from the board than honesty and objectivity is no help at all!

- The audit committee must function separately from executive management, even though the CEO occupies a dual role as the board's chairman (This is a normal requirement for listed companies; but all companies aren't listed.)

- Audit committee members and board members should be aware that reluctance on their part to measure executive performance objectively is common. Boards have difficulty giving their CEO the honest results of their reviews of him and his executives. However, open, objective boardroom analysis is what the CEO and the company need, and should want. Loyalty and support are misconceived if the board's review committee does otherwise. Corporate loyalty involves commonality of commitment to an ideal and an objective, not merely to a person; loyalty does not demand or require agreement on every issue, nor should it be personalized by the board to the point of lost perspective.

- The audit committee should play a major role in selecting and monitoring counsel and outside auditors. CPAs and attorneys represent the company, not the executive officers. There should be no doubt that these professionals are directly accountable to the board for their corporate activities.

- The audit committee should be sensitive to, and aware of, the upward lines of communication, both formal and informal, within the corporation. The audit process should not block the upward flow of information to executive management or to the board.

• When the business of the company is regulated, the audit committee should appoint one of its members to serve as an observer of the regulatory examination process. Management may feel threatened; however, if focus is maintained on the objective — the development of facts that compliment strengths and point out weaknesses in time, that threat can be kept to a minimum.

Inside the Park

The importance of audit committee members having full information was illustrated to me in our experience with the FDIC regulators at Park Bank. In banking, when a regulatory examination is completed, examiners do not report directly to the board of the examined bank unless a certain level of negative data is developed during the examination. Early signs, visible before conditions are severe, are conveyed only to management.

Furthermore, examiners may make field notes from conversations with bank officers that do not find their way into the examination report that finally gets to the board. In a sense, it is a system similar to that used in public schools. When a child receives a failing grade, his or her parents are called, but not before.

Prior to the time I became CEO, during an examination in which Park Bank got good marks, the FDIC noted in its internal papers that it had made comments to Park's executive vice president in charge of lending that the FDIC was concerned about Park Bank's loan quality, standards, and growth. That comment, and the thrust of the regulator's concern, were not conveyed to the board.

Would the presence of a member of Park's audit committee attending FDIC meetings with Park's management have picked up that stray fact? There is no doubt in my mind that the presence of a Park Bank board member would have been helpful, not only to the board, but to the executive officer who handled the examination and was threatened by its implications.

In addition to the traditional audit committee, the formation of at least three other audit-type board committees should be considered. They are nominating (keeping fresh blood on the board), compensation (establishing and reviewing compensation of executive officers down to a specified level) and executive (taking care of boardroom legalities and details that would use an inordinate amount of board time) committees. The SEC, NASD, and the major stock exchanges consider these committees important boardroom tools and recommend that memberships contain a majority of unaffiliated, outside directors. Consideration should also be given to a strategic planning committee. Strategic planning, however, in my view, should be directed by the CEO. The board committee has an important role to play as planning mentor.

Chapter 15

Completing the Task

*There is no greater waste of human resources to be
found in American corporations than the way boards
of directors are typically used.*

James O'Toole

In this chapter, we conclude our discussion about boardroom transformation.

Evaluating the CEO

The fourth, and perhaps most difficult, boardroom crisis task: *The board
must determine whether the CEO can deal successfully with the Black
Hole environment, and if he cannot, replace him.*

Making sure that a company has an extraordinary leader is a board
responsibility of unquestionable importance. Crisis will test the board's
judgment in the exercise of that responsibility. The directors must not
become panicky in their evaluation of the CEO's performance. There is a
tendency, once trouble is identified, for the board to act, or react, too
quickly. During its uncontrolled stages, the terror of the crisis can cause
a board of directors to take precipitous actions that can be more damaging
to the corporation than the underlying causes of the crisis itself.

When it comes to the CEO of a company on the rim, directors are prone to make one of two errors: They either refuse to face the fact that there is a need for leadership change, or they scapegoat, replacing the CEO prematurely, as a symbolic way of dealing with troubled times without understanding the fundamental reasons for the crisis or what is required for the company to turn around.

Directors should strive to answer the question: Can the CEO handle the crisis? If, after a careful evaluation, the board believes the CEO cannot, then the board has the responsibility to act on its conclusions, difficult and unpleasant as that action may be.

Hopefully, the board has evaluated the CEO long before the crisis appeared; but, unfortunately, periodic executive reviews are superficial, particularly when business is going well. Leadership characteristics required of a CEO to handle crisis are typically ignored by a board in good times. Peter Drucker has pointed out that even if crisis-handling characteristics have not been ignored, predicting how a particular executive will react in the rim's environment is something that cannot be accurately measured in advance. Yet, a board cannot escape its responsibility to judge how its CEO likely will perform if their company is on the rim.

In evaluating the CEO, directors need to consider several of the leadership and management issues discussed in this book and in other management literature. However, certain factors that influence board evaluation deserve special mention.

- Whether or not the CEO can tolerate ambiguity may be his most important crisis management characteristic. CEOs who can tolerate ambiguity are challenged by a crisis, not threatened by it. Being challenged, they exude strength and confidence and become a resource to others.

Most business crises appear to be financial in nature; consequently, as noted in chapter 9, a financially oriented person is most likely to be selected by the board as a turn-around CEO. Choosing a leader for his financial acumen alone may be a grave mistake, particularly if the crisis lasts for some time.

Why?

First, people in troubled situations concentrate on what they know best, regardless of what is needed. Financial people concentrate on finance, cash flow, and cost controls, often to the exclusion of other essentials. Financial difficulties may be the result of crisis; rarely are they the cause of the crisis. Dealing with the results of crisis is certainly critical; not dealing with crisis causes, however, is usually fatal.

Second, and most important, a financial person's approach to issues is apt to be inappropriate for leading others through the crisis. What is required is not autocratic cost-cutting and numbers-crunching; what is required is inspiring and motivating leadership from a person who has the ability to *link* up, bond, with the people he leads. *Linkage* and the *charisma connection* between leader and followers during crisis are the subject of Part VI of this book.

Psychologists Harrison and Bramson point out that ambiguity-tolerant people use the thinking styles of the synthesist or pragmatist, often coupled with that of an idealist. Those styles are appropriate for leaders in crisis situations. Thus, board understanding of the CEO's thinking style, his approaches to problem-solving, and his ability to handle the rim's muddled environment, as well as his ability to juggle multiple options and provide inspirational leadership, is important.

- Whether factors, particularly financial factors, in the CEO's outside life place him under stress should not be ignored.

If, for example, the CEO's life is leveraged, he will focus on his personal solvency and be unable to concentrate. The board must consider the cumulative weight of outside pressures. Personal factors could press the CEO to the point where he might not be strong enough to deal with the crisis or resist the ethical dilemmas he will face on the rim.

We explained in earlier chapters that a CEO who measures his self-worth by the trappings and possessions of life will see the crash of his business as an obliteration of his personality and values. Crisis-overload can quickly crush him; and when it does, his otherwise acceptable personality traits will yield to the press of chaos.

- Whether or not the relationship of the board itself with the CEO is healthy should also be considered.

Part of the board's evaluation of the CEO should include its examination of the nuances of its relationship with the CEO — the board itself may have some changing to do.

During its evaluation, the board should remember that there is a romance about leadership and that romance can cause the CEO to receive too much credit when things go well and too much discredit when things go bad. This kind of bias is most likely to occur in the crises environment, and the board must be cautious in its first conclusions. After the board has completed its evaluation of the CEO, using the best information available, it will be in a position to be the CEO's active mentor and counselor, or it will be in position to replace him.

Replacing the CEO

What considerations confront the board if it decides to replace the CEO?

A new CEO, especially one selected from outside the company, should be less burdened by the baggage associated with a troubled company. He will have a honeymoon period in which he has the opportunity to act decisively. However, he will have to undergo an adjustment period while he learns the company and its personnel. Learning periods can be dangerous. The crisis may be so deep by the time he starts that he may not have the time he requires to bring himself up to maximum performance.

In fact, the company's situation may be so far gone that new management is not a reasonable alternative for the board to consider. I found this to be true when I attempted to hire a new CEO after I assumed control at Park Bank.

Inside the Park

One of my first efforts after becoming Park's CEO was to recruit a person with banking and loan workout experience to serve as Park's chief operating officer. I found an ideal candidate and started negotiations. He had a senior position with another bank. Unfortunately, his investigations of us, his meetings with board members and senior officers, as well as our contract discussions, took painfully long. He was intrigued with the challenge and he liked our people. His reputation and knowledge were respected by our officers. He would have been a strong manager, a solid leader.

Finally, after two months of negotiations, in early July 1985, we agreed on a package and a hand-shake deal was struck. In mid-July, he came in for final discussions. By then, the first RICO lawsuit had been filed and anticipated second quarter operating losses and loan delinquencies were quantified at levels higher than we had projected. We continued to experience balance sheet deterioration, and our planned capital offering, filed with the SEC months before, was blocked and no longer practical.

At an early breakfast, he finally declined, saying, "You know, this is a real challenge. With the stock options offered, it looks like a real entrepreneurial opportunity; but people who take measured *risks are the real entrepreneurs, not people who just take risks. The way things are happening, there is no way to make an evaluation. I am sorry; I wish it felt right."*

Time is required for leadership to establish itself, whether the company is troubled or not. John J. Gabarro wrote in *The Dynamics of Taking Charge* that, with rare exceptions, two years pass before new CEOs establish themselves as strong, trusted leaders. The new CEO will have to develop understanding of the company's strengths and weaknesses. He will have to develop his interpretation of the corporation's culture and shared values. He will have to convert his ideas into effective strategies. He will have to develop and communicate his version of the corporation's mission.

If the new leader comes from outside the industry, the adjustment may take even longer, and the chance of his successfully altering the course of the troubled business is greatly diminished.

Executive change shocks the corporate system, particularly when the new CEO is brought in to sweep it clean. A CEO change, like any other corporate change, must be digested, tentatively at first, until participants understand the extent their occupational safety will be disturbed.

What does a new CEO attempt at the start? Gabarro concluded that the problems the CEO focuses on initially will be those he recognizes from his prior experiences, and the actions he is most likely to choose will be the ones he has tried before. His judgment base is his prior experience, his own history. Time will pass before he focuses beyond immediately recognizable problems.

If the board is knowledgeable about the status of the company, its periodic consultations with the new CEO will be invaluable. Open, active board support, evidenced to employees, suppliers, and customers, tying together the old with the new during the CEO's transition period, will also make a substantial difference.

The board must remember, however, that the new CEO is operating with an inherited corporate history he might not be able to change. The CEO will have to cope with momentum effect — the tendency of his inherited company to continue in the direction it has been headed, despite the new leader's attempts to alter its course.

In November 1987, professors Chung, Rogers, Lubatkin, and Owers published the collective results of their research on the effect of management changes on future company performance. Among their conclusions, they found that leaders have an almost impossible time changing the course of events already set in motion! They wrote: "Those who inherit low-performing firms are on a tightrope in their efforts to reverse declining profitability in the face of dwindling financial resources, unprofitable product lines, and deteriorating employee morale."

Stated another way, there is a good chance that any new leader, no matter how strong, will be overwhelmed by the negative performance of a company bound for a Black Hole, particularly if the crisis was not recognized at a very early stage. Iacocca's initial experience at Chrysler was clearly the exception.

Chung and his colleagues observed that, when CEOs of troubled companies are replaced, boards of directors tend to replace them with someone from within the company itself. However, their research indicates that a CEO brought in from the outside is better able to influence strategies and effectuate recovery programs.

The research described, coupled with my Park Bank experience, support the following conclusions:

- When a troubled business reaches the rim of the Black Hole, the pull of gravity — momentum effect — is almost irreversible; a new CEO, if available, may not be able to help.

- The personality and thinking styles of the person selected by the board to lead the company's efforts away from its rim-bound course are important; the wrong person is often selected. The best chances for recovery come from executives who: (1) have been hired from outside the company, (2) are from within the same industry, (3) possess tolerance for ambiguity, and (4) have exceptional leadership skills.

Although armed with information that its CEO must be replaced, a board may, nevertheless, remain frozen in inaction, its members reluctant to confront the CEO openly. Most likely, the CEO had a hand in placing them on *his* board. They may be friends, investment bankers, suppliers, customers, or lawyers who value the company's business or whose business is valued by the company. Or, as it was at Park Bank, the directors' mind-sets may block change of long-held conceptions of reality, even in the face of compelling facts.

A challenge to the status quo requires that someone on the board rise to the occasion and face the CEO, a task potentially easier if the CEO is not also the board chairman. The vice chairman or perhaps the chairman of the audit committee must seize the moment and tell their corporate emperor he has no clothes. For a time, the scene in the boardroom might parallel that on the Serengetti Plain when two warring lions engage in a territorial dispute, at least until the challenger builds sufficient support. It is small wonder that directors, part-time participants in a struggle perceived as not of their own making, and rarely fully understood, are reluctant to face their CEO and replace him.

There can come a time, however, as it did at Park Bank, when the CEO must be challenged, head-on, in the boardroom (groupthink pressures notwithstanding). There is no more difficult position for a board member to be in than that of whistle-blower, a perceived "trouble-maker" in the boardroom. He must fight pressures that have led the board, above reason, to embrace conformity and acquiescence to the CEO's position.

Inside the Park

No single task was as difficult for me as convincing the board at Park Bank that John Kearney should resign as CEO. For the first few months of 1984, after his admonishment to the board that Park Bank was different and beyond understanding by the regulators, it appeared as if substantial progress was made in reducing Park's loan quality problems. In mid-1984, the Division of Banking for the State of Florida examined Park Bank as a follow-up to the earlier hyper-critical FDIC examination. The Division of Banking reported to Park's board that good progress had been made and that it appeared that Park Bank was headed toward recovery.

However, in the latter half of 1984, troubling indicators kept surfacing amidst Park's loan workouts. Those indicators caused me to doubt that Park Bank was headed for recovery. Kearney, as CEO of the bank and chairman of the loan committee, and Matthews, as senior lender, still discounted the continuing trouble signs.

I began to realize that lending problems were being met with solutions that offered no permanent cures. Quick restructurings or extensions and additional financings were band-aid fixes that couldn't last.

In addition, Kearney's other business interests were continuing to suffer, sapping his time and attention. They were jeopardizing his financial standing and distorting his own judgment.

I tried to convince Kearney that changes were needed, but I was unsuccessful. That kind of confrontation was very difficult. Not only had we known each other for years through our work together as lawyer and accountant prior to our Park Bank days, but, as I noted in an earlier chapter, I felt reluctant to believe what my intuition was telling me. After all, I was flying in the face of executives with greater bank lending experience and their favorable analysis of Park's circumstance and progress.

Finally, I could no longer ignore the signs. I believed an open challenge of Kearney as CEO before the board was necessary. Emotions were high. It was traumatic standing up against a business companion of fifteen years in front of seven other long-time business friends on Park's board who did not believe, or perhaps did not want to believe, that Park Bank was headed for a Black Hole.

The challenge involved long, exhausting meetings and frustrating conversations during the last quarter of 1984 and into the first quarter of 1985. Meetings were held with the board and with individual board members as I tried to develop understanding that would be sufficient to build a coalition of director support. I was thwarted until it seemed that my resignation was the only logical solution.

But I could not resign.

Near the end of December 1984, Park's perplexed board suggested that a director meet with Kearney and me to "arbitrate our differences." The board continued to believe that those differences were nothing more than divergent opinions and personality differences. After three hours of confrontation, jawbone to jawbone, I refused to back down.

The initial reaction of the board was disbelief. To this day, more than five years later, I can picture where each board member sat at the board meetings that followed and what they said.

"You're making a power move!"

I told them I didn't want to run the bank. But someone had to grab control and point the bank in the right direction. There simply was no one else around to do it.

"Why are you putting Kearney under an inquisition?"

"It's not an inquisition," I replied. "He's wrong! It's our responsibility."

"You've got no right to say that! Kearney's got things under control!"

"Things aren't under control! Look at them!"

Throughout the confrontation period, Park's senior managers could not help but sense what was going on. Though the board tried to calm the managers, their efforts did little good. The confrontation between Kearney and myself brought Park's progress to a virtual standstill while they waited the outcome.

Then, at the confrontation's most frustrating moment, the majority of the bank's officers rallied behind me, supporting my concerns and saying they would leave if Kearney stayed and I went. Several executive officers called individual board members to solicit their support.

At the next directors' meeting, board support solidified, and Kearney resigned. His resignation was unanimously accepted. But there were tears. The experience was emotional to the end.

I never want to go through that kind of confrontation again. It is more than "tight gut-square jaw" time. It is hell. For everybody.

Clearly, however, the important role of the board in serving as a transforming resource for its company in crisis will be thwarted unless the board is willing to:

- become educated about their company's situation; and,

- evaluate the ability of the CEO to lead the company through the crisis and then, without delay, replace him or actively support him.

The Mentor Role

The fifth recommendation to the board is: *The board must facilitate the CEO's ability to deal with crisis by consulting with him and by insisting that communications be open and interactive.*

The board fulfills one of its most valuable transforming roles when it performs as consultant and mentor to its CEO. Hopefully, a careful evaluation of the CEO will have been made so that the advice and counseling are on target.

One or more board members serving as mentors, informal consultants to the CEO, can be invaluable. The mentor relationship, open, built on trust and respect, helps the CEO avoid the damage withdrawing into himself can cause, both to his health and by being broadsided by his blind spots. Because the relationship is built on trust and respect, there is less pressure on either participant to prove himself. An experienced, down-to-earth director, 8 to 12 years older than the CEO, best fills the CEO mentor role. A quiet, informal talk with one who has already accumulated his battle scars is an opportunity for the CEO to benefit from experience and to develop perspective, wisdom, and sensitivity.

Inside the Park

I was fortunate to have a Park Bank board member, Bill Zemp, who filled the role of mentor. I was able to talk with him almost any time of the day or night about Park's problems, about various theories for handling them, as well as about proposals for dealing with customers, the public, the press, and our other constituencies. I found the relationship to be invaluable, not only because of the advice received and the perspective developed, but because of the stress-relief it provided. His office was near mine, and I was able to slip in for his opinion on a wide variety of issues.

Semi-retired now, at one time Bill Zemp had had the largest marketing and public relations firm in Florida. Shortly after assuming the role of CEO, I approached him for advice about how Park Bank could re-establish credibility with the press. John Kearney had viewed the press as the enemy not to be trusted. The press had responded in kind.

Bill and I discussed an early experience he had with a troubled corporate client. His conclusion from that experience was that the CEO and company should always be open, frank, and truthful in media communications. If potentially dangerous facts existed, Bill recommended that I discuss their background with the media off the record and rely on their integrity.

A few days later, I nervously met with the press for the first time, reporting Park's first major annual loss. I gave the reporter copies of our reports and SEC filings and answered questions in as straight forward a manner as possible. The press responded favorably to my openness. The information was reported accurately and tactfully. My request to respect certain background disclosures was respected. A follow-up article about the positive steps we were taking to deal with Park's affairs appeared in the St. Petersburg Times. *Employees and customers called me enthusiastically with favorable comments.*

I was relieved. Bill was right. His advice set the tone for my dealings with the media from then on. As often as we were in the press during our crisis, never did their reporting suggest that we suffered lack of credibility. In fact, the Tampa Bay Business Journal *reported in a February 8, 1986, article that, throughout Park's dark days, I had been "uncommonly forthright." Not only was that credibility immensely important outside Park Bank, it was vital for our internal self-image.*

Much of the advice and counseling by board mentors will be shaped by the kind of crisis confronting the company and its management and after evaluation of the CEO and his needs. However, at least two questions of universal applicability should be considered.

- Is the CEO concentrating on the most important aspects of the crisis, the ones that make a difference?

Focusing on specific crisis problems is difficult because the CEO feels forced by circumstances and by the demands of his people to jump from one issue to another, rarely spending enough time on any one problem and its solution. The use of task forces and proper delegation by the CEO are essential if he is to concentrate on priorities, even though his natural tendencies will be to be involved in everything. The CEO, however, must focus his energies on those fundamental issues that make the difference, and he must avoid diverting his attentions to half-solving a vast array of lesser problems that others can handle or that are not vital to the health of the organization.

- Is the CEO getting the right kind of performance from his executives?

Sometimes crises bring out what consultant Charles M. Kelley has identified as the executive *Destructive Achiever* mentality. A Destructive Achiever, a DA, is an executive whose actions provide illusory support for his verbalization of high values. His CEO is misled into believing that the DA "thinks just like me."

However, the DA's focus and his value-orientation are short-term, dedicated toward immediate results or at least the appearance of results. In terms of the Harrison and Bramson research on thinking styles the DA is probably a deformed realist. Band-aids, corner-cutting, repackaging, restructurings, and fads are his approach. His solutions are fundamentally cosmetic, accomplishing little and only delaying the inevitable. His solutions require nearly impossible outside conditions to succeed, and he pays no heed to Drucker's boundary conditions or philosopher Mencken's admonition that "for every problem there is a solution that is quick, easy and wrong."

Within a bank, for example, workout solutions proffered by a lender who originally had responsibility for a currently troubled loan can take on the characteristics of a DA solution: restructuring by adding an interest reserve when there is no ability to repay interest, deferring a maturity date when there is no better prospect that the loan can be repaid tomorrow, or tying repayment projections into overly optimistic economic trends.

The DA's long-term effect on the company is negative. He sacrifices the company's future to the present. His performance also has another important, less obvious, but decidedly negative, effect. People in the organization who work for him see what he does, and if what he does seems to impress executive management or the board, what he does is interpreted as the thing to do. The effect is to compound the disaster.

While the CEO concentrates on the major issues facing the company, board members, through committee work, have an opportunity to observe other managers in action; thus, the board can supplement the CEO's impressions and evaluations of his executives and can assist in identifying potential trouble-spots and DA-solutions before it is too late.

To maximize mentoring and communication skills, board members and executive officers need frequent get-togethers and executive retreats that permit interaction. These are "time-outs" in the sense of formal boardroom activities. However, time-out periods furnish opportunities to develop philosophic coherency between participants through the exchange of experiences brought up in gossip and small talk.

The goal, of course, is to develop director and executive officer sensitivity to each other and to what each is observing about the company. Board members and executives committed to transforming a company must take the time to develop interrelationships that produce common understandings from shared words whose deeper meanings are otherwise conflicting and diverse because of the diverse backgrounds and unshared perceptions of the directors who use them.

Plan for the worst

The sixth, and final, boardroom crisis point is: *Insist that the corporation develop strategies and plans to deal with the potentialities of Black Holes.*

Pay heed to the admonition offered by an ancient Japanese saying, "when you're thirsty, it's too late to dig a well." The board of directors should insist that management develop, during calm times, plans for chaotic times.

What are reasonable objectives for a corporation to consider when developing its crisis management plan?

- Its primary objective is for management and employees to be sufficiently prepared so that they are not overwhelmed by the unexpected.

- Its secondary objective is to understand the crisis and its requirements sufficiently so that the limited resources of the company can be allocated efficiently and effectively.

- Its third objective is to minimize the effects of stress and uncertainty so that its people can be productive and will not be destroyed by, or flee in the face of, crisis.

In addition to the basics (i.e., who will be the spokesperson to the press, and who should be responsible for transmitting any crisis alert within the company), there are fundamental issues that should be considered to support these objectives.

Any crisis plan should:

- Include a company credo that clearly sets out fundamental corporate values, recognizing that people adopt the credo of their company as they see it enacted by its executive officers and directors. The company's credo must be more than high-sounding words; the credo must express the company's deepest values, and must be reflected in the way people live in the corporate environment, from the top to the bottom. Values will be the corporation's most important reservoir of "capital" during crisis, permitting it to work its way through troubled times without resorting to short-cuts or other self-destructive activity.

- Emphasize the importance of prompt communication, upwards, sideways, and downwards. There should be no doubt that facts — what is really happening — can safely be conveyed upwards without threat to the messenger. The CEO and the board set the stage for good communications through their demeanor and by the way they respond to communications.

- Clarify which constituencies of the corporation are to be involved in crisis communication and in the design of crisis solutions. No longer are stockholders the only concerns of the company and its board and executives, either legally or pragmatically. Furthermore, the stockholders survive best when every interest is considered and addressed.

- Provide for board participation with management in selecting the objectives to be accomplished when crisis arises.

- Educate people within the company about the difficulties in recognizing early warning signs of trouble and about their probable reactions to crisis. People will perform best when they have some advance idea about the pressures and feelings they will experience in both the external and internal environments. Educate management about how to deal with those reactions.

- Encourage "what if" conceptualizing. What could go wrong within our company? What is the worst that can happen? What are possible turns of events? What can we do to influence, or change, those events? What is the effect of those events on operations? On morale? What are the options available?

- Be certain that there will be crisis support systems available to the company's people by assuring accessibility to consulting psychologists experienced in stress management.

The company's crisis planning procedure should be more than a perfunctory fire drill. The life of the corporation depends on it.

The Boardroom Alive

It should now be clear that the board of any company has more than a passive role to play. When the company is on the rim of the Black Hole, its war room — its boardroom-come-alive — must assume positive responsibility for the company's destiny in time for it to escape from momentum effect.

The board, the CEO, and his executive management should each be strong personalities. An interaction of strong people, independent and respectful of each other, should produce optimum results. The CEO and the board need each other and the contributions each can responsibly make to their corporation. Their collective influence has been given too little attention in management lore.

Part VI

Doing the Right Thing

Managers are people who do things right and leaders are people who do the right thing.

Bennis and Nanus

Chapter 16

The Charisma Connection and the Concept of Linkage

Whatever the style, taking over and turning around a troubled organization requires that the leader start, not with the "things" of the organization (machines, numbers, or plans), but with people.

Clemens and Meyer

Prior to *Leadership*, the definitive work by James MacGregor Burns, leadership literature had been elitist. Followers were portrayed as helpless, powerless, almost invisible bland, masses of humanity — immobile except when leaders are able to uplift them. In that same vein, the success of an enterprise was viewed as falling on the Herculean shoulders of its chief executive, as if he alone were the important performer. Ralph Waldo Emerson expressed the persuasion: "An institution is simply the length-ened shadow of a single individual."

Burns, however, described leadership as an interaction between leader and followers. Burns created the idea of *transformational leadership,* the interaction in which the leader identifies the "potential motives within his followers" and blends them with his own aspirations, resulting in "mutual stimulation and [an] elevation that converts followers into leaders and may convert leaders into moral agents."

Burns described heroic, or charismatic, leadership (the form of transforming leadership arising during crisis) as the sum of the qualities possessed by the person fulfilling the hero role and the interactions between that person and his followers. Heroic leadership manifests itself when followers, trusting the ability of the leader to overcome obstacles, grant him leadership power and commit themselves to him.

Despite Burns's focus on the interactive character of leadership, writers, particularly authors of pop management books produced since Burns's work, have concentrated on the dimensions of a leader's transforming qualities (as if his qualities alone shaped results) and on leadership "how to." The effect has been to idolize charismatic CEOs, distancing them from followers, endowing them with qualities bordering on the mystical.

In contrast, the effective crisis leader has the ability to sense emotional needs, anticipate responses, and harmonize leader-followers interactions within a framework that has been engineered out of commonly held motives, goals, and values. The purposes of both leader and followers fuse, and they bond — leader and followers become *connected*.

The importance of Burns's observations is that one of the strengths of an effective crisis leader is his ability to perceive the motives and needs of his people. He is able to understand followers' goals and desires and to synthesize or connect them with his objectives for the organization.

People buy into the charismatic leader's cause because they see his mission in harmony with theirs. Thus he is able to build trust and engage the full personalities of those involved with him.

Charismatic leadership can therefore be characterized as a connection — a charismatic connection — between leader and followers. That connection builds in a process that can be identified as *linkage*.

The Concept of Linkage

Linkage is the process whereby leader and followers connect to each other through the interplay of their values, beliefs, needs, perceptions, and strengths. Linkage connections begin when the leader is seen by his followers as having moved toward them, in spirit and in understanding. As a result, the leader is trusted and embraced. Followers accept his leadership, commit themselves, and empower him to act. The leader responds to followers' needs, resulting in a two-way relationship, a commitment between leader and followers to each other and in a perceived common cause.

Linkage is energizing. Linkage provides strength to endure hardships and to perform at levels beyond expectations. Linkage builds on the mutual willingness of participants to risk, to give of themselves for each other and for their cause. Like musketeers, leader and followers are committed "all for one and one for all."

Inside the Park

The importance of linkage became apparent to me during my struggles to gain control of Park Bank. It was detected quite by accident.

I explained it to Professor William R. Boulton of the University of Georgia during an interview providing him with materials for a business school case study about Park's crash landing.

Boulton asked me what we did to keep everyone together. I answered:

I lucked into some things. . . . The bank had not been around long enough to build a corporate culture. The culture came out of the ads. But the culture wasn't around long enough to withstand Park's crisis pressures. The loyalty that developed was between myself and [Park's people]. It happened and I acted by instinct. . . . We started a company newsletter and they asked me to write something. While I was in New York, I got an idea for a motivational story about Frank Sinatra. The story came to me at his Carnegie Hall concert and was entitled "One More Time." It was about Sinatra's comeback from his mid-life failures. Later I organized that story and the motivational stories that followed into a book entitled One More Time, *and gave it to the employees as a Christmas gift.*

I explained that the stories had a positive, cohesive effect, so I kept writing messages each month and giving talks as often as I could.

People in a crisis crave a charismatic relationship. I didn't know that then; but I started to let more of the emotional side of myself appear; I got more involved with the employees. Instead of being a benevolent dictator, as I had been in the law firm, I told the managers I wanted to have a go-to-hell relationship with them — an open, participative relationship. I said we don't have time for ceremony. If you see something wrong, come in and tell me to go to hell. Our human resources director was the first to walk in and say, "Dick, you said that if I didn't like what you were doing, I could tell you to go to hell. Well, . . . !" I laughed about it, but our openness developed a close relationship.

Time and time again, under stress, when I was about to go over the cliff, one of Park's officers or employees stuck their hands out to help. Park's people became an emotionally supportive team. . . . There was a time when [a group of the officers] held hands in a meeting, because they weren't going to let [anyone] down and they vowed to stick together.

That taught me that a charismatic relationship can arise out of circumstances, and people want it. If you let yourself go, it can happen and it can be very helpful. . . . I developed a close and emotional relationship with everybody.

In retrospect, Park's officers and employees joined in and supported me when we became connected — linked — when they sensed that our values and goals, though perhaps not identical, were in harmony, when they learned they could trust me, when they believed that I was, in fact, committed by deed as well as word to the scripts I had written and exhibited — scripts they, too, believed.

One of the officers said in a meeting after our final successful clash with the board: "We know you're not a banker; but we're behind you. We'll take care of operations — you work on our capital problems and the regulators and stockholders. We'll pull Park out together."

Tragically, Park Bank was, by then, too close to its Black Hole; there was no saving the bank. Yet, as Park approached the fatal edge, Park's people continued to perform beyond expectations. They were bound together in heart and soul, despite the fact that they were being pulled toward a destiny from which, unfortunately, there was no escape.

It has become clear to me from the Park Bank experience that, in crisis times, leadership is a relationship, a deep, emotional relationship between leader and followers. That relationship becomes their sustaining connection, built through the process of linkage which is, in reality, team play.

The Beginnings of the Charisma Connection

How does the CEO forge linkage with his followers when he and his company are on the rim?

Mao Tse-tung has been characterized by James MacGregor Burns as a transforming leader who had the genius to understand the emotions of his followers. Mao's understanding of his followers, Burns has said, enabled him to mobilize them into a positive force serving a common cause. The CEO on the rim must start where Mao began — with the needs and emotions of followers. From that understanding, the CEO will build his linkage and create the future.

Chaos and Lost Meaning

Trapped and fearful on the chaotic edge of a Black Hole, people can become paralyzed. They can feel lost, their sense of meaning and purpose gone, their "why," as Nietzsche put it, is lost. Thus, coping with the present, their "how," becomes intolerable.

Much of our understanding about man's need for a "why" in his life has come from psychiatrist Victor E. Frankl, who wrote about his concentration camp experiences. Man, Frankl concluded, lives by looking toward the future; there is a close connection between the orientation of a man's mind and his hope and courage. When a man has lost his belief in the viability of his future, Frankl observed, he has "also lost his spiritual hold; he let himself decline, and became subject to mental and physical decay."

Search for meaning is man's primary driving force. Meaning itself is discovered by man in his encounters; its source is factual, experiential, found in the nuances of the particular life. Yet experiences alone do not provide meaning. Meaning turns on interpretation, what man makes out of his experiences. That interpretation depends upon how he applies his values to his particular circumstances.

Meaning in Chaos

For the person trapped on the rim, meaning must be found in the chaos itself; drawn out of the ordeal's encounters and sufferings. Unless meaning can be found, however, the rim experience can be devastating. Why?

- The rim experience shakes the foundations underlying the corporate culture and shatters the cultural maps that had provided stable guides for people. Thus, people lack appropriate reference points.

- The company's sufferings cause employees who have measured their worth by its successes to experience identity crisis. They anguish unless reoriented.

- Identity crisis increases anxieties and fears, blocking or distorting visions of the future, driving people into survivor-type behavior. "First comes the belly" conduct takes over.

The crisis leader's task is to direct and guide interpretation of the latent *why* within the rim experiences of each person involved. Interpretation of the *why* leads to a glimpse of the future and a self-discovery of the essential *how*. The *why* and the *how* emerge through the *linkage experiences*.

Linkage Experiences

Suresh Srivastva and David L. Cooperrider have described the leadership-empowerment process as paradoxical: Executives are ineffective until followers empower them with authority to lead; followers are powerless until executives deliver power to them to perform. When the empowerment paradox — from followers to leader and from leader to followers — comes full circle, the followers-leader team takes responsibility for the welfare of the organization. Order emerges from chaos. Shared responsibilities and efforts merge into shared goals.

Goals that are shared objectively form visions that are shared emotionally. Visions evolve into meaning, meaning into renewal, renewal into commitment, commitment into sustained effort. The process involves the whole of the personalities of the leader and followers.

Without linkage, empowerment is not possible. As the leader-followers empowerment process unfolds, their shared experiences — their linkage experiences — move the rim's participants from Maslowian self-protective activity to higher levels of self-actualization, intensifying commitment and building dedication, providing the best opportunity for the rim-bound company to escape from its Black Hole.

Linkage experiences are the contexts in which the leader-followers relationship are shaped. They include:

- *Linkage Interaction* — which converts "leader caring" into "followers courage";

- *Linkage Vision* — which divines meaning and leads to commitment;

- *Linkage Self-Direction* — which unlocks potential and develops tenacity;

- *Linkage Accomplishment* — which produces self-esteem and efficacy and re-enforces commitment;

- *Linkage Learning* — which endows wisdom and insight.

Linkage interaction and linkage vision are the subjects of this chapter.

Linkage Interaction

Armed with data and fiscal analyses, the finance-oriented crisis leader, it is said, coolly takes charge of his company's crisis. He defines the problem, ranks options, moves decisively, eliminates the crisis causes, and prevents recurrence — quickly, efficiently, even ruthlessly. Like a captain of a listing ship whose gaping hull is flooding, as the editors of *Success* magazine advocate. ". . . The leader must be ruthless, even dictatorial. In the first months of the crisis, he orders more and more baggage overboard, allowing no questions, no hesitation. . . . Failed turnarounds have basic things in common: The companies lack true strategies or lack a ruthless chief executive who will slash costs, employees and facilities."

Cutting is required in crisis. But ruthless slashing is neither courageous nor bold nor, in the long run, successful. Brutal, ruthless leadership, in fact, results in ultimate burnout and breakdown of any prolonged recovery effort. It should not be part of the actions the crisis leader is required to take because of circumstances.

There will be times, particularly during the early stages of a deep, prolonged crisis when people are immobilized, that a crisis leader must act with dramatic, seemingly audacious power and authority. He will be decisive, disciplined, occasionally difficult, as he neutralizes the rim's shock waves, but it will always be painful for him.

Iacocca, for example, wrote: "The toughest assignment in the world is for the doctor who's at the front during battle. . . . They would pick the ones who had the best chance of survival. . . . To cut expenses, we had to fire a lot of people. It's like a war — we won, but my sons didn't come back."

A crisis leader, then, can be tough-minded and focused; but he is also concerned and compassionate, for he knows he must also heal what crises destroy.

He knows that the people within the troubled company bear the burden of turning its course and saving it from the Black Hole. He knows no leader can bring about recovery of a crisis-ridden company without the concerted efforts of people willing to commit themselves to performance beyond all reasonable expectations.

The first revitalizing steps any crisis leader must take have less to do with grasping statistics on how badly his troubled company is doing than with winning the loyalty of demoralized employees. By unlocking the frozen hands and shell-shocked minds of followers, the leader unlocks the door to the future.

How does the crisis leader go about winning loyalty and unlocking minds and hands of followers? He does it by initiating the process of linkage interaction. He is ever alert to the unsatisfied needs and emotions of his followers, and he reaches out and links their needs to his at the first opportunity.

The leader moves toward his followers, giving himself to them as he does to his mission. Giving is evidenced by his openness, inquiry, listening, and empathy, as well as by his presence and willingness to risk for the common cause.

By his linkage movement, he tells his unsure followers: "Yes, you can trust me. Yes, I care about you."

Consultant Harry Levinson, predicting followers' corporate leadership needs from populous reactions to presidential candidates, has written that effective leaders "find a path to our soul."

That is what the charismatic leader does, first and foremost: he finds a path to the souls of followers. Linkage movement opens that pathway and creates the conditions necessary for his followers to identify with their company through their linkage with him.

With linkage movement, the leader reveals his values and personality to followers. As followers respond, linkage interaction occurs. The charismatic leader's caring and presence, revealed in his linkage movement, intensifies followers' beliefs, solidifies trust, renews self-confidence, increases willingness to risk, and inspires courage. Leader-caring, then, converts into followers'-courage and, ultimately, as courage evolves into hope about the future, into commitment.

Don Shula, coach of the National Football League's Miami Dolphins has been described as a "mercurial mix: bullheaded, brilliant, devout, abusive, caring, combative, proud and self-effacing." In an interview with *Florida Trend* magazine about the Dolphins tough times, Shula spoke about what I have called linkage movement: "The things that are most important are credibility and communication. . . . For some people the tendency would be to circle the wagons or just draw into a shell. That's the wrong way. You've got to open the doors, make players feel they can approach you when something is on their minds. . . . You've got to realize that it takes something different to get inside each guy."

An understanding of linkage movement and interaction can also be gained from studying the heroic leader-followers relationship of T. E. Lawrence and his Arab guerrillas during World War I. Lawrence, an Englishman known as Lawrence of Arabia, single-handedly organized and led Arab tribes in desert victories against the German-affiliated Turks. Lawrence was described by admiring followers as "corsair supreme, a desert pirate and guerilla leader of the utmost daring and cool courage." Lawrence's ability to lead undisciplined, disorganized Arab tribes grew out of his sensitivity to Arab mentality and values and his willingness to fuse his spirit and heart with theirs.

As biographer Anthony Nutting described: "The extent to which Lawrence had become an Arab was evident not only in his dress — Bedouin robe, head-dress and sandals — and in his ready acceptance of the Spartan and unsavory living conditions of those long marches, but also his entire mental approach. He had become a creature of the desert, a guerilla fighter, an Arab chieftain." Arabs called him *El Aurens*. He was their transforming desert leader.

Is leadership movement toward followers a primary element of charismatic leadership, a distinct quality uncharacteristic of leadership as otherwise practiced?

The idea that leadership at any stage involves charismatic qualities has been difficult for many to accept. A survey by Bennis and Nanus of top executives indicated that none of them saw the leadership role, their role, as involving charisma. Rather, survey participants viewed leadership as a bundle of qualities made up of persistence, self-knowledge, willingness to take risks and endure, commitment, consistency, and learning.

Charismatic leaders are described by Jay A. Conger and Rabindra N. Kanungo in *Charismatic Leadership* as those who "demonstrate a concern for followers' needs rather than their own self-interest." They "transform concern for followers' needs into total dedication and commitment to the common cause they share with the followers in a disinterested and selfless manner and . . . engage in exemplary acts that followers perceive as involving great personal risk, cost and energy." After you review the linkage experiences, and the role the chief executive plays in shaping those experiences, I think you will agree that chief executives perceived in the Bennis and Nanus survey and in Conger and Kanungo's description are separated in degree and not in kind.

The differences between the surveyed leaders and crisis-bred charismatic leaders are in the intensity of leader-followers interaction, the energy expended, the personal risks taken, and the dedication of the leaders and their followers to their common cause. Those attributes are reflections, not of the wills of the gods, but of the intense human effort and commitment involved, of those who rise to the crisis occasion.

The first step for building the charismatic connection — movement toward followers — can be learned. In fact, all the linkage parts involved in the charismatic connection are available to us all.

Linkage Vision

The charismatic leader's movement toward his followers unquestionably helps followers develop courage. Followers on the rim, however, need more than courage. They need hope, some glimpse of the future to be courageous about. Without hope, there is no commitment. Without commitment, there is no sustaining effort.

What kind of vision best grabs the hearts and minds of people trapped on the rim? It is one that is:

- experiential, materializing out of circumstances;

- justifiable, sustaining varying viewpoints under a variety of conditions; and

- emotional, changing ideals into dedicated commitment.

Experiential Vision

The process of envisioning, that is, creating idealized images about the future state of a company, and empowering followers through communication of those images, has been described in management literature as a distinct, three-step process.

Conceptualized in that sense, vision might be conceived of as springing abstractly from the mind and heart of the crisis leader who, like Moses descending from Sinai with the tablets of the Covenant secured in his arms, delivers the word to his followers, who embrace it and its literal efficacy. However, vision that begins abstractly and is maintained rigidly does not last and eventually is destroyed by confrontations or compromises with life's experiences.

Fortunately, the vision of the promised land held by the lost tribes of Israel did not disintegrate. Why? Because the Israelite vision was shaped by desert experiences accumulated over forty years of wanderings. The people who left Egypt were transformed by their desert experiences.

The original vision of the peoples enslaved in Egypt was sculptured, and constantly redesigned, by life itself. Their vision became an experientially based vision, growing from life and subjected to continual reinterpretation. Reinterpretation of a vision can provide renewal and recommitment.

Experientially based vision can be described as today's version of the end of the story. Rarely, however, is that version of the end of the story likely to be present at the end.

The end of the story, to survive over time, must be continually redefined, like the Constitution of the United States, which serves today's needs not because it is rigidly bound to its "original meaning," as some legal scholars suggest, but because it is a living document, continually renewed by the insights of each succeeding generation. Historical roots provide an anchor, but Constitutional interpretation grows out of the experiences of each new generation, a step at a time.

Contributing authors for *Charismatic Leadership*, Frances R. Westley and Henry Mintzberg, compared the development of strategic vision of former Canadian Prime Minister René Levesque with that of Chrysler's Lee Iacocca. Levesque's vision of Quebec sovereignty disintegrated when his plan, abstractly visioned and rigidly implemented, failed to cope with events. In contrast, Iacocca's vision grew out of process, out of his ability to create wholeness from the bits and pieces he was able to put together through his daily interactions with people and events and his exposure to ideas.

Levesque's approach, according to Westley and Mintzberg, was deductive. "He began with an ideal and attempted to construct or find a mirror image in reality."

Iacocca's approach was inductive, "his vision or ideal growing from and in response to the stream of his operational decisions and day-to-day encounters."

The ability to assemble linkage vision out of chaos is similar to Notre Dame's Lou Holtz's use of what he has described as "adjustment coaching" — opportunistic changes implemented in response to a football game's unfolding events. The process is reactive, but in a proactive way. Charismatic leaders create the future as they adapt to it.

Inside the Park

The original dream for Park Bank was that it be a strong, vibrant, locally owned bank, responsive to the needs of its business community, able to withstand future takeover attempts by regional or national banks. When the FDIC's report card shocked Park's management and board, Park's building process became derailed, but its dream remained on track, believed achievable through a few strategic adjustments and asset improvements.

Soon, however, Park's struggle on the rim began. Our dream had to change from creating a bank to restoring a bank to its rightful place within the community. In April 1985, I spoke to our staff about our belt-tightening, our tough decisions, tying our revised future into our historic past. The speech, reproduced for shareholders, said, in part:

What we have done reflects our attitude about our times, our company and our responsibilities to our communities of stockholders and customers. In reality, it reflects our attitude about ourselves. Healthy, self confident people can make tough decisions. Healthy, self confident businesses, such as Park Bank, also can make tough decisions. . . .

We took market share from our older, more established competitors. We went on to locate our expansion preferences in other key West Coast cities. Those were good decisions. Our franchise locations are very important to us, particularly with interstate banking around the corner.

But there is a cost in achieving this objective of market position and dominance. Frankly, a little more cost than we expected. . . .

This year we tidy things up. We complete our computer conversion. We get to know and accept all our new faces. We take care of some troubled loans. All in all, we pull things together. We settle down. We switch our emphasis from growth to profitability.

But Park's dream was not to be. On November 15, 1985, I called our staff together and announced our decision to sell the bank. I said that we would have to pull ourselves together again; that we would work to preserve our assets and the jobs of our people. With heavy hearts, but with renewed effort, we began to shape ourselves into a worthy acquisition.

A "Shareholder's Report" was sent to Park's stockholders. It said, in part: "We have reluctantly concluded that in order to obtain additional capital we must sell the bank. . . . Our efforts are now directed toward preserving Park Bank so that it may continue to serve this community."

A meeting was held with the press. I said, "The truth is right now there probably is not another solution to the financial problems of the bank. They're deeper than we thought they were. It comes to the point where you need to just preserve the asset base the best you can, and that requires a sale."

That sales effort, too, became blocked. Park's most likely purchasers were money-center banks looking for entry into the Florida market. However, they were prohibited under existing banking rules from acquiring us unless we failed.

In mid-February, our options exhausted, I called Park's staff together again. We must pull ourselves together one more time, I said; we must prepare Park Bank for an FDIC takeover. All would not be lost, however; likely purchaser-candidates would be the money-center banks. A money-center bank would want our staff and its knowledge of the market. We had to show them that we were made of the right stuff.

Though scared, uncertain about any future, we prepared. We held on to customers. We negotiated on loans to improve our portfolio. We created an information book about Park Bank, its people, and business, to enlighten the bidding victor and smooth the transition. Our operations executive vice president had colored name tags prepared for the final event — blue for us, yellow for the FDIC officials who would walk in, and red for the takeover purchasers. Everyone would know the players.

At 11:00 P.M., on Friday, February 14, 1986, five hours after Park's official closing, as the FDIC bids were being opened, a tired, but still-able-to-joke bank staff got together a betting pool on who Park's takeover bidder would be.

Chase was the betting favorite.

Justifiable Vision

The early efforts of leadership on the rim are often directed toward filling spiritual voids brought about by the rim's chaos, toward helping people whose lives have been emptied by the crisis experience discover a future.

The vision of the crisis leader, however, whether directed at changing views or filling the rim's voids, is unfinished until it has been completed by the interpretations of followers. The leader's vision, once adopted, is held by each follower in his own way, through varying levels of consciousness, nuances in understanding, and differences in personally pursued goals.

Followers' interpretations of the leader's vision create possible differences in meaning. Michael Walzer, author of *Exodus and Revolution,* described such a dualism between leader and followers in the desert experiences of the Israelites. The promise of milk and honey represented the materialistic interest the oppressed tribes had in escaping Egyptian bondage. On the other hand, the holy promise of deliverance held by

Moses was spiritual, idealistic. Walzer also reported that, during the Russian revolution, Lenin similarly described two levels of responses among his followers. The Russian masses focused on a better life, and he and his vanguard focused on a new society. During both of these historic struggles, the two levels, materialism and spiritualism, were closely entwined, supporting each other.

It is that kind of different interpretation of the vision by followers that is likely to justify the goals of the leader to followers and motivate each to a commonality of purpose and action.

Inside the Park

At one point I was frustrated that I was not communicating our vision throughout the bank with sufficient clarity. I felt the senior officers shared my zeal to save the bank. But what did our effort mean to our younger employees? What would it take to encourage them to be willing participants in our now holy crusade?

In one of those "by-the-way" conversations that often provide the bits of information upon which vision is built, a senior officer told me of a young employee who, contrary to some, had become turned on by his workout experience; he viewed it as a great opportunity to learn, making him invaluable in whatever he would end up doing if Park Bank failed.

That conversation gave me an idea that I used to communicate a different aspect of our vision, appealing, I hoped, to our younger employees. I used it in the bank's next newsletter, Inside the Park. *It was entitled "Challenge at Cape Bojador."*

Five hundred years ago the Portuguese were the world's pioneers of the sea. Under the direction of Prince Henry (known as Henry the Navigator), Portuguese mariners ventured into unchartered waters, expanding man's knowledge and utilization of our world.

Five hundred years ago, our earth was known to be flat, the Mediterranean Ocean at its center. South, East, West and North of the known Mediterranean world was the Sea of Darkness: the world's end into which no man dare enter. . . .

Worldwide explorer, Marco Polo, reported from "reliable sources" that certain of the islands at the edge of the Sea were the home of an enormous eagle, with feathers 12 paces (about 36 feet) long—strong enough to seize an el-

ephant and smash it to pieces. No wonder ancient mariners dared not to penetrate the Sea of Darkness.

The map makers placed the southern edge of the known world just past Cape Bojador, an indistinguishable bulge on the West Coast of Africa slightly south of the Canary islands. . . .

Fifteen expeditions went out from Portugal between 1424 and 1434. But none would pass Cape Bojador. Fear turned the ships back. Beyond the Cape there would be no race of man; there were stark, desert-like cliffs on the visible coast of Africa, deathly currents in the seas, and Marco Polo's "reliable information" on giant eagles preying on any mariner foolish enough to penetrate further into the unknown. It was no wonder that, in 1433, the Portuguese captain, Gil Eannes, returned and told Prince Henry that Cape Bojador could not be passed. . . .

But Prince Henry wanted one more try. Was Eannes up to it? Yes, he would face the Gates of Hell, the giant eagles. He would try. In 1434, off Africa's coast, Eannes approached Cape Bojador very wide at sea, away from the threatening currents. Suddenly and unexpectedly as his caravel emerged from the fog, Eannes found himself past the Cape. Bojador was behind him. The Gates of Hell did not exist!

Europe ultimately found its eastward sea route to India.

Boorstein, describing these events in his fascinating book, The Discoverers, *quotes ancient historian Zurara who reported that Portuguese mariners had been blocked, ". . . not only by fear but by its shadow. . . . So he [Eannes] performed, . . . despising all danger, and found the lands quite contrary to what he, like others, had expected. And although the matter was a small one in itself, on account of its daring it was reckoned as great."*

An event, small in itself. But, because of its daring, it became great.

The experiences and challenges of each of us that architect our lives — events small in themselves. . . . How many times have we been immobilized not only by fear, but by our "shadows of fear"? Our concocted versions of reality. Our Marco Polo's eagles swooping down on us, dashing us in our minds on the rocks below before we begin to try.

Some of us approach our personal Cape Bojadors like the Portuguese mariners who would not venture into the Sea of Darkness. And we miss the challenge, the opportunity and the learning experience that venturing on an unchartered course can provide.

Others of us are up to it. Each day's experiences are a trip on our own Portuguese caravel rounding Cape Bojador. A romantic, mind-expanding opportunity. . . .

I remarked to one of our young officers the other day how excited he appeared, how upbeat he seemed despite his stressing workout responsibilities for us at Park Bank.

He answered: "You know, I was really scared when you said the bank was in trouble. I was afraid for my job. I couldn't face customers who criticized us. I felt really bad. But I thought about it. I listened to the things you said."

He continued: "Now I wouldn't miss the challenge. What a great opportunity. I'm handling tough situations. Real problems. I'm getting a million dollar education! I wouldn't leave Park now for anything."

A Portuguese seafarer reincarnated. He has found opportunity in his personal Cape Bojador. An event small in itself, but an event that by its nature has become great! For him. For Park Bank.

Emotional Vision

Vision becomes the source for commitment when it can be seized by the heart. To be seized by the heart, vision must find its expression in imagery. Westley and Mintzberg state that "analogy, as a rhetorical device, bridges unlike contexts and works to mobilize energy and emotion. Iacocca may or may not have 'believed' in his own analogies, but they seemed to work powerfully for those around him. His choice of metaphor/analogy was vivid and created rich justification for discrete strategic initiatives."

Iacocca's use of imagery peaked during his attempt to convince the federal government that Chrysler's loan should be guaranteed. Iacocca compared Chrysler as a company to America as a nation, saying: "We are a microcosm of what was going wrong in America." When he took his salary cut to $1.00 a year, done at a time when he was negotiating pay concessions from Chrysler's unions, he said, "I didn't take one dollar a year to be a martyr. I took it because I had to go into the pits."

Iacocca's use of emotional imagery provided linkage to Chrysler's people, permitting a range of related interpretive meanings arising from Chrysler's chaos to be fused into a vision of a common cause.

Inside the Park

There is little doubt in my mind that vision, emotionally shared vision, is at the heart of commitment. Joe O'Neill of the Tampa Bay Business Journal *wrote after an interview with me during the last month of Park Bank's life:*

While Jacobs pursues potential purchasers — the most viable are out of town interests — and regularly updates the regulators, his day-to-day routine entails a lot of crisis management and morale building.

"You have to communicate more," Jacobs explains. . . . "You must remain empathetic with your people, and it's very important that everyone understands that we are all part of the same team — that we are all helping each other. You've got to carry the message."

That message is also carried in the bank's monthly newsletter, Inside the Park, *which typically contains inspirational, anecdote-laced articles by Jacobs. He's prone to quote from sources as varied as Aristotle, Santayana, Schweitzer, Thoreau, Voltaire and Getty. He pulls homilies out of visits to places as diverse as Peru, Carnegie Hall, Israel and Wimbledon.*

My Park Bank experience taught me that a leader's vision becomes the source of commitment when that vision becomes linked with the followers' hearts, sparking at least a corner of the private dreams of each of them.

The crisis leader's principal task is to grab bits and pieces off the rim's scrap piles and, through his use of a wide variety of symbolic language and communicative techniques, mold them into hope, vision, and, ultimately, commitment.

Chapter 17

From Commitment to Sustained Effort

The qualities of greatness become manifest only when times are bad.

James O'Toole

People on the rim respond with intense feelings and fervor when they become linked with their leader. According to Sigmund Freud, it's like being in love. Motivated by lofty expectations about their leader's ability to create order out of chaos, followers commit themselves to him and his cause with enthusiasm and emotion, imbuing him with extraordinary, mystical qualities projected from their personal needs and ideals.

But highly charged emotions fade when disenchanted by reality. No leader in the rim's environment, no matter how omnipotent, can fulfill followers' ideals and satisfy their needs without occasionally faltering.

When reality's disillusionment sets in, what happens to followers' commitment?

To a large degree, the answer to that question will depend on the three remaining *linkage experiences* — self-direction, accomplishment, and learning — and whether they are part of the leader-followers' charisma connection.

Linkage Self-Direction

After Park Bank failed, I had an opportunity to consult with the president of a manufacturing company that was on the verge of bankruptcy. Following a brief orientation meeting, in which I received an overview of his perception of the company's crisis, I toured its facilities and visited with several of his staff. It was obvious that the company was on the rim, about to explode. It was also obvious that the president was exhausted and that his staff was frozen into inaction. When I returned to the president's office, I told him in words painfully learned: "You're trying to save this company all by yourself. For the most part, your people are standing around watching you. You can't do it. Not only will the stress kill you, there's too much to do — you'll blow it. Decide what has to be done. Pick out the most important things *you* can do. Tell everybody that this is what you are going to do. Let them know you need their help to do the rest. Then trust them, get everybody involved!"

In chapter 9, I pointed out that executive pride, feelings of embarrassment, and fear of failure and power disintegration combine to discourage executives from involving others in the management of a crisis. As the crisis deepens, power, control, and authority become increasingly concentrated at the top. This, however, may be the most serious mistake a crisis leader can make.

During the early stages of the crisis, particularly if he is new to the company, the crisis leader may centralize control and authority. He centralizes to size up the rim environment in a hurry and to develop accurate information about the nature of the crisis and its probable causes; the capabilities and capacities of the staff; the relationships between customers, suppliers, regulators, stockholders, the public, and the press; and the strengths and weaknesses of various parts of his company.

He also centralizes control during the early stages because the rim-bound company lacks verve. His decisive, aggressive, dramatic, sometimes autocratic, action may be the only way a dying organization's heart can be energized.

Followers consent to a leader's dictatorial authority for a time; passive consent gives them an opportunity to judge *him* without commitment on their part. The leader's take-charge style becomes part of his IM (impression management) delivery, communicating to followers that he has the wisdom, strength, and heart required to lead them through the rim's erupting chaos.

The first lesson crisis teaches a leader, however, is that it is almost impossible to control anything, much less everything. A leader may anticipate, coach, mentor, and inspire, but, ultimately, he has little choice but to rely on the performances of his people.

Inside the Park

Somewhat ironically, in an interview with Tampa Bay Business Journal, *one of Park's directors likened me to former President Jimmy Carter saying that I wanted to master all the details. That was somewhat true early-on when I was trying to develop an overview of Park's strengths and weaknesses to decide where I should concentrate my efforts and where Park's people were strong. Also, the comment was quite accurate in relation to control of Park's communication with customers, regulators, stockholders, and the press. Crisis communication is the one task, I am convinced, that must stay with the chief executive of the troubled company. Time and again, regardless of what was going on, I would take calls from unsettled bank customers. The CEO's attitude and demeanor are, for most people, the signs of the rim-bound organization's health, and everyone involved, internally and externally, wants to know how he is and what he is doing.*

I quickly learned, however, regardless of what I might have liked to do, that I had little direct control over the wide varieties of daily activities of bank employees or the many interactions of customers with our tellers or loan personnel at a half dozen branch locations.

The Park Bank seen by customers on an everyday basis was its employees at its branches and lending offices — not me or anyone else at the executive offices. When a skittish customer appeared at a teller-window in any of our branches several miles from our executive offices, the customer's comfort with Park Bank and the outcome of the teller-customer interaction was at that decisive moment in the hands of the teller.

Placing people in a position to accomplish results on their own is a prime objective of a crisis leader. The crisis leader places his people in that position through linkage self-direction . He does this both by:

- developing autonomous followers; and

- developing team players.

Autonomous Followers

Robert H. Waterman, Jr., wrote in *The Renewal Factor* that every renewing company has a "clearly-in-charge chief executive." A clearly-in-charge chief executive does not control, because he knows that in the final analysis, he cannot control, but can only influence. A clearly-in-charge executive is in charge — his influence is felt and shapes events — because he has prepared people to function on their own, minimizing crisis panic and bunker mentalities.

Preparation Through Factual Communication

The in-charge chief executive prepares people by communicating information, frequently and accurately, about the true state of affairs, arming followers with knowledge about what can be expected, what the public with whom they will deal is going to hear and read in the press, how the public will feel, and, most likely, how they will react. Under no circumstances should people within the company read about its state of affairs in the paper before being informed of it by the CEO.

Preparation by Communicating Attitude

The in-charge crisis leader, by his words and deeds, communicates from his inner self, his attitude, and by so doing, interprets the rim's events. His conduct — his deliberate risk of himself, his complete dedication to the cause, and his willingness to jump in and, as Geneen puts it, pull an oar — serves as symbolic representation of the effort needed. He inspires others, creating within followers a if-he-can-do-it-so-can-I spirit and a "he's-okay,-so-I'm-okay,-so-we're-okay" attitude.

Inside the Park

Park's director of Human Resources expressed the consequences of all-out effort — the "it's okay" feeling picked up by followers — when she was interviewed by a reporter: "There's a feeling that as long as Dick's still here, it's OK. . . . No one works harder, is under more stress, or has more to lose. He leads by example. He's terribly concerned but always optimistic."

The effective crisis leader communicates confidence by betting on people, by delegating decision-making and responsibility at every chance, giving others within the organization an opportunity to extend themselves. The leader directs the orchestra, as Peter Drucker has described it, but he lets his people know that the orchestra's performance is theirs. He encourages people to extend themselves, communicating corrective visions when correction is appropriate. He does not scapegoat.

Inside the Park

The attitude of management toward the people they deal with and toward each other can deteriorate dangerously when tensions mount. Shortly after replacing several of Park's loan officers, those attributed with making many of its bad loans, I found that new loan officers, dealing with the perceived mess created by the discharged lenders, chose to vent their feelings on customers with the bad loans.

I called a meeting of the new loan officers, and we discussed the importance of positive attitudes, of maintaining our solution-orientation, of not identifying scapegoats, and of keeping ourselves on a high plane. Attitudes expressed toward others, after all, express what we feel about ourselves.

The idea of keeping everything on a high plane, even when stress made it unbearably difficult, became the subject of some good-natured joking, but the idea took hold. And, I think, that attitude helped us feel better about ourselves during very difficult times.

The effective crisis leader is also aware that not everyone can operate on the rim without close support. People come from a variety of background experiences and are armed with different strengths and weaknesses, varying levels of self-confidence, and competing interests. Anxiety and shock affect people in diverse ways. So the leader, too, should communicate that requiring help is okay; and he should find ways to give help when it's needed. But, wherever possible, his help should assist people in succeeding on their own. He should mentor, teach, prod, suggest, but not, unless it is absolutely necessary, step in and substitute his performance for theirs.

The effective crisis leader treats people, and encourages his managers to treat people, individually. He writes and talks of team work, of each person's contribution and role, always creating images about future outcomes. He describes, in direct and symbolic terms, what must be done, raising followers' expectations, identifying them as the solution, not as the problem. He talks to groups within the company, large and small, and he talks to people, one-on-one.

The effective crisis leader also communicates by his willingness to listen. As much as he writes and talks, he listens, not just to the words but to the subtle, perhaps contradictory, messages intimated in by-the-way conversations and body language.

By listening, by seeking opinions, and by acting on suggestions, he lets people know that they and their ideas matter; they are important to the company and its recovery.

Using Charisma Extenders

The crisis leader also should identify people within the organization who are *charisma extenders* — natural communicators, independent and strong enough in their own right to help carry the message. The leader should make sure that the charisma extenders know his expectations, his dreams, what he is doing, and where the company is headed. He should ask for their help to carry the message, not through the company's formal communication channels but, more importantly, through informal communications, which are the primary attitude-builders during the company's troubled times. Charisma extenders are themselves mentors, team players who, directly by words and vicariously by example, encourage others to find strength within themselves.

Inside the Park

   I was fortunate. As I circulated among various offices and departments of Park Bank, over time, I sensed certain people had communicative
influence with others working within the bank. I learned that, after my visit
with any of those people, others would soon know what we talked about
and that communication from those people would carry with it a ring of
authority.
   As I continued my visits with the branches and departments, I increasingly began to make certain that, if time constraints did not allow me
to visit with everyone, I at least talked to Park's charisma extenders.
Bringing those persons in on our plans and current developments assured
that the informal communication channels, normally ripe with rumors,
would also carry information I felt should be communicated to Park's
staff.

Communications and Consistency

   Communication of information, attitude, and hope also require linkage to reality. All communications, internal and external — even advertising — relate to and interpret the rim's environment for those involved.

Inside the Park

   During the summer of 1985, I suggested that our ad agency prepare
a series of advertisements designed to bring to the public the message:
Park Bank was back on track, ultimately to be recognized as one of the
excellent. The advertisement series tied into the Peters and Waterman
book, In Search of Excellence.
   At the time the advertising campaign was conceived, I felt that Park
Bank had turned the corner (we had finally been able to publicly report
nonperforming portfolio loan improvement); however, I was wrong. I had
stretched hope into fact. Park Bank was, in reality, in the quiet eye of its
Black Hole storm.
   The advertisements turned out to be a disaster; the public perceived
Park's statements as unwarranted puffing. There was not enough support-
ing evidence to back up Park's advertisements.

Resentment, open hostility, was expressed by several customers. Who were we to flaunt ourselves? Did we think so little of our customer's intelligence? Employees reacted to customer feedback and the whole effort produced a negative effect within and without the company. We quickly pulled the ads.

In retrospect, I realize that, in my zest to tear Park Bank away from the rim, I had ignored the importance of earning one's way out of trouble — of performance being the statement.

Communication and Courage

Abraham Zaleznik has written that the "real work" of company leadership could be allocated between two persons, a task leader (an operations officer whose job is to attain achievement) and a social leader (a chief executive officer whose job is to develop team work and cooperation). True, as we have said, leadership tasks can, and must, be delegated or shared. But ultimate verification of the vital signs of the troubled company must come from the CEO. Followers' faith in the vitality of the company is inseparable from his visible courage and willingness to communicate. Charisma extenders may promote and implement the CEO's message, but the CEO must first — courageously — walk his talk and — cogently — talk his walk.

Simply put, it is impossible for the crisis leader to walk courageously without communicating courage; it is impossible for him to communicate courage without walking courageously.

That kind of walk-talk combination is infectious. Tom Peters wrote in *Thriving on Chaos*: "People in all organizations are boss-watchers, especially when external conditions are ambiguous. For better or worse, what you spend your time on (not what you sermonize about) will become the organization's preoccupation."

Unlocking Potential

If a leader is viewed as worthy of emulation, if he has communicated strength and values, followers are more willing to commit themselves. Commitment becomes the source of self-mastery and efficacy, unlocking potential and encouraging each person to be accountable for himself. As a result, followers facing the rim's daily disasters will be able to maintain a stronger sense of self-worth and direction. They "buy in" because they believe not only in their cause and their leader, but, more importantly, in themselves and in their ability to contribute. They become willing, committed participants. Followers and leader become mutual participants in the recovery effort. Together, they unlock the potential so necessary for their troubled company.

Team Players

Studies have shown that the differences between the leader and follower lessen as the relationship intensifies. Harry Levinson, writing for the *Academy of Management Executive,* reported that leader-crew interactions on space missions indicate that hierarchy and status play lesser roles as relationships intensify and extend over time. Task-oriented, somewhat aloof, leaders rated high on short missions; however, democratic leaders who were concerned with the emotions and well-being of their crews carried the day on longer missions.

The crisis leader must remain anything but aloof as he implements his game plan. In the long-run, it is the team that performs.

The team relationship differs from a hierarchic relationship. The continuing performance of each person remains significant, but there is less concern about the self and more concern about the team and its accomplishments. There is camaraderie and devotion.

People have a need to direct their personal destiny. That is why linkage self-direction works; there is separateness with togetherness. Peters and Waterman refer to this dualism in *In Search of Excellence:* "With equal vehemence, we seek self-determination and security."

Autonomous followership is the balance necessary for all-out performance. Being an accomplished member of a team provides the opportunity for self-determination against a background of security. Each person is responsible for his own assignments; but those assignments are part of a greater whole. Each person is responsible to himself; yet, others depend upon him and at the same time look out for him. He is counted on, a worthwhile contributor to a cause with which he identifies. He is responsible to — linked with — those working with him.

The charismatic crisis leader should focus his efforts both on individual performance and on team-building. He should strive for team performance, for socialized, not personalized, power.

The differences?

Professor Jane M. Howell compared socialized and personalized forms of leadership in *Charismatic Leadership.* Socialized leadership relates goals to followers' needs, the common good, and high ideals, not to the leader's private motives. Socialized leadership encourages followers to develop in their own right, empowering them to perform at their potential; personalized leadership seeks dominance and blind obedience. Socialized leadership builds internalized values; personalized leadership seeks behavioral conformity.

Professor Howell concludes that followers become independent, self-directing, and more altruistic when their leader expresses goals followers want and when he communicates his confidence that they can reach those goals.

The process of linkage self-direction builds follower confidence in themselves and develops their inner strength. The process is guided by crisis leadership, which builds on we, not me; on thy, not I.

Linkage Accomplishment

Search for Meaning

I started our discussion about linkage describing Victor Frankl's observation that man's driving force is his search for meaning — man's search for the *why* of his life which makes the *how* understandable. Ultimately, rim experiences and interpretations of them become the source of feelings about the self.

The Importance of Real Work

Frankl wrote that man detects existential meaning in three ways: by doing a deed, by experiencing a value, and by suffering. The most significant is doing a deed; that is, accomplishment.

In "Leadership: The Art of Empowering Others," Jay A. Conger describes four ways a transforming leader provides empowerment information to followers: through words of encouragement and persuasion, through positive support in situations imposing anxiety or stress, through mentoring (providing others with a role model), and through the experience of mastering a task — through accomplishment (the conclusions of researcher Alfred Bandura).

Abraham Zaleznik calls accomplishment *real work*. Though no leader should overlook the importance of meaning gained through bonding and by exhibition of courage, the crisis leader must always look for results — accomplishment — Zaleznik's real work.

Research indicates clearly that people's greatest motivations come through their achievement, and achievement reaches its high point when personal accomplishments and company requirements synchronize.

The charismatic crisis leader may arouse people to action, he may stand as their admired hero, he may unite them around inspiring goals, but, ultimately, his aspirations and leadership must produce results.

Achievement and Avoidance of Failure

How is accomplishment achieved on the rim when disaster is imminent and chaos is the rule of the day?

- By identifying important activities that can be accomplished successfully, even if these activities are not determinative of ultimate success.

- By identifying people who can achieve results, placing them in visible positions and endowing them with the freedom to perform.

- By redefining accomplishments to fit situations.

Identification of Success Potentials

One of the primary tasks of the crisis leader is to identify potential situations for success within the company. There will almost always be success-potentials to exploit. Results will permeate the company. Success engenders energy, strength, and confidence, even if, for some, its experience comes vicariously through people operating in less troubled parts of the rim's landscape.

Inside the Park

We were blessed with opportunities in several areas within Park Bank. Through the dedicated efforts of those involved, major accomplishments were achieved right to the end, minimizing the ultimate destruction. Those efforts and successes were a strength to others in more troubled areas of the bank. Here are three examples:

- *Finance. Liquidity management is critical for a troubled bank. Banks traditionally maintain a large investment portfolio of tax-exempt bonds and government securities. Short-term bonds or securities provide earning cash reserves and liquidity. Long-term bonds and securities are held for tax-equivalent yield and diversification. Of course, a troubled bank has little use for tax-equivalent yield. It needs cash flow and liquidity. The long-term strategy of tax-equivalent yield produces disastrous results during troubled times. If a troubled bank cannot convert its long-term tax-equivalent yield bonds and securities to short-term cash flow producing equivalents without substantial principal loss, the bank can suffer a fatal liquidity crisis and a cash flow disaster. Through careful planning and skillful management of maturities and market opportunities, Park's Finance Department was able to avoid a liquidity and cash flow crisis, converting Park's long-term securities to cash equivalents over a relatively short time period without destructive portfolio loss. Through the process, Park's depositors who had had certificates of deposit in excess of the FDIC insured amount were all quietly placed into a position of full insurance coverage; there were no uninsured depositors on the day Park Bank crashed.*

- *Human Resources. Park's Human Resources Department was able to maintain staff training, so essential to skills and morale, and was able to offer counselng to those we asked to leave, minimizing pain and possible repercussions. Some of the specialized programs put on by Human Resources were vital in communicating to Park's staff how to treat customers during crisis. We were able to avoid a disastrous run on deposits, mass exodus of employees, and lawsuits by employees who were painfully discharged before the final crash.*

- *Operations. Park's Operations Department accomplished an almost impossible computer conversion while managing Park's branches (deposit acquisition sites and customer service centers) and opening our new operation's center during the midst of the crisis. Construction of the center and the conversion process had started under prior management before our loan troubles surfaced. Had the conversion not been handled with deft skill, our systems would have crumbled into chaos and, with them, the confidence of customers and staff who relied on them.*

Each of these departments was lead by a manager who was brought in as part of our reorganization. Each manager had had prior crisis experience and moved quickly and professionally to establish his or her credibility and competence, identifying the departmental problems that had to be solved, accomplishing results essential for Park's continued survival.

Each manager was a skilled communicator, not only within his or her department, but also interdepartmentally, sensing where and when others required support and encouragement.

The people in those departments, perhaps two-thirds of Park's employees, were proud of their accomplishments and their role in giving Park Bank the best chance it could have for survival. And rightfully so. As one person in the Finance Department said to me after the crash, "Now I know I can handle anything."

Identification of Achievers

As we pointed out earlier, one of the more important tasks any crisis leader has is to identify key people within the organization who spread the word through gossip and rumor, the informal channels of communication in the company. These same people can also communicate achievement and accomplish major results for the rim-bound company.

These *charisma extenders,* as I call them, are usually attracted to challenge and have a high tolerance for a troubled environment. The rim's landscape provides them a chance to overcome difficult obstacles — their definition of accomplishment.

Charisma extenders typically are self-confident and self-directed, bent on controlling their environment and managing their own courses. They can possess a mastery over their work that, through emulation, increases the confidence and productivity of those around them.

Typical extenders respond to openness. They speak out and express their ideas. They do not provide the crisis leader with manipulated information, which sounds good but lacks substance. Extenders have no time for circumlocution and will let any leader know (and every crisis leader must be willing to know) when a proposal is a lousy idea.

The more aggressive charisma extenders can be mavericks. They can appear to be anything but team players because they are not compliant actors cementing their jobs through corporate gamesmanship. Their language is one of substance, not form; their focus is achievement.

The maverick charisma extender's priority is his job — *first*. This charisma extender identifies with what he does, not who he is with. His independence comes from the fact that his job commitment precedes his company commitment. He can speak out and operate with a freedom the less secure lack. He has self-confidence and strength, which permit him to deal with outside adversity with little fear of self-destruction.

A paper by professors Gary J. Blau and Kimberly B. Boal about organizational commitment, turnover, and absenteeism makes some relevant observations. The professors created a research model to measure rates and frequency of corporate turnover and absenteeism among a variety of personalities. They categorized employees as:

- *Institutionalized Stars* — people with high levels of job involvement and organizational commitment. Their commitment is such that they exert a high level of job effort and support maintenance of the organization.

- *Lone Wolves* — people who experience a high level of job involvement and a low level of organizational commitment. Their commitment is primarily directed toward the tasks they perform rather than to the organization. They serve as mentors to others who also have a high degree of affinity for task performance, and to others who are mystified by them. Their problem, from the perspective of the organization, is that they follow personal agendas.

- *Corporate Citizens* — people who exhibit a low level of job involvement and a high level of corporate commitment. Their work usually is not important, but they are committed to the company and its objectives. They focus on corporate group harmony and group maintenance (group politics) rather than on task performance. Their behavior fits into roles, into "expectations." A problem for a company dominated by *corporate citizens* is that it has a high number of people who are willing to attend meetings and too few who are willing to assume responsibilities.

- *Apathetic Employees* — People who have a low level of task performance and of company involvement. These people are most apt to do enough to get by, but little more. They will contribute little to the efforts of the rim-bound company. In trouble, their bunker mentality is hard to shake.

The *institutional stars* and the *lone wolves* within the organization must be earmarked by the crisis leader as "keepers." These people will be the charisma extenders and the primary source of mentors who energize the organization.

The *lone wolves* will be the mavericks. Throughout history, war stories have been spun from the substance of their heroics. Their ability to focus on the rim's demands without being overwhelmed by its chaotic conditions makes them invaluable. Their flair for accomplishing the seemingly impossible, their apparent nonchalance and conspicuous independence, ignites the spirits of those with whom they work, motivating everyone to higher levels of accomplishment. Every troubled company can use at least one *lone wolf*. Park Bank was blessed in this regard.

Inside the Park

One Park Bank maverick in particular, a workout-lender, stands out in my mind. He followed his own drum beat; he would rarely maintain the schedule we asked others to follow. He was energetic, driven, brutally frank, intuitive about people and situations, uncompromisingly honest.

He would work twenty hours straight for days on end. Then he would disappear without a word until he refueled. It was frustrating.

Yet, the toughest of workout challenges were his. He insisted. And he was good, the best we had. On more than one occasion, he reached out and pulled us back from disaster. Other lenders admiringly called him the Jet-Man. He operated with a mystique they honored and sought to emulate.

One troubled corporate loan in particular showed the Jet-Man's stuff. He insisted on a meeting with the business owners whose fighting amongst themselves had left their company in disarray and its loans delinquent. They were belligerent toward any settlement of the company debt. The meeting was followed by a series of threats directed toward the bank. The threats were followed with bombings that destroyed trucks and equipment that had been part of Park Bank's collateral.

As broad-shouldered and courageous as he was smart and tenacious, the Jet-Man was not to be deterred. He went back into the rubble and persuaded the owners to convey Park Bank substantially all of their real estate properties in settlement of their debts. He then tirelessly worked out a sales plan and was able to dispose of several of the properties before Park's final crash.

Redefining the Situation

Peter Drucker has written that "management exists only in contemplation of performance;" that management is a means to an end, its task is "to make work productive and the worker achieving." The rim's environment provides an ultimate challenge in that regard.

Locating pockets of success potentials and identifying charisma extenders will not be enough. The rim will continue to take its toll. The crisis leader must remember that *productive achievement* is a principal way, if not *the* principal way, that most people realize meaning. Followers seek achievement as verification of their efficacy and leaders seek followers' achievement for the success of their enterprises.

Achievement cannot always be measured in absolute terms, however. Just as vision is defined by circumstances, so is achievement. As vision of the future grows out of the ashes of the rim's encounters, so does the measure of achievement.

Inside the Park

One of the articles for Inside the Park *that I wrote in late 1985, when Park's potential for turning itself around was at its lowest, was designed to encourage us to throw ourselves into our performance at Park Bank, to bring about the all-out effort Park so desperately needed at that time. The article was published coincidentally with a speech to Park's staff that carried a parallel message. It was entitled, "The Zen of Hard Work."*

I'm into "Zen." Don't worry, I haven't joined some Far East Cult.

Zen is not a far out philosophy aimed at placing us into a state of passive harmony with our otherwise stress-filled world. Zen deals with our highly developed sense of understanding about our personal environment gained through "throw-yourself-into-it" participation in whatever we are doing.

It's the old "lose yourself to find yourself" philosophy. It's life lived to its fullest by one who is really tuned in. Being tuned in is Zen.

Let's take a couple of examples. The Zen of seeing. There is a difference between looking and seeing. For example, when we are in a park we may look at a tree and step out of the way. Looking is coping, surviving. But looking is not experiencing. Seeing is experiencing, feeling and comprehending. When we see, we experience; we feel a part of our very personal environment. We enjoy an exhilaration, an awareness of the marvelous unity of all of life. . . .

An athletic effort, when we throw ourselves into it, is also a Zen experience. For example, there is a Zen in running. Running is more than physical exertion. It's a form of self-discovery, definitely beneficial to our emotional well-being, as well as our physical state. When we jog we "get into it." We lose ourselves in the experience. When that occurs our subconscious takes over, we digest our daily experiences and we fine-tune our perspective. We feel good about life and about ourselves.

Now to the point of my story. Work can be a Zen experience. Work can be more than earning a living, more than just a job.

When we realize we're participating in a productive process, and others rely on us, we understand that each of us has a contribution to make and we get involved. When we really get involved with what we do, it is a Zen experience.

We concentrate on the quality of our performance. We settle only for the performance that meets our highest ideals. Quality for the sake of quality. We literally lose ourselves in what we are doing.

We don't worry about comparing ourselves with others. After all, that's a losing experience. (There is always someone doing better. There is always someone doing worse. So if we spend our time comparing we either unduly flatter ourselves or unduly criticize others.) Thus, the Zen work experience is obtained when we perform all out to our own high ideals. We gain from the exhilaration of the feeling of a job well done. Done by us. For us. To our specifications. Our ideals.

When we at Park see ourselves as part of the solution, when we really put ourselves into what we are doing, when customers and co-workers feel and sense the magic of our enthusiasm, the quality of our performance, our job is a Zen experience.

An experience in which we find ourselves by losing ourselves. When we go a little further to be the best we can be, we are into Zen.

To quote Lee Iacocca ". . . Hard work. Commitment. They are the stuff we're made of. Without them there is no future."

The crisis leader's continual reinterpretation and communication of the latent *why* within today's meager triumphs are his highest responsibility and most difficult task.

Linkage Learning

In their work, *Leaders*, Bennis and Nanus conclude that leaders, above all, are perpetual learners. They write: "Learning is the essential fuel for the leader, the source of high-octane energy that keeps up the momentum by continually sparking new understanding, new ideas, new challenges."

The ability of the leader to instill the spark of learning among followers converts their present experiences into future possibilities; possibilities which will serve them beyond the present chaos, regardless of its ultimate outcome.

Bennis and Nanus differentiate between two types of organizational learning, maintenance learning and innovative learning. Maintenance learning deals with the acquisition of information about existing systems, rules, and procedures. It is useful during periods of stability, but hardly suitable by itself on the rim. Innovative learning is related to renewal, restructuring, and reformulation of problems; it provides new insight, the potential for catalytic reactions.

Thus, innovative learning involves reinterpretation, experimentation, reeducation, as well as observation and analysis. Innovative learning can also involve unlearning, sometimes a frightening and unsettling experience, for it calls into play a reappraisal of basic assumptions.

The crisis leader demonstrates the significance of learning by its influence on his life — by his curiosity, his interactive-openness, his willingness to innovate, his willingness to listen and share ideas. Most important, he demonstrates the importance of learning through his role as mentor and teacher, in his recognition of talent and his love to develop others.

Those who have worked with a mentor can say, "I have gained from this relationship. It has stretched me, I have grown. I have experienced an ideal. The experience has been painful, but I am better because of it. I have learned and now I will teach others."

As Levinson and Rosenthal said in *CEO*, "Though leaders may demand more of their subordinates than other bosses do, their followers willingly give their best because they know they are doing more, learning more, and growing more than they thought possible."

The person who can express those feelings has achieved the ultimate *linkage experience*. It is he who understands that, beyond the ordeal itself, the rim's experiences provide a level of wisdom essential to understanding and coping with life.

Inside the Park

I will not forget the note I received from our vice president of Park Bank's International Division during the last days of Park's life.

"Thanks so much for your support and compassion for me as an individual above and beyond my role as manager of the International Division. I look forward to facing the challenges ahead with your guidance and I only hope I can share the same degree of support and compassion with my staff that you have shared with me."

Beyond Charisma?

In this and the preceding two chapters we have described crisis leadership as a connection between leader and followers, arising out of mutual need during the rim's encounters, bonded through their linkage experiences. The charismatic crisis leader, empowered to lead his followers by their confidence, trust and dedicated support, in turn guides his followers, empowering and strengthening them as they move through the rim's volcanic landscape.

Within much of today's management literature, however, charisma is equated with shallow personality and showmanship.

Selwyn Feinstein, author of a *Wall Street Journal* article entitled "Charisma is Costly in the Executive Suite," stated that psychological research indicates that many business managers got their positions based "more on charm than on skill or inclination to work productively." Not being able to meet expectations in productivity, the "peter principle" sets in, and those managers eventually fail.

Feinstein concluded that charming managers "self-destruct" and are sandbagged by employees. He equates charm with charisma, as if charisma were a matter of a shallow, pleasing personality, not substance.

In that same vein, in an article entitled, "Beyond Charisma," appearing in the January 1989 issue of *The President*, American Management Association president Thomas R. Horton wrote: "Charisma isn't the key to leadership; there are, however, other 'C' words essential to leadership."

Horton described his "C's" as:

- Character — "Integrity is the bedrock on which effective leadership is built."

- Courage — "It is the leader who. . . drive(s) a stake in the ground and take(s) the responsibility and the risk (and that's the issue) of really having it not work."

- Capabilities — "The leader sees to it that the organization develops or acquire(s). . . capabilities and resources."

- Consistency — "There must be consistency of purpose and values. Otherwise, a leader will lose. . . followers."

- Communication — "To avoid surprises, the leader must share information widely and quickly. . . and must seek information from people at all levels of the organization."

- Collaboration — "The sharing of information is only a start in collaboration. More important is sharing of power."

- Commitment — "Leadership is the will to overcome any challenge, a determination — in short, a commitment."

- Credibility — "Good leaders are believed in."

After dismissing charisma as an attribute of leadership, Horton concluded, however, that leadership is related to its affect on followers: "If you want to know whether you are a leader, look over your shoulder to see whether anyone is following you."

Separating substance from semantics, Horton's "C's," which go "beyond charisma," are essentially the same characteristics leaders possess who have made their charisma connection.

Charismatic leadership is not merely a matter of pleasing others or having personality or charm. Rather, charismatic leadership is the result of an intense, personal, demanding, high-energy relationship between leader and followers that is especially developed in troubled times.

The charismatic relationship can create superhuman, often impossible, expectations in both leader and followers. And it should. Crisis is a time for adrenaline to flow, for survival instincts to dominate, for hope to well up. The function of leadership in those times is to shape hope and meaning, intensify efforts, and improve expectations.

Charismatic relationships are rarely permanent. They typically rise and fall with the winds that fan a crisis. Charismatic relationships are not likely to survive failure if the crisis ends in failure; nor will they endure with the same intensity during periods of success and tranquility if there is crisis recovery.

But the *charisma connection* and its *linkage experiences* produce deep, very powerful forces forever affecting the lives of those involved. And *momentum effect*, the unrelenting tightening, destructive pull of the Black Hole — so difficult to overcome even with charismatic leadership, can never be overcome without it.

Chapter 18

After Zen the Laundry

*If you bring forth what is inside you, what you bring
forth will save you.*

Gospel of Saint Thomas

A hundred or so years ago, Ralph Waldo Emerson bragged to Henry
Thoreau, "At Harvard they teach all branches of learning. . . ."

Thoreau responded, "Yes, but they don't teach the roots."

Throughout this book, I have attempted to explore business crisis at
its roots, because I am convinced it is here that business in crisis is
salvaged or is lost.

In this last chapter, I focus on the major roots I believe must not be
overlooked by an effective CEO during his crisis leadership. What is the
ultimate crisis-objective? Save the company? Of course. But that is not
always possible. He may not be able to prevent the destruction of material
values. So he must set an additional, perhaps higher, objective. He must
seek to prevent destruction of the spiritual values of those involved: crisis
may destroy what man has created, but it must not destroy who those men
are.

Taking Charge

The Effective CEO Leads Through the Crisis Without Reservation

Remember that management and leadership are not the same. Management is predominantly a left brain, non-emotional activity, involving analysis, planning, prioritizing, evaluating, and directing. As important as those functions are, if they are performed without leadership, there is unlikely to be any escape from the Black Hole.

Leadership involves the emotions. Leadership raises people who have retreated into security-seeking forms of behavior toward self-actualization efforts in the face of tremendous, frightening odds. There should be no doubt among those trapped on the rim that their leader leads and leads affirmatively. Without demonstration of his faith and his strength, the *charisma connection* we have advocated as essential for rim survival will not materialize.

The effective crisis leader enters the battle totally, without reservation. He wastes no time in recrimination; he accepts the challenge and, above all, is willing to risk himself — and to fail.

He maintains his composure, optimism, and sense of humor. And he encourages risk-taking and achievement in others. He does this by defining problems as opportunities, by praising the efforts of those trapped on the rim with him, by allowing mistakes as fair exchange for the all-out effort required in the unpredictable environment. He delegates so that others are involved and are able to contribute, allowing no idle standers-by. He knows he cannot go it alone.

Expressing Concern

The effective crisis leader takes charge by the way he expresses concern. The leader's concern is reflected in everything he does, including how he discharges people. There is no more difficult rim activity than letting people go. He is careful not to use discharged people as scapegoats or as vindictive targets. He is careful to insist on a human resources program designed so that people who leave have an opportunity to proceed with their lives with as little residual damage as is possible. To minimize impact within the community, his discharge plan will involve termination pay, job opportunity, and family counseling. He knows that the way employee discharges are processed makes a statement to those who continue — who could be next.

Dealing With Communication Constituencies

The effective crisis leader takes charge by quickly identifying and communicating with his company's constituencies. He seeks to communicate with each of his company's constituencies regularly about the all-out effort under way, and he seeks support whenever possible.

Employees. He communicates frequently, timely, factually, and yet, optimistically with employees. He understands that the rim's environment is anything but clear and that he must interpret events, define meaning, offer hope and opportunity.

He knows that it is essential that he communicate that "the CEO's okay!" He knows that as long as he is perceived as okay, the rim-bound company's efforts will be perceived as okay. He communicates that he is okay by demeanor and presence, by walking around, by encouraging others, by writing messages, by formally and informally talking, by listening and seeking advice, by developing and encouraging charisma extenders, and by sharing himself in every way he can.

His communications explain what can be expected on the rim. Careful, anticipatory communications go a long way toward building morale. The effective CEO is the first to advise employees about the rim's events. Reading or hearing about the rim-bound company's troubles in the media without advance warning sets up shock waves that are debilitating and disastrous. So he communicates up front about planned SEC filings, press releases and conferences, major events, departure of key people, as well as his analysis of rumors.

The effective CEO also communicates immediately when stories or events catch him by surprise to let everyone know what is happening. His accurate communication about the situation he and his followers are in builds employee confidence and places them in a position to take responsible action. Employees need a sense of mastery in their lives, and communications can provide them with information to enhance those abilities. One result is that employees are able to handle troubled customers and suppliers more knowingly and deftly.

When the effective CEO has communication meetings with his people, he follows up with written summaries to minimize miscommunication and to apprise those employees who could not attend. The written word, supplementing the spoken word, minimizes stress and misunderstanding. A summary serves as a useful reference tool when employees explain the company's efforts to customers and suppliers, or when they discuss rim experiences with their families.

Media. The effective CEO understands that bad press accelerates crisis damage. He knows that, if the media first learns about rim troubles from others, the results can be disastrous. The story they hear is apt to lack balance and fail to present a fair story. If the CEO is not a participant in the initial distribution of crisis information, he will waste time and energy explaining misinformation and rebuilding faith among constituencies. Thus, the effective CEO communicates with the media openly, fast, and factually. Dishonest communications create crises of their own. The effective CEO is willing to risk "off-the-record" conversations with the media to provide background information. The risk that off-the-record communications will be misused is likely to be less than the risk of damage from otherwise misleading communications.

The effective leader is careful to time press releases so that various elements of the media do not gain an unfair advantage and so that he can prepare his employees for damaging news. He is also careful to provide the media with a road map, similar to that provided to employees, about where the rim-bound company is headed in its recovery efforts.

The effective leader does not hide from the press nor rely on "no comment." Bad information will not disappear because he chooses to avoid or ignore it. If there is information to be had, the media will obtain it, with or without him. It's better if he is part of the process.

The effective CEO can use public communications as his forum for constituency communication. Working with the press shows his openness and demonstrates that his company's actions during its crisis are responsible and trustworthy. The company's constituencies want to hear about the crisis *from him.* Others within the company can assist him in communication, particularly when he cannot be available, but he understands that crisis communication is one of his prime responsibilities.

Regulators. The effective crisis leader communicates with regulators with the same degree of frequency, openness, and frankness as he has employed with his followers. He is sensitive to the negative effects bad press can have on the regulatory process, so he makes sure regulators do not first learn of any rim dilemmas in the press. He seeks regulator advice when his courses of action are unclear and might run afoul of applicable law.

Customers and suppliers. The effective crisis leader understands that the impression customers and suppliers obtain about recovery efforts comes primarily from employees. He knows that, to the extent employees are informed about and trusting of their company's crisis efforts, they will communicate confidence to customers and suppliers. Occasionally, even the most motivated employees will not be able to calm irate customers and suppliers. He arranges an open line to himself and to his charisma extenders to provide reassuring backup and support. He knows that this kind of communication is time-consuming, and viewed by some as a misuse of his time; but any business exists only because of customer and supplier support, so this kind of communication has a high priority.

Creditors. The effective leader knows that the Black Hole experience can precipitate its own liquidity crisis. Without liquidity, rim survival is impossible. So he insists that liquidity be planned and monitored and that communication with creditors and other liquidity sources be maintained on the same open and frank basis as are communications with other constituencies. He involves his liquidity sources in his recovery plan. He needs their cooperation and participation and he openly solicits it, giving them the best available information about his company's chances. He is sure to communicate his company's plan, even if vague and, more important, his and his company's all-out, fully committed, survival effort.

Insurers. The effective crisis leader is aware that insurers often cancel coverage when companies get into trouble. Risk monitoring and direct communications with insurers and risk-management consultants are thus essential. Particularly vulnerable during an extended crisis period are products liability and officer and director liability coverage. Those two forms of coverage bear the brunt of much of the crisis-induced litigation. Timing of events and selection of crisis solution alternatives are often influenced by availability of insurance coverage; thus, insurers remain one of the important communication constituencies.

Investors. The effective crisis leader is aware that communications with stockholders and other investors is also essential, and delicate. Individual investor communications from public companies can be sensitive; company communications with public or quasi-public security-holders are regulated by the Securities Exchange Commission and state regulatory agencies. Private communications with select investors will make the recipients insiders, unable to act on their information. Thus investor communications, essential during crisis, are colored by regulatory requirements that insist that all investors be given the same essential information at the same time without any advantage being granted to any particular investors. These requirements affect the timing of employee and other constituency announcements. The effective crisis leader is aware of the communication dilemma and handles telephone calls from investors and others in such a way that an additional crisis, the result of violation of securities' laws, will be avoided.

Families. The effective crisis leader is aware that crisis does not stop at the rim-bound company's door. Crisis follows each employee home. Thus, he includes families among his communication constituencies. He knows employees who are not supported at home will be unable to perform with the energy required on the rim.

Communication Methods

Each effective crisis leader takes charge through his own particular communications methods. Each leader will have his favorite form of communication; however, every available method should be considered. Information meetings, the grapevine and other forms of down-time conversations, notes to employees expressing appreciation, newsletters, shareholder information meetings, fireside chats with employees — all should be utilized, along with an open door, so that he remains approachable.

Visual tools, things people touch, take with them, reread, and share with others, are especially effective. News stories are often more effective than advertising. Advertising as a method of communication requires special consideration, depending upon the nature of the crisis. The rim-bound company's need for continuous visibility compared to the advantage of dignified silence also must be balanced.

The atmosphere of each communication meeting should be planned. Each meeting's setting should exemplify the walk the effective crisis leader is talking.

The effective crisis CEO also remembers the importance listening plays in communication. He listens carefully, not only to the spoken word but to the symbolic communication that accompanies it. By listening he will be able to interpret events from the points of view of his audiences, and he will be better able to deal with their concerns.

Manage the Crisis

The effective crisis leader must not overlook that, though management without leadership will not work, neither will leadership without management. Though the crisis leader will bear primary responsibility for his company's tone and pace, others will bear principal responsibility for implementation.

Identification of Key People

The effective crisis leader identifies the company's key people early on and devises methods to assure that they do not become rim casualties. The best people are attractive to competitors who will not be above using the rim-bound company's disaster to their advantage. Because key people have alternative career opportunities available, they could become the first to leave, particularly if family pressures become overwhelming. However, key people are proud, professional, and usually inner-directed; thus, if they can be a part of the solution, rarely will they want to become part of the problem. The effective CEO will involve them early, quickly, and completely. He lets them know that he and the rim-bound company need their input and will not survive without their contribution. He consults with them, and they with him, creating an experience from which everyone benefits.

Prioritizing

The effective crisis leader chooses priorities. All crisis issues are not of equal importance, and certain crisis tasks are better performed by others than himself. He understands the ultimate importance of action and the danger of overanalysis — *analysis paralysis* — and he watches for tell-tale signs in himself and in his employees so that inclinations toward inaction can be avoided. He is willing to rely on intuitive judgment, his and his staff's, after he has obtained the best data and counsel available. He knows that decisions must be made without clarity as to outcomes, and he is willing to risk action rather than to be overwhelmed by inaction.

Positive Objectives

The effective leader understands that, under the best of circumstances, the crisis atmosphere results in loss of personal esteem for himself and his employees. He recognizes that efforts to balance damaged egos often take the form of scapegoating or a bunker-mentality; so he directs energies and efforts toward objectives that bear positive potentialities.

Self-Management

The effective CEO remembers the danger of making critical decisions when fatigued or stressed-out. Actions taken when one is overwrought are excessively risky and often wrong. He thus manages his health and stress levels to maintain his effectiveness.

Setting Up to Be Lucky

Along with everything else, the effective crisis leader positions himself to be lucky. He knows that leading, planning, managing, keeping up morale, controlling stress, focusing, and concentrating may not be enough to break the Black Hole's momentum effect. He may need a "Hail Mary" pass during the final seconds of the game.

He knows that luck, however, is not raw chance; luck comes to the bold, and to the prepared. Louis Pasteur was right: "Chance favors the prepared mind." The effective crisis leader retains an intuitive openness to fleeting offerings — deviations to his plans not visible when his initial strategies were implemented. He is able to do so because he has prepared and can extract data from his mental computer banks, allowing him to interpret the new events with reasonable competence. The attitude he holds toward chance sets his willingness to risk himself when risk may be the only alternative. And it may determine the ultimate outcome of his rim journey.

On a PBS television series, in response to a question by Bill Moyers about the place chance plays in human life, mythologist Joseph Campbell responded, "The ultimate backing of life is chance — the chance that your parents met, for example! Chance, or what might seem to be chance, is the means through which life is realized. The problem is not to blame or explain, but to handle the life that arises. Another war has been declared somewhere, and you are drafted into an army, and there go five or six years of your life with a whole new set of chance events. The best advice is to take it all *as if* it had been your intention — with that, you evoke the participation of your will."

And so it is on the rim.

Planning for Chaotic Times

I have pointed out that management must develop its plans for chaotic times during calm times. What, however, is the key ingredient of a corporate plan for the rim's unpredictability?

Tylenol Crisis

Within American industry, Johnson & Johnson's 1982 handling of the Tylenol crisis has been considered the premier handling of an episodic crisis.

A death in the Chicago area caused by poison identified as coming from a Tylenol capsule, was followed by 80,000 news stories, a Congressional investigation, the withdrawal of Tylenol (a major J&J product) from the market, decimated consumer confidence and anguished, disbelieving employees. Johnson & Johnson's successful handling of the crisis has been attributed by Steven Fink, author of *Crisis Management*, to three key points:

- openness with the press and public;

- prompt withdrawal of Tylenol from the market place without regard to cost; and

- demonstration by conduct and communicative candor that J&J was trustworthy.

J&J had no formal crisis management plan at the time of the Tylenol incident, yet it handled the crisis in role-model fashion. J&J's culture provided the key ingredient — a powerful, ethical, fundamental *credo*. The credo, ingrained through 40 years of corporate history, provided that J&J's employees have responsibility to J&J constituencies in the following order: to the consumers, to the employees, to the communities they serve, and to the stockholders.

J&J's fundamental business philosophy prepared it for handling the crisis properly.

Nonlinear Dynamics

Historically, scientific experience with our universe has, for the most part, been described through precise, mathematical, linear equations. A beginning circumstance, quantified by calculable variables, ends up at a predictable conclusion. When an apple falls from a tree, science can calculate, by linear equations, when and where the apple will fall.

But as in-depth knowledge about nature grows, linear equations provide fewer accurate answers and more approximations. Nature, it seems, is not totally linear. Systems interact, amplify, and feed on each other. Weather, for example, is not predictable in linear fashion. Minute variations in any of the components of a weather system produce radically different, unpredictable results. Nature's systems, it turns out, are chaotic, not quantifiable by linear equations. Henry Adams was right: "Chaos is the law of nature; order is the dream of man."

As scientists study chaos, they find that the apparent disorder within nature appears to have, at its roots, a simplicity indicating that even the unpredictable is not irrational. What appears to be disorder is, fundamentally, a different kind of order, a chaotic order, a disorder within an orbit of possibilities, but always within the orbit. Gary Taubes wrote in *Discover* magazine:

> Weather has become the quintessential example of a chaotic system. It never repeats itself precisely, and in the not too distant future it always diverges from what meteorologists can forecast. . . . Nevertheless, one can safely say that the temperature in Kansas City this summer will not be 900 degrees, as it is on the surface of Venus; Earth's weather always stays on the strange attractor known as climate. Stretching the attractor metaphor a little, one might find another example in human behavior: it is rarely predictable from day to day or even from minute to minute, but it always hovers around the strange attractor we call character. It may seem random on occasion, but when you delve deep enough, it usually is not.

Physiologists and cardiologists are finding that chaos also plays a dynamic role within the human body. The heart does not beat with metronome consistency; rather, beat rates fluctuate, but within a predictable range. Previously thought to be random experiences, researchers now believe that the human nervous system deterministically produces chaotic heart beat fluctuations. Furthermore, healthy hearts produce greater variation than do diseased hearts. Taubes quotes Dr. Ary Goldberger, a Harvard cardiologist: "To be healthy, you need to be able to cope with an environment that's throwing you curveballs and sliders and knuckleballs. And if you're wrapped up in some periodic, monotonous dynamic, you're in no shape to contend with the environment. Chaos is the only mechanism I know for generating that necessary variability. . . ."

Linear and Nonlinear Business Dynamics

Is there a similarity between nature's chaotic systems and man's business systems?

Historically, the thrust of business strategy has been linear, a function of computers and MBA programs designed to develop measurable values of performances through internal rates of return, present values, and trend analysis. Planning, strategic planning, utilizes similar dynamics. Quantifying who we are, where we are, where and how we are going, is fundamental to corporate planning processes; they become performance benchmarks.

Yet, the business environment is, under the best of times, chaotic. Business forecasts, prepared with linear precision, have turned out to be, for the most part, megamistakes. Steven P. Schnaars, author of *Megamistakes: Forecasting and the Myth of Rapid Technological Change*, concluded that more than 80 percent are totally off base. Five-year strategic plans, developed over months, typically become obsolete before they are published. Inventions, technology, consumer preferences, population movements, changing financial markets, government policies rarely interact with straightforward precision.

Instead, today's effective business leaders are substituting umbrella plans, broad strategic overviews with few details, and an abundance of latitude so that today's built-in uncertainties can be met proactively, not reactively.

It is probably no accident that the best selling business book of 1988 was Tom Peters's *Thriving on Chaos*. Peters describes today's business environment as an upside down world filled with generic uncertainties, requiring unbelievably short responses given international competition, and faced with discriminating customers and changing technology.

Peters predicts, as did Peter Drucker before him, that the successful 1990s business will have fewer management layers (it will be flatter), will utilize more decentralization and delegation (it will have autonomous units), and will concentrate on product differentiation (it will serve market niches). Peters's version of a winning organization will be training-oriented, quality-conscious, service-conscious, and response-driven. The company can be described in an oxymoron — a *disorganized organization* — chaotic in terms of volatility, constant change, demands, flexibilities imposed upon it, but able to respond effectively in a dynamic way to the environmental demands of the 1990s.

The same thing is being said by Peters about American business and by Dr. Goldberger about the heart: success comes from adaption to chaos. The successful heart and the successful business operate within a range of unpredictability that strengthens and quickens their responses to precarious and unstable environments.

The healthy heart and successful business have each succeeded because they have mastered nonlinear dynamics. Both succeed during chaotic times because those times fit within the range of skills available and, thus, are no longer viewed as chaotic by the systems that must adapt.

Nonlinear dynamics should dominate corporate crisis planning. That means that a corporation organized to handle the rim country will, like J&J, have a philosophic credo established in its mission, belief statements, and cultural maps. The credo must be strong enough to hold everyone's heart when all else fails.

A crisis plan may specify external and internal communication procedures, identify helpful lawyers, and assign various aspects of corporate responsibility under a variety of "what ifs." But the mechanics of the plan will work no better than a fire drill procedure tacked nonchalantly on the wall of the employee's lounge, if the company's people are not steeped in fundamentals solid enough, and flexible enough, to carry them through the rim's chaotic, and nonlinear, experiences.

The World Is As We Are

One day, near the end of Park Bank's aftermath, I was enjoying coffee on the porch of our condominium on the island of Tierra Verde, Florida, engrossed in the morning paper. My wife, Joan, turned to me and said, "Look at the sun — how beautiful it is this morning!"

I looked up from my paper as the sun's rays seemingly meandered their way through a covey of early morning cumulus clouds that were rapidly losing their violent greys as their burdens of rain scattered over Tampa Bay.

"The sun is always the same," I threw out nonchalantly. "It is the earth's atmosphere that makes the sun beautiful! It's the interruptions — the way the earth and the weather interfere with the sun's rays — that create the beauty."

And then I reflected, "You know, human experiences are the same. There are no good times and bad times; it is we who paint our experiences that way."

I sat straight up in my chair. "The Oriental Proverb I have in my office is right; problems *are* disguised opportunities! When we open ourselves to the potentialities in each experience, life's journey unfolds and takes on meaning, even when we find ourselves in the rim country. It's our choice."

We are continually faced by great opportunities brilliantly disguised as insoluble problems.

Epilogue

To have worked is to have succeeded — we leave the results to time.

Elbert Hubbard

In June, 1988, I received a call from Charles Ruff, my attorney, informing me that the lawyers for the defendants and plaintiffs in the stockholder's lawsuit and the FDIC suit had agreed on a settlement of the pending litigation with Park Bank's directors and officers.

Preparation of documents and approval of the details by the FDIC and the other parties involved took over 13 months. Finally, in the late summer of 1989, the last threads were sewn into the settlement documents, and the officer and director litigation was settled.

By the time our settlement was reached, more than one-half of available directors' and officers' insurance proceeds had been utilized in defense costs. To facilitate the settlement, our insurance carrier (as anxious as we were to terminate litigation) agreed to contribute funds in excess of its policy limits. The six directors who were financially able, including myself, contributed supplemental funds. The over-all settlement amounts remain confidential, but the stockholders and their lawyers received less money than the directors' and officers' insurer had already spent on legal fees.

When asked by reporter Jeff Smith of the *Tampa Tribune* whether or not I thought the settlement vindicated me and the board, I replied that there is never vindication in litigation. I was then 58 years old. I was 54 when the bank failed. I was not anxious to continue litigation until I was 65 to prove a point — if there was a point to prove.

Former Directors Frank Byars, Bill Zemp, Vern and Phil Vineyard have retired, while Dr. Peter Dawson continues to enhance his international reputation through his dental seminars and the latest revision of his text on reconstructive dentistry. I understand he now includes some recently learned (Park Bank experience-based) philosophy in his lectures. Former director Gary Froid has his life insurance business booming on a national scale again. And Lloyd Williams is back in the real estate development business in other Florida markets.

Harold Kelley, Park Bank's first CEO and chairman, is selling insurance and investments. Park's former senior lender, Jim Matthews, is winding through his probation. John Kearney, continues to consult in the real estate field.

My old law firm reorganized and is now substantially smaller in size. I have returned to the practice of law in St. Petersburg — wiser, more realistic in my evaluations, more empathetic, hopefully more perceptive and forceful in my advice. I have plenty of personal examples to sprinkle throughout the course of my recommendations. I have also been writing and speaking on crisis management and leadership issues, and another book is in the works.

Chase Bank, after preserving all of Park Bank's depositors intact, moved its Florida headquarters to Tampa. Several of Park's people continue with Chase. In November 1990, Chase appointed a new president for its Florida operations and announced expansion plans, stating that Florida is expected to be a very attractive state for Chase's operations.

The federal government adopted the Financial Institutions Reform, Recovery and Enforcement Act of 1989 (known as "FIRREA"). FIRREA expands the RICO Act to a wide variety of director and officer situations when financial institutions fail. Also, financial institutions recovery efforts centralized in the newly-created Resolution Trust Corporation; and the

FDIC became the sole provider of deposit insurance, for thrifts as well as banks.

FIRREA preempts a variety of state laws that had been implemented in the 1980s. The state laws had been adopted to limit boardroom liability in connection with directors' management responsibilities. The idea was to make corporate directorships more attractive. To the contrary, FIRREA increases officer and director liability when financial institutions are involved. In addition to directors and officers, FIRREA also creates new responsibilities and liabilities for consultants, lawyers, and accountants advising financial institutions. The Act also offers whistle blowers rewards for providing information leading to a financial institution's recovery.

Frustrated by mega-lawsuits, open-ended risks, and responsibilities of board of director memberships, Harvard Professor William A. Sahlman wrote a provocative article in the May-June 1990 *Harvard Business Review* entitled "Why Sane People Shouldn't Serve on Public Boards." A few months later, the *Wall Street Journal* reported that major law firms were backing away from representing banks and thrifts; their malpractice carriers, now wary of multimillion-dollar law suits being filed by regulators, had begun canceling their insurance coverage.

In late 1990, faced with increasing failures of financial institutions and a sagging economy, the federal government announced it was considering requiring solvent banks to buy stock in the FDIC to bolster capital for its depleted deposit insurance fund. In the meantime, as loan failures and writeoffs mounted, and as thrift and bank failures spread from the southeast and west to the rest of the country, banks in the northeast devised accounting techniques permitting them to report their troubled loans as if they were performing loans. Using the accounting techniques for its restructured workouts, a Bank of Boston executive was quoted by *Wall Street Journal* reporter Ron Suskind as saying (as any Master of the Universe would say) that his bank was at the "leading edge of bank accounting." A CPA bank specialist commented to the reporter that "you have banks with desperate people doing desperate things." A federal bank regulator said simply that a bank's use of the new "leading edge" accounting method had the effect of concealing problems in its loan portfolios.

So there are still lessons for the learning. Again.

And, again this morning, the sun's rays, today a harvest-orange, radiated through towering cumulus clouds, silhouetting the mangroves that grow behind our condominium on the edge of Tampa Bay.

December 15, 1990

References and Further Reading

Preface

Rosener, Judy B. "Ways Women Lead." *Harvard Business Review* (November-December 1990).

Introduction

Blundell, W. E. "Failure: Spotlight on a Neglected Side of Business." *Wall Street Journal* (December 15, 1986).
Dessauer, John P. "Debt Equals Disaster, or Does It?" *World Monitor* (December 1990).
Jensen, R. H. "Scenes From a Breakup." *National Law Journal* (February 8, 1986).
Prokesch, S. "Remaking the American CEO." *New York Times* (January 25, 1987).
Schlesinger, J. M. "Park Bank: From Triumph to Turmoil." *St. Petersburg Times* (January 19, 1986).
Simpson, J. C. "Business Schools — and Students — Want to Talk Only About Success." *Wall Street Journal* (December 15, 1986).
Smith, Roy C. *Money Wars: The Rise and the Fall of the Great Buyout Boom of the 1980s.* New York: Dutton, 1990.
Toffler, Alvin. *Powershift: Knowledge, Wealth and Violence at the Edge of the 21st Century.* New York: Bantam Books, 1990.

Chapter 3, Black Hole Blinders

Adams, James Ring. *The Big Fix.* New York: John Wiley & Sons, Inc., 1990.
Anders, George. "Junk King's Legacy." *Wall Street Journal* (November 20, 1990).

Associated Press. "Space station report adds to NASA woes." *St. Petersburg Times* (July 11, 1990).

Brown, Warren, and Frank Swoboda. "Iacocca feels heat from investors, UAW." *St. Petersburg Times* (October 29, 1990).

Cohen, Eliot A., and John Gooch. *Military Misfortunes: The Anatomy of Failure in War*. New York: The Free Press, a division of Macmillan, Inc., 1990.

College Notebook. "Ex-Notre Dame player alleges rampant steroid use." *St. Petersburg Times* (August 21, 1990).

Cooper, Richard C., and Ann E. Covey. "Whistle-Blower Protection Acts Broaden Rights of Employee." *National Law Journal* (July 3, 1989).

Diamond, Jared. "The Price of Human Folly." *Discover* (April 1989).

Drucker, Peter F. "The effective decision." *Harvard Business Review* [reprinted in special *Harvard Business Review* series: "Leadership, Part I."] (January-February 1967).

Drucker, Peter F. *People and Performance: The Best of Peter Drucker on Management*. New York: Harper & Row Publishers, Inc., 1977.

Drucker, Peter F. "The Coming of the New Organization." *Harvard Business Review* (January-February 1988).

Farnsworth, Clyde H. "Survey of Whistle Blowers Finds Retaliation But Few Regrets." *New York Times* (February 22, 1987).

Fink, Steven. *Crisis Management*. New York: AMACOM, a division of American Management Association, 1986.

Ford, Jeffrey D., and David A. Baucus. "Organizational Adaption to Performance Downturns: An Interpretation-Based Perspective." *The Academy of Management Review* Vol. 12 No. 2 (1987) pp. 366-380.

Galloway, Joseph L. "Fatal Victory." *U.S. News & World Report* (October 29, 1990).

Giap, General Vo Nguyen. "A talk with General Giap: 'There are limits on power'." *U.S. News & World Report* (October 29, 1990).

Harrison, Allen F., and Robert M. Bramson, Ph.D. *Styles of Thinking*. Garden City: Anchor Press/Doubleday, 1982.

Hector, Gary. *Breaking the Bank*. Boston: Little, Brown & Company, 1988.

Hornstein, Harvey A. *Managerial Courage*. New York: John Wiley & Sons, 1986.

Jakobson, Max. "EURO Future." *World Monitor* (December 1990).

Jordan, Nick. "When to Lie to Yourself." *Psychology Today* (June 1989).

Kantrow, Alan M. *The Constraints of Corporate Tradition*. New York: Harper & Row Publishers, 1987.

Keen, Sam. "The Stories We Live By." *Psychology Today* (December 1988).

Leatherwood, Marya L., and Edward J. Conlon. "Diffusibility of Blame: Effects on Persistence in a Project." *Academy of Management Journal* Vol. 30 No. 4 (1987) pp. 836-847.

Levinson, Harry. "Management by Whose Objectives?" *Harvard Business Review* [reprinted in special *Harvard Business Review* series: "Motivation: Part I."] (July-August 1970).

Liden, Robert C., and Terence R. Mitchell. "Ingratiatory Behaviors in Organizational Settings." *Academy of Management Review* Vol. 13 No. 4 (1988) pp. 572-587.

Los Angeles Times (special). "NASA blamed for Hubble flaw; report says errors were ignored." *St. Petersburg Times* (November 28, 1990).

Luthans, Fred. *Organizational Behavior*. New York: McGraw-Hill Book Company, 1985.

Mathews, Jessica Tuchman. "America still hasn't learned its energy lessons." *St. Petersburg Times* (September 1, 1990).

McCaskey, Michael B. "The Hidden Messages Managers Send." *Harvard Business Review* (November-December 1979).

Merriam, John E., and Joel Makower. *Trend Watching*. New York: A Tilden Press Book, AMACOM, a division of American Management Association, 1988.

Meyers, Gerald C. *When it Hits the Fan*. Boston: Houghton Mifflin Company, 1986.

Mitchell, Constance. "Mellon's Chairman Pearson Says Extent of Bad Loans Shocked Outside Directors." *Wall Street Journal* (April 21, 1987).

Mitroff, Ian I., Paul Shrivastava, and Firdaus Udwadia. "Effective Crisis Management." *The Academy of Management Executive* Vol. 1 No. 4 (1987) pp. 283-292.

People, "Rivers says she missed suicide warning signs." *St. Petersburg Times* (August 24, 1987).

Peters, Thomas J., and Robert H. Waterman Jr. *In Search of Excellence*. New York: Harper & Row Publishers, 1982.

Rowen, Hobart. "Trump's troubles are linked to bank irresponsibility." *St. Petersburg Times* (June 17, 1990).

Saffold, Guy S., III. "Culture Traits, Strength and Organizational Performance: Moving Beyond 'Strong' Culture." *Academy of Management Review* Vol. 13 No. 4 (1988) pp. 546-558.

Shear, Jeff. "Japan Upsets Computer Applecart." *Insight* (October 22, 1990).

Sinetar, Marsha. *Do What You Love, the Money Will Follow*. New York: Paulist Press, 1987.

Tichy, Noel M., and Mary Anne Devanna. *The Transformational Leader*. New York: John Wiley & Sons, 1986.

Toffler, Alvin. *Powershift: Knowledge, Wealth and Violence at the Edge of the 21st Century*. New York: Bantam Books, 1990.

Weiner, Edith, and Arnold Brown. "Human Factors: The Gap Between Humans and Machines." *The Futurist* (May-June 1989).

Wiener, Yoash. "Forms of Value Systems: A Focus on Organizational Effectiveness and Cultural Change and Maintenance." *Academy of Management Review* Vol. 13 No. 4 (1988) pp. 534-545.

Wilkins, Alan L. , and W. Gibb Dyer Jr. "Toward Culturally Sensitive Theories of Cultural Change." *Academy of Management Review* Vol. 13 No. 4 (1988) pp. 522-533.

Chapter 4, Masters of the Universe

Adler, William M., and Michael Binstein. "The Speaker and the Sleazy Banker." *Bankers Monthly* (March 1988).

Batten, Joe D. *Tough-Minded Leadership*. New York: AMACOM, a division of American Management Association, 1989.

Benderly, Beryl Lieff. "Everyday Intuition." *Psychology Today* (September 1989).

Bennis, Warren, and Burt Nanus. *Leaders*. New York: Harper & Row Publishers, 1985.

Blotnick, Srully. *Ambitious Men*. New York: Viking Penquin, Inc., 1987.

Chatsworth, W. Rushton, III. "Ego Maniacs." *M* (July 1987).

Cole, Diane. "The Entrepreneurial Self." *Psychology Today* (June 1989).

Conger, Jay A. *The Charismatic Leader*. San Francisco: Jossey-Bass Publishers, 1989.

Craddock, John. "How the Gatsby of St. Petersburg Got to the Top." *Florida Trend* (December 1984).

Drucker, Peter F. *People and Performance: the Best of Peter Drucker on Management*. New York: Harper & Row Publishers, Inc., 1977.

Drucker, Peter F. "The coming of the new organization." *Harvard Business Review* (January-February 1988).

Fitzgerald, F. Scott. *The Great Gatsby*. New York: Bantam Books, 1980.

Freudenberger, Dr. Herbert J. *Burnout*. New York: Bantam Books, 1980.

Garfield, Charles. *Peak Performers*. New York: William Morrow & Company, Inc., 1986.

Geneen, Harold. *Managing*. Garden City: Doubleday & Company, Inc., 1984.

Goleman, Daniel. "Dash of unreality may be good for us." *New York Times* (___, 1987).

Goodson, Peter D., and Donald J. Gogel. "Managing as if shareholders matter." *Harvard Business Review* (May-June 1987).

Gordon, Maynard M. *The Iacocca Management Technique*. New York: Ballantine Books, 1985.

Hanson, Peter G., M.D. *The Joy of Stress*. Kansas City: Andrews, McMeel & Parker, 1986.

Hilder, David B. "Lender's Lament, FCA's Rapid Growth Got Out of Hand and Regulators Failed." *Wall Street Journal* (June 23, 1987).

Horton, Thomas R. *What Works For Me*. New York: Business Division of Random House, 1986.

Hyatt, Carole, and Linda Gottlieb. *When Smart People Fail*. New York: Simon and Schuster, 1987.

Johnson, Bonnie. "The Avalanche Death of a Friend has Prince Charles Grieving — and England Pondering — his Love of Risk." *People* (March 28, 1988).

Kotter, John P. *The Leadership Factor*. New York: The Free Press, a division of Macmillan, Inc., 1988.

Lachia, Eduardo. "Foreign Applicants Got Almost 50% of Patents in 1987." *Wall Street Journal* (February 26, 1988).

Leatherwood, Marya L., and Edward J. Conlon. "Diffusibility of Blame: Effects on Persistence in a Project." *Academy of Management Journal* Vol. 30 No. 4 (1987) pp. 836-847.

Levinson, Harry, and Stuart Rosenthal. *CEO: Corporate Leadership in Action.* New York: Basic Books, Inc., 1984.

Levinson, Harry. "When Executives Burn Out." *Harvard Business Review* (March-April 1990).

Luthans, Fred. *Organizational Behavior.* New York: McGraw-Hill Book Company, 1985.

Maugham, W. Somerset. *The Razor's Edge.* New York: William Henemann Ltd, Great Britain, 1944. Penguin Books [by arrangement with Doubleday & Co., Inc., 1963], 1984.

McCall, Morgan W., Jr., Michael M. Lombardo, and Ann M. Morrison. *The Lessons of Experience.* Lexington: Lexington Books, 1988.

Miller, Michael M., and Patricia Bellew Gray. "Why Businesses Often Sink in Decisional Quicksand." *Wall Street Journal* (December 15, 1986).

Mitchell, Terence R., and William G. Scott. "America's Problems and Needed Reforms: Confronting the Ethic of Personal Advantage." *Academy of Management Executive* Vol. 4 No. 3 (1990) pp. 23-35.

Mitroff, Ian I., Paul Shrivastava, and Firdaus Udwadia. "Effective Crisis Management." *The Academy of Management Executive* Vol. 1 No. 4 (1987) pp. 283-292.

Mitroff, Ian I., and Susan A. Mohrman. "The Slack is Gone: How the United States Lost its Competitive Edge in the World Economy." *The Academy of Management Executive* Vol. 1 No. 1 (1987) pp. 65-70.

O'Neill, Joe. "Park's Leader Stands Tall Amid Trouble." *Tampa Bay Business Journal* (February 2-8, 1986).

Peters, Thomas J., and Robert H. Waterman Jr. *In Search of Excellence.* New York: Harper & Row Publishers, 1982.

Peters, Tom. "Prometheus barely unbound." *Academy of Management Executive* Vol. 4 No. 4 (1990) pp. 70-84.

Pomice, Eva. "Back Behind the Wheel." *U.S. News & World Report* (November 5, 1990).

Reich, Robert B. "Lean and Mean May Hurt." *St. Petersburg Times* (February 8, 1987).

Rowan, Roy. *The Intuitive Manager.* Boston: Little, Brown & Company, 1986.

Schaef, Anne Wilson. *When Society Becomes an Addict.* San Francisco: Harper & Row Publishers, 1987.

Schlesinger, Jacob M. "Park Bank sees light at end of problem-loan tunnel." *St. Petersburg Times* (May 15, 1985).

Sicilia, David B. "Was Tucker Really Torpedoed?" *Harvard Business Review* (November-December 1988).

Skrzycki, Cindy. "Risk Takers." *U.S. News & World Report* (January 26, 1987).

Smith, Adam. "Wall Street's Outrageous Fortunes." *Esquire* (April 1987).

Staw, Barry M., and Jerry Ross. "Good Money After Bad." *Psychology Today* (February 1988).

Stertz, Bradley. "Failure of a bank: the survivors still suffer." *St.Petersburg Times* (November 30, December 1, 1986).

Taylor, John. "Putting its house in order." *St. Petersburg Times* (April 22, 1985).

Touche Ross. "Ethics in American Business." (Special Study, Touche Ross, 1988).

Viscott, David, M.D. *Risking*. New York: Pocket Books, a division of Simon & Schuster, Inc , 1977.

Waterman, Robert H., Jr. *The Renewal Factor*. New York: Bantam Books, 1987.

Winter, Ralph E. "Myopic Managers?" *Wall Street Journal* (January 8, 1987).

Wolfe, Tom. *The Right Stuff*. New York: Farrar, Straus, Giroux, 1979.

Wolfe, Tom. *The Bonfire of the Vanities*. New York: Farrar, Straus, Giroux, 1987.

Chapter 5, Boardroom Blocks

Baum, Laurie, and John A. Byrne. "The Job Nobody Wants." *Business Week* (September 8, 1986).

Boulton, William R. "The Evolving Board: A Look at the Board's Changing Roles and Information Needs." *The Academy of Management Review* Vol. 3 No. 4 (1978) pp. 827-836.

Bratter, Herbert. *A Bank Director's Job*. New York: The Journal of the American Banker's Association, 1970.

Burns, James MacGregor. *Leadership*. New York: Harper Torchbooks, Harper & Row Publishers, 1978.

Cabbot, Louis W. "On an Effective Board." *Harvard Business Review* [reprinted in special *Harvard Business Review* series: "Boards of Directors: Part 1."] (September- October 1976).

Craddock, John. "How the Gatsby of St. Petersburg Got to the Top." *Florida Trend* (December 1984).

Crudele, John. "Board Games." *New York* (January 25, 1988).

Drucker, Peter, F. *People and Performance: the Best of Peter Drucker on Management*. New York: Harper & Row Publishers, Inc., 1977.

Ellue, Jacques. *The Technological Society*. New York City: Knopf, 1964.

Geneen, Harold. *Managing*. Garden City: Doubleday & Company, Inc., 1984.

Jacobs, Richard O. "Business Crisis 101: Why Boards Miss Looming Black Holes." *Director's Monthly of the National Association of Corporate Directors* (August 1990).

Janis, Irving L. *Victims of Groupthink*. Boston: Houghton Mifflin, 1972.

Lorsch, Jay with Elizabeth MacIver. Pawns or Potentates: *The Reality of America's Corporate Boards*. Boston: Harvard Business School Press, 1989.

Luthans, Fred. *Organizational Behavior*. New York: McGraw-Hill Book Company, 1985.

Mace, Myles L. "The President and the Board of Directors." *Harvard Business Review* [reprinted in special *Harvard Business Review* series: "Boards of Directors: Part 1."] (March-April 1972).

Mueller, Robert Kirk. "The Hidden Agenda." *Harvard Business Review* [reprinted in special *Harvard Business Review* series: "Boards of Directors: Part II."] (September-October 1977).

Peck, M. Scott, M.D. *A Different Drum*. New York: Simon & Schuster, 1987.

Ross, Joel E., and Michael J. Kami. *The Crisis in Management: Why the Mighty Fail*. Engelwood Cliffs: Prentice Hall, 1973.

Sahlman, William A. "Why Sane People Shouldn't Serve on Public Boards." *Harvard Business Review* (May-June 1990).

Schnaars, Steven P. *Megamistakes: Forecasting and the Myth of Rapid Technological Change*. New York: The Free Press, a division of Macmillan, Inc., 1989.

Stertz, Bradley. "Failure of a bank: the survivors still suffer." *St. Petersburg Times* (November 30, December 1, 1986).

Straw, Barry M., and Jerry Ross. "Understanding Behavior in Escalation Situations." *Science* (October 13, 1989).

Whyte, Glen. "Groupthink Reconsidered." *The Academy of Management Review* Vol. 14 No. 1 (1989) pp. 40-56.

Wiener, Yoash. "Forms of Value Systems: A Focus on Organizational Effectiveness and Culture Change and Maintenance." *The Academy of Management Review* Vol. 13 No. 4 (1988) pp. 534-545.

Chapter 6, The Rim People

Editor. "Unjust Prosecution." *St. Petersburg Times* (May 27, 1987).

Editor. "Prosecutorial Indiscretion — II." *Wall Street Journal* (May 27, 1987).

Editor. "Consumer Fraud." *Wall Street Journal* (November 9, 1990).

Feldman, Paul. "Twilight Zone: The Acquittal." *National Law Journal* (June 15, 1987).

Gurung, K. K. *Heart of the Jungle*. London: André Deutsch Limited, 1983.

Hammer, Armand. *Hammer*. New York: G. P. Putnam's Sons, 1987.

Iacocca, Lee, with William Novak. *Iacocca*. New York: Bantam Books, 1984.

LaBier, Douglas. *Modern Madness*. Reading: Addison-Wesley Publishing Company, Inc., 1986.

Low, Charlotte. "In pursuit of Crime, They Find New Glory." *Insight* (July 6, 1987).

Luthans, Fred. *Organizational Behavior*. New York: Mc Graw-Hill Book Company, 1985.

Maslow, Abraham H. "A Theory of Human Motivation." *Psychological Review* (July 1943).

Meyers, Gerald C. *When it Hits the Fan*. Boston: Houghton Mifflin Company, 1986.

Pear, Robert. "Panel would include suspects in computer file." *St. Petersburg Times* (June 11, 1987).

Peck, M. Scott, M.D. *The People of the Lie*. New York: A Touchstone Book, Simon and Schuster, Inc., 1983.

Schlesinger, Jacob M. "Switching From Park to Chase." *St. Petersburg Times* (February 17, 1986).

Siegel, Barry. "System on Trial: wrong man on death row." *St. Petersburg Times* (August 1, 1987).

Thomas, Paulette, and Thomas E. Ricks. "Just What Happened to All That Money Savings & Loans Lost?" *Wall Street Journal* (November 5, 1990).

Time-Life. *Volcano*. In The Planet Earth Series edited by Time-Life. Chicago: Time-Life Books, 1982.

Yang, John E. "California S&Ls Fail by Fraud, U.S. Study Says." *Wall Street Journal* (June 18, 1987).

Werner, Leslie Maitland. "Justice Department Says Prosecutor Law Should Be Vetoed." *New York Times* (June 17, 1987).

Chapter 7, Volcanoes of Litigation

Abramson, Jill. "High-Powered Bid to Gut RICO Law Is Derailed By Unrelated Scandals, Backers' Seeming Greed." *Wall Street Journal* (November 9, 1989).

American Bar Association Journal. "Quotes" (August 1, 1987).

Berton, Lee. "Accountants Battle a Move to Widen Rico's Coverage." *Wall Street Journal* (April 29, 1988).

Committee On Government Operations. "Combating Fraud, Abuse and Misconduct in the Nation's Financial Institutions: Current Federal Efforts are Inadequate." 100th Congress. (October 13, 1988).

Cox, Gail Diane. "Study Finds Plaintiffs More Successful in California, Illinois." *National Law Journal* (March 9, 1987).

Drucker, Peter F. "Management: The Problems of Success." Speech given at the Academy of Management, Chicago. August 14, 1986.

Eisler, Kim Isaac. *Shark Tank*. New York: St. Martin's Press, 1990.

Fink, Steven. *Crisis Management*. New York: AMACOM, a division of American Management Association, 1986.

Geyelin, Milo. "Fired Managers Winning More Lawsuits." *Wall Street Journal* (September 7, 1989).

Gordon, Maynard M. *The Iacocca Management Technique.* New York: Ballantine Books, 1985.

Kalette, Denise. "Lawyers reap windfall profits as S&L legal woes mount." *USA Today* (March 14, 1989).

Mayfield, James R. "Legal Malpractice: a trend for the future." *Paraclete (St. Petersburg Bar Association)* Vol. 12 No. 7 (1988)

McCarthy, Michael J. "Stressed Employees Look For Relief in Worker's Compensation." *Wall Street Journal* (April 7, 1988).

Naylor, Bartlett. "Banks May Face a Rash of Triple Damage Suits." *American Banker* (July 2, 1985).

Sahlman, William A. "Why Sane People Shouldn't Serve on Public Boards." *Harvard Business Review* (May-June 1990).

Sanders, Alain L. "Showdown at Gucci Gulch." *Time* (August 21, 1989).

Sansing, John. "First, Kill All the Lawyers." *The Washingtonian* (November 1990).

Schaef, Anne Wilson. *When Society Becomes an Addict.* San Francisco: Harper & Row Publishers, 1987.

Stertz, Bradley. "Failure of a bank: the survivors still suffer." *St. Petersburg Times* (November 30, 1986).

Stertz, Bradley. "Citrus County Developer Sues Park Bank Officials in Fraud Case." *St.Petersburg Times* (January 9, 1987).

Strasser, Fred. "Prosecutors, Private Bar Finds New Uses for RICO." *National Law Journal* (September 28, 1987).

Stricharchuk, Gregory. "Fired Employees Turn the Reason for Dismissal Into a Legal Weapon." *Wall Street Journal* (October 2, 1986).

Verespej, Lawrence R. "Was Rehnquist Right For a Change?" *National Law Journal* (March 30, 1987).

Verespej, Michael J. "Boardroom Roulette." *Industry Week* (August 10, 1987).

Waldman, Peter, and Brenton Schlender. "Falling Chips." *Wall Street Journal* (February 17, 1987).

Chapter 8, Black Ashes of Publicity

Barnes, Andrew. "President's failure was in not knowing what was going on." *St. Petersburg Times* (__, 1987).

Committee On Government Operations. "Combating Fraud, Abuse and Misconduct in the Nation's Financial Institutions: Current Federal Efforts are Inadequate." 100th Congress. (October 13, 1988).

Goldstein, Alan, and Bruce Vielmetti. "Convictions aren't the end of Park Bank investigation." *St. Petersburg Times* (May 5, 1989).

LaBier, Douglas. *Modern Madness.* Reading: Addison-Wesley Publishing Company, Inc., 1986.

Miller, Michael W., and Laurie P. Cohen. "'I Am Not a Crook' Image Problem Dogs Investment Bankers." *Wall Street Journal* (March 9, 1987).

O'Neill, Joe. "Park's Leader Stands Tall Amid Trouble." *Tampa Bay Business Journal* (February 2-8, 1986).

Pogrebin, Letty Cottin. *Among Friends*. New York: McGraw-Hill Book Company, 1987.

Schlesinger, Jacob M. "Park Bank: a dream derailed." *St. Petersburg Times* (January 19, 1986).

Chapter 9, The Crew's Experience

Ashforth, Blake E., and Fred Mael. "Social Identity Theory and the Organization." *Academy of Management Review* Vol. 14 No. 1 (1989) pp. 20-39.

Bass, Bernard, M. *Leadership and Performance Beyond Expectations*. The Free Press, a division of Macmillan, Inc., New York, 1985.

Bolton, Phillip P. "Park's Rapid Growth Leads to Failure." *Southern Banker* (April 1986).

Buono, Anthony F., and James L. Bowditch. *The Human Side of Mergers and Acquisitions*. San Francisco: Jossey-Bass Publishers, 1989.

Cameron, Kim. S., David A. Whetten, and Myung U. Kim. "Organizational Dysfunctions of Decline." *Academy of Management Journal* Vol. 30 No. 1 (1987) pp. 126-138.

D'Aveni, Richard A. "The Aftermath of Organizational Decline: A Longitudinal Study of the Strategic And Managerial Characteristics of Declining Firms." *Academy of Management Journal* Vol. 32 No. 3 (1989) pp. 577-605.

Eisler, Kim Isaac. *Shark Tank*. New York: St. Martin's Press, 1990.

Feinstein, Selwyn. "Labor Letter." *Wall Street Journal* (May 30, 1989).

Geneen, Harold. *Managing*. Garden City: Doubleday & Company, Inc., 1984.

Harmon, Frederick G., and Garry Jacobs. *The Vital Difference*. New York: AMACOM, a division of The American Management Association, 1985.

Luthans, Fred. *Organizational Behavior*. New York: McGraw-Hill Book Company, 1985.

Meindl, James R., and Sanford B. Ehrlich. "The Romance of Leadership and the Evaluation of Organizational Performance." *Academy of Management Journal* (March 1987).

Meyers, M. Scott. "Who Are Your Motivated Workers?" *Harvard Business Review* [reprinted in special *Harvard Business Review* series: " Motivation: Part I."] (January-February 1964).

Miller, Lynn E., and Joseph E. Grush. "Improving Predictions in Expectancy Theory Research: Effects of Personality, Expectancies and Norms." *Academy of Management Journal* Vol. 31 No. 1 (1988) pp. 107-122.

Nelson, Reed E. "The Strength of Strong Ties: Social Networks and Intergroup Conflict in Organizations." *Academy of Management Journal* Vol. 32 No. 2 (1989) pp. 377-401.

Peck, M. Scott, M.D. *The Different Drum.* New York: Simon & Schuster, 1987.

Peters, Tom. *Thriving on Chaos.* New York: Alfred A. Knopf, 1987.

Peters, Thomas J., and Robert H. Waterman Jr. *In Search of Excellence.* New York: Harper & Row Publishers, 1982.

Prichett, Price. *After the Merger: Managing the Shock Waves.* Homewood: Dow Jones Irwin, 1985.

Randall, Donna M. "Commitment and the Organization: The Organization Man Revisited." *Academy of Management Review* Vol. 12 No. 3 (1987) pp. 460-471.

Reich, Robert B. "Entrepreneurship reconsidered: the team as hero." *Harvard Business Review* (May-June 1987).

Riesman, David. *The Lonely Crowd.* New Haven: Yale University Press, 1961.

Romzek, Barbara S. "Personal Consequences of Employee Commitment." *Academy of Management Journal* Vol. 32 No. 3 (1989) pp. 649-661.

Sprankle, Judith K., and Henry Ebel, Ph.D. *The Workaholic Syndrome.* New York: Walker and Company, 1987.

Srivastva, Suresh, and Associates. *Executive Power.* San Francisco: Jossey-Bass Publishers, 1986.

Sutton, Robert I., and Anita L. Callahan. "The Stigma of Bankruptcy: Spoiled Organizational Image and Its Management." *Academy of Management Journal* Vol. 30 No. 3 (1987) pp. 405-436.

Wartzman, Rick. "Nature or Nurture? Study Blames Ethical Lapses on Corporate Goals." *Wall Street Journal* (October 9, 1987).

Whitney, John O. *Taking Charge.* Homewood: Dow Jones-Irwin, Inc., 1987.

Wilkins, Alan L., and Nigel J. Bristow. "For Successful Organizational Culture, Honor Your Past." *Academy of Management Executive* Vol. 1 No. 3 (1987) pp. 221-229.

Woodward, Harry, and Steve Buchholz. *Aftershock.* New York: John Wiley & Sons, Inc., 1987.

Chapter 10, The Costumes of Man

Bass, Bernard M. *Leadership and Performance Beyond Expectations.* New York: The Free Press, a division of Macmillan, Inc., 1985.

Bennis, Warren. *On Becoming a Leader.* Reading: Addison-Wesley Publishing Company Inc., 1989.

Flach, Frederic, M.D. *Resilience.* New York: Fawcett Columbine, 1988.

Forward, Dr. Susan, and Joan Torres. *Men Who Hate Women & The Women Who Love Them.* New York: Bantam Books, 1986.

Gardner, William L., and Mark J. Martinko. "Impression Management: An Observational Study Linking Audience Characteristics with Verbal Self-Presentations." *Academy of Management Journal* Vol. 31 No. 1 (1988) pp. 42-65.

Hyatt, Carole, and Linda Gottlieb. *When Smart People Fail.* New York: Simon and Schuster, 1987.

LaBier, Douglas. *Modern Madness.* Reading: Addison-Wesley Publishing Company, Inc., 1986.

Lee, Cynthia, Susan J. Ashford, and Philip Bobko. "Interactive Effects of 'Type A' Behavior and Perceived Control on Worker Performance, Job Satisfaction, and Somatic Complaints." *Academy of Management Journal* Vol. 33 No. 4 (1990) pp. 870-881.

Naifeh, Steven, and Gregory White Smith. *Why Can't Men Open Up?* New York: Warner Books Edition, Crown Publishers, Inc., 1984.

Nelson, Debra L., and Charlotte Sutton. "Chronic Work Stress and Coping: A Longitudinal Study and Suggested New Directions." *Academy of Management Journal* Vol. 33 No. 4 (1990) pp. 859-869.

Peck, M. Scott, M.D. *The Different Drum.* New York: Simon & Schuster, 1987.

Pogrebin, Letty Cottin. *Among Friends.* New York: McGraw-Hill Book Company, 1987.

Quick, James Campbell, Debra L. Nelson, and Jonathan D. Quick. "Successful Executives: How Independent?" *The Academy of Management Executive* Vol. 1 No. 2 (1987) pp. 139-145.

Schechter, David. "Complex Characters Handle Stress Better." *Psychology Today* (October 1987).

Schellhardt, Timothy D. "What Bosses Think of Ethics." *Wall Street Journal* (April 6, 1988).

Shepard, Sam. *A Lie of the Mind.* Reprint. New York: New American Library, 1986.

Sinetar, Marsha. *Do What You Like, The Money Will Follow.* New York: Paulist Press, 1987.

Viscott, David, M.D. *Risking.* New York: Pocket Books, a division of Simon & Schuster, Inc., 1977.

Wolfe, Tom. *The Bonfire of the Vanities.* New York: Farrar, Straus, Giroux, 1987.

Chapter 11, Strong at the Broken Places

Bass, Bernard M. *Leadership and Performance Beyond Expectations.* New York: The Free Press, a division of Macmillan, Inc., 1985.

Baum, Andrew. "Disasters, Natural and Otherwise." *Psychology Today* (April 1988).

Benson, Herbert, M.D. "Your innate asset for combatting stress." *Harvard Business Review* (July-August 1974).

Birren, James E. "The Best of All Stories." *Psychology Today* (May 1987).

Bricklin, Mark. "Walking: Sport of Geniuses." *Prevention* (August 1986).

Brouwer, Paul J. "The Power to See Ourselves." *Harvard Business Review* [reprinted in special *Harvard Business Review* series: "Leadership: Part 1."] (November-December 1964).

Burns, James MacGregor. *Leadership*. New York: Harper Torchbooks, Harper & Row Publishers, 1978.

Charles, Sara C., M.D., and Eugene Kennedy. *Defendant*. New York: Vintage Books, a division of Random House, 1986.

Drucker, Peter F. *The Frontiers of Management*. New York: Truman Talley Books, E. P. Dutton, 1986.

Frank, Frederick. *Zen and Zen Classics*. New York: Vintage Books, a division of Random House, 1987.

Freudenberger, Herbert J., Ph.D., with Geraldine Richelson. *Burn-out*. New York: Bantam Books, 1980.

Hanson, Peter G., M.D. *The Joy of Stress*. Kansas City: Andrews, McMeel & Parker, 1985.

Harrison, Allen F., and Robert M. Bramson, Ph.D. *Styles of Thinking*. Garden City: Anchor Press/Doubleday, 1982.

Holmes, T. H. , and R. H. Rahe. "Social Readjustment Rating Scale." *Journal of Psychosomatic Research* Vol. 11 No. — (1967) pp. 213-218.

Kantrow, Alan M. *The Constraints of Corporate Tradition*. New York: Harper & Row Publishers, 1987.

Luthans, Fred. *Organizational Behavior*. New York: McGraw-Hill Book Company, 1985.

Meyers, Gerald C. *When it Hits the Fan*. Boston: Houghton Mifflin Company, 1986.

Nutting, Anthony. *Lawrence of Arabia*. New York: Signet Books, 1961.

Ogilvy, David M. *The Creative Organization*. Chicago: The University of Chicago Press, 1965.

Palmer Testing Service. *ESSII System's Stressmap Report*. Andover: Palmer Testing Service, 1987.

Quick, James Campbell, Debra L. Nelson, and Jonathan D. Quick. "Successful Executives: How Independent?" *Academy of Management Executive* Vol. 1 No. 2 (1987) pp. 139-145.

Reibtein, Larry. "What is the Worst Age to be Fired?" *Wall Street Journal* (March 4, 1988).

Rippe, James M. "CEO Fitness: The Performance Plus." *Psychology Today* (May 1989).

Saddler, Jeanne. "Entrepreneur's Support Group Eases Stress." *Wall Street Journal* (April 27, 1989).

Safran, Claire. "You Are What You Think." *Reader's Digest* (August 1987).

Sintar, Marsha. *Do What You Like, the Money Will Follow*. New York: Paulist Press, 1987.

Smith, Jeff. "Park's final days marked by battles." *Tampa Tribune* (April 30, 1987).

Suzuki, Shunryu. *The Zen Mind, Beginner's Mind*. New York: Weatherhill, 1985.

Viscott, David, M.D. *Risking*. New York: Pocket Books, a division of Simon & Schuster, Inc., 1977.

Zaleznik, Abraham. "The Leadership Gap." *Academy of Management Executive* Vol. 4 No. 1 (1990) pp. 7-22.

Chapter 12, Bracing Against the Sirens

Anders, George, and Constance Mitchell. "Junk King's Legacy." *Wall Street Journal* (November 20, 1990).

Andrews, Kenneth R. "Ethics in Practice." *Harvard Business Review* (September-October 1989).

Bass, Bernard, M. *Leadership and Performance Beyond Expectations*. New York: The Free Press, a division of Macmillan, Inc., 1985.

Bhide, Amar, and Howard H. Stevensen. "Why Be Honest if Honesty Doesn't Pay." *Harvard Business Review* (September-October 1990).

Blanchard, Kenneth, and Norman Vincent Peale. *The Power of Ethical Management*. New York: William Morrow and Company, Inc., 1988.

Blotnick, Srully. *Ambitious Men*. New York: Viking, 1987.

Bok, Sissela. *Lying: Moral Choice in Public and Private Life*. New York: Vintage Books, a division of Random House, 1979.

Burns, James MacGregor. *Leadership*. New York: Harper Torchbooks, Harper & Row Publishers, 1978.

Clancey, Paul. "1 Month to 2 Years left: 'It ain't bad.'" *USA Today* (March 25-27, 1988).

Drucker, Peter F. "The Effective Decision." *Harvard Business Review* [reprinted in special *Harvard Business Review* series: "Leadership: Part I."] (January - February 1967).

Drucker, Peter F. *People and Performance: The Best of Peter Drucker on Management*. New York: Harper & Row, Publishers, Inc., 1974.

Frankl, Victor E. *Man's Search For Meaning*. New York: Washington Square Press, 1963.

Homer. *The Odyssey*. Chicago: Britannica Great Books Edition, Encyclopaedia Britannica, Inc., 1952.

Horton, Thomas R. *What Works For Me*. New York City: Business Division of Random House, 1986.

Howard, Robert. "Values Make the Company: An Interview With Robert Haas." *Harvard Business Review* (September-October 1990).

Kets de Vries, Manfred F. R. "Leaders Who Self-Destruct: The Causes and Cures." *Organizational Dynamics* (Spring 1989).

Kwitny, Jonathan. "The Wrong Stuff: Space Agency Lets Contractors Off Easy If They Overcharge." *Wall Street Journal* (April 6, 1988).

Luthans, Fred. *Organizational Behavior*. New York: McGraw-Hill Book Company, 1985.

Maslow, Abraham H. "A Theory of Human Motivation." *Psychological Review* (July 1943).

Maslow, Abraham H. *Eupsychian Management*. Homewood: Dorsey-Irwin, 1965.

Milgram, Dr. Stanley. "Some Conditions of Obedience and Disobedience to Authority." *Human Relations* (February 1965).

Milgram, Dr. Stanley. "Obedience to Authority." *Psychology Today* (June 1974).

Mitroff, Ian I., Paul Shrivastava, and Firdaus Udwadia. "Effective Crisis Management." *The Academy of Management Executive* Vol. 1 No. 4 (1987) pp. 283-292.

Muczyk, Jan. P., and Bernard C Reimann. "The Case for Directive Leadership." *Academy of Management Executive* Vol. 1 No. 4 (1987) pp. 301-311.

Nierenberg, Gerard I. *Workable Ethics*. New York: Nierenberg & Zeif Publishers, 1987.

O'Neill, Joe. "Park's Leader Stands Tall Amid Trouble." *Tampa Bay Business Journal* (February 2-8, 1986).

Peck, Scott M., M.D. *The Road Less Traveled*. New York: Touchstone Books, Simon and Schuster, 1978.

Romzek, Barbara S. "Personal Consequences of Employee Commitment." *Academy of Management Journal* Vol. 32 No. 3 (1989) pp. 649-661.

Schlesinger, Jacob M. "Park Bank: a dream derailed." *St. Petersburg Times* (January 19, 1986).

Taylor, John. "Putting its house in order." *St. Petersburg Times* (April 22, 1985).

Toffler, Barbara Ley. *Tough Choices*. New York: John Wiley & Sons, 1986.

Whitney, John O. *Taking Charge*. Homewood: Dow Jones-Irwin, Inc., 1987.

Zerbe, Wilfred J., and Delroy L. Paulhus. "Socially Desirable Responding in Organizational Behavior: A Reconception." *Academy of Management Review* Vol. 12 No. 2 (1987) pp. 250-264.

Chapter 13, The CEO As Catalyst

Andrews, Kenneth R. "The Roundtable statement on boards of directors." *Harvard Business Review* [reprinted in special *Harvard Business Review* series: "Boards of Directors: Part II."] 1978).

Bailey, Dan A., and William E. Knepper. *Liability of Corporate Officers and Directors*. Charlottesville: The Michie Company, 1988.

Boulton, William R. "The Board of Directors: Beware of Those Tigers That Cause Board Change." *The Journal of Business Strategy* (19__).

Burns, James MacGregor. *Leadership*. New York: Harper Torchbooks, Harper & Row Publishers, Inc., 1978.

Cabot, L. W. "On an Effective Board." *Harvard Business Review* [reprinted in special *Harvard Business Review* series: "Boards of Directors: Part I."] (September-October 1976).

Crudele, John. "Board Games." *New York* (January 25, 1988).

Dooley, Michael P. *A Practical Guide For the Corporate Director*. Washington: KPMG Peat Marwick and National Association of Corporate Directors, 1990.

Fleisher, Arthur, Jr., Geoffrey C. Hazard, and Z. Klipper. "The Parsley on the Fish." *Director's Monthly of the National Association of Corporate Directors* (September 1988).

Geneen, Harold. *Managing*. Garden City: Doubleday & Company, Inc., 1984.

Jacobs, Richard O. "Business Crisis 201: What Directors Can Do." *Director's Monthly of the National Association of Corporate Directors* (September 1990).

Kotter, John P. "Why Power and Influence Issues Are at the Very Core of Executive Work." In *Executive Power* edited by Suresh Srivastva and Associates. San Francisco: Jossey-Bass Publishers, 1986.

Lorsch, Jay with Elizabeth MacIver. *Pawns or Potentates: The Reality of America's Corporate Boards*. Boston: Harvard Business School Press, 1989.

Mace, Myles L. "The president and the board of directors." *Harvard Business Review* [reprinted in special *Harvard Business Review* series: "Boards of Directors: Part I."] (March-April 1972).

Meyers, Gerald C. *When It Hits the Fan*. Boston: Houghton Mifflin Company, 1986.

NACD, Editor. "Outside Directors Underestimate Liability Risk." *Director's Monthly of the National Association of Corporate Directors* (October 1987).

Nash, John M., and Alexandra R. Lajoux. *A Corporate Director's Guide*. Washington: National Association of Corporate Directors, 1988.

Palmieri, Victor H. "Corporate responsibility and the competent board." *Harvard Business Review* [reprinted in special *Harvard Business Review* series: "Boards of Directors: Part II."] (May-June 1979).

Patton, Arch, and John C. Baker. "Why won't directors rock the boat?" *Harvard Business Review* (November-December 1987).

Prince, George M. "How to be a better meeting chairman." *Harvard Business Review* [reprinted in special *Harvard Business Review* series: "Leadership: Part II."] (January-February 1969).

Rand, Ayn. *Atlas Shrugged*. New York: Random House, Inc., 1957.

Sherwin, Douglas S. "Strategy for winning employee commitment." *Harvard Business Review* [reprinted in special *Harvard Business Review* series: "Executive Power-Its use and Misuse."] (May-June 1972).

Waterman, Robert H., Jr. *The Renewal Factor*. New York: Bantam Books, 1987.

Zaleznik, Abraham. "Power and politics in organizational life." *Harvard Business Review* [reprinted in special *Harvard Business Review* series: "Executive Power-Its Use and Misuse."] (May-June 1970).

Chapter 14, The Ingredients of the Director's Job

American Banker's Association, Editor. "Rating Directors the 4-I way." *ABA Banking Journal* (May 1987).

Banker's Monthly, Editor. "Safeguarding Your Bank—A Word to CEOs and Directors." *Bankers Monthly* (November 1988).

Baysinger, Barry, and Robert E. Hoskisson. "The Composition of Boards of Directors and Strategic Control: Effects on Corporate Strategy." *Academy of Management Review* Vol. 15 No. 1 (1990) pp. 72-87.

Bechmann, Mary. "Getting Tough: How Directors Can Spot the Seven 'Early Warning Signs' of Trouble — and What to Do About It." *Director's Monthly of the National Association of Corporate Directors* (October 1989).

Boulton, William R. "The Evolving Board: A Look at the Board's Changing Roles and Information Needs." *Academy of Management Review* Vol. 3 No. 4 (1978) pp. 827-836.

Business Roundtable. "Corporate Governance and American Competitiveness." *The Business Lawyer* Vol. 46 No. 1 (1990) pp. 241-252.

Cabot, Louis W. "on an effective board." *Harvard Business Review* [reprinted in special *Harvard Business Review* series: "Boards of Directors: Part I."] (September-October 1976).

Cullen, John B., Bart Victor, and Carroll Stephens. "An Ethical Weather Report: Assessing the Organization's Ethical Climate." *Organizational Dynamics* (Autumn 1989).

Drucker, Peter F. *The Effective Executive*. New York: Harper & Row Publishers, Inc. 1967.

Drucker, Peter F. *People and Performance: the Best of Peter Drucker on Management*. New York: Harper & Row Publishers, Inc., 1977.

Drucker, Peter F. *The Frontiers of Management*. New York City: Truman Talley Books, E.P. Dutton, 1986.

Feinstein, Selwyn. "Director Certification." *Wall Street Journal* (February 17, 1987).

Geneen, Harold. *Managing*. Garden City: Doubleday & Company, Inc., 1984.

Hrindac, William G. "Failed Banks: The Buck Stops with Directors." *Southern Banker* (July 1985).

Kesner, Idalene F. "Directors' Characteristics and Committee Membership: An Investigation of Type, Occupation, Tenure, and Gender." *Academy of Management Journal* Vol. 31 No. 1 (1988) pp. 66-84.

KPMG Peat Marwick. "The Audit Committee." (special study for clients and friends of firm, KPMG Peat Marwick, January, 1988).

Lorsch, Jay, and Elizabeth MacIver. *Pawns or Potentates:The Reality of America's Corporate Boards*. Boston: Harvard Business School Press, 1989.

Luthans, Fred. *Organizational Behavior*. New York: McGraw-Hill Book Company, 1985.

Mace, Myles L. "The president and the board of directors." *Harvard Business Review* [reprinted in special *Harvard Business Review* series: "Boards of Directors: Part I."] (March-April 1972).

Mace, Myles L. "Becoming more aware and knowledgeable." *Harvard Business Review* [reprinted in special *Harvard Business Review* series: "Boards of Directors: Part I."] (September-October 1975).

Mace, Myles L. "Legal guidelines for directors." *Harvard Business Review* [reprinted in special *Harvard Business Review* series: "Boards of Directors: Part I."] (September-October 1975).

Mace, Myles L. "Management information systems for directors." *Harvard Business Review* [reprinted in special *Harvard Business Review* series: "Boards of Directors: Part I."] (November-December 1975).

Patton, Arch, and John. C. Baker. "Why won't directors rock the boat?" *Harvard Business Review* (November-December 1987).

Saunders, Carol, and Jack William Jones. "Temporal Sequences in Information Acquisition for Decision Making: A Focus on Source and Medium." *Academy of Management Review* Vol. 15 No. 1 (1990) pp. 29-46.

Schlesinger, Jacob M. "Park Bank: a dream derailed." *St. Petersburg Times* (January 19, 1986).

Stedman, Michael J. "When a Crisis Hits Your Bank: Stonewall or Stroke the Press?" *Banker's Monthly* (March 1988).

Tichy, Noel M., and Mary Anne Devanna. *The Transformational Leader.* New York: John Wiley & Sons, 1986.

Wartzman, Rick. "Nature or Nurture? Study Blames Ethical Lapses on Corporate Goals." *Wall Street Journal* (October 9, 1987).

Waterman, Robert H., Jr. *The Renewal Factor.* New York: Bantam Books, 1987.

Whyte, Glen. "Groupthink Reconsidered." *Academy of Management Review* Vol. 14 No. 1 (1989) pp. 40-56.

Chapter 15, Completing the Task

Bass, Bernard M. *Leadership and Performance Beyond Expectations.* New York: The Free Press, a division of Macmillan, Inc., 1985.

Chung, Kae H., Ronald C. Rogers, Michael Lubatkin, and James E. Owers. "Do Insiders Make Better CEOs than Outsiders?" *Academy of Management Executive* Vol. 1 No. 4 (1987) pp. 325-331.

Drucker, Peter F. *The Frontiers of Management.* New York: Truman Talley Books, E. P. Dutton, 1986.

Ernst & Whinney. "The Audit Committee: Functioning in a Changing Environment." (A special study for clients and friends of the firm, Ernst & Whinney, 1988).

Gabarro, John J. *The Dynamics of Taking Charge*. Boston: Harvard Business School Press, 1987.

Harmon, Frederick G., and Garry Jacobs. *The Vital Difference*. New York: AMACOM, a division of the American Management Association, 1986.

Harrison, Allen F., and Robert M. Bramson Ph.D. *Styles of Thinking*. Garden City: Anchor Press / Doubleday, 1982.

Kelley, Charles M. "The Interrelationship of Ethics and Power in Today's Organizations." *Organizational Dynamics* (Summer 1987).

KPMG Peat Marwick. " 'Interdependent Independence' Seen as Premise for Board/ Management Balance." (Executive Newsletter, KPMG Peat Marwick, February 12, 1988).

KPMG Peat Marwick. "The Audit Committee." (special study for clients and friends of firm, KPMG Peat Marwick, January, 1988).

Mace, Myles L. "The President and the board of directors." *Harvard Business Review* [reprinted in special *Harvard Business Review* series: "Boards of Directors: Part I."] (March-April 1972).

Meindl, James R., and Sanford B. Ehrlich. "The Romance of Leadership and the Evaluation of Organizational Performance." *Academy of Management Journal* Vol. 30 No. 1 (1987) pp. 91-109.

Meyers, Gerald C. *When it Hits the Fan*. Boston: Houghton, Mifflin Company, 1986.

O'Neill, Joe. "Park's Leader Stands Tall Amid Trouble." *Tampa Bay Business Journal* (Feb 2-8, 1986).

Patton, Arch, and John C. Baker. "Why won't directors rock the boat?" *Harvard Business Review* (November-December 1987).

Rogers, Carl R., and F. J. Roethlisberger. "Barriers and Gateways to Communication." *Harvard Business Review* [reprinted in special *Harvard Business Review* series: "People: Managing Your Most Important Asset."] (__ 1986).

Sullivan, Jeremiah J. "Three Roles of Language in Motivational Theory." *Academy of Management Review* Vol. 13 No. 1 (1988) pp. 104-115.

Tichy, Noel M., and Mary Anne Devanna. *The Transformational Leader*. New York: John Wiley & Sons, 1986.

Whitney, John O. *Taking Charge*. Homewood: Dow Jones-Irwin, Inc., 1987.

Chapter 16, The Charisma Connection and the Linkage Experience

Archdeacon, Tom. "How Don Shula Motivates In Bad Times." *Florida Trend* (January 1989).

Bass, Bernard M. *Leadership and Performance Beyond Expectations*. New York: The Free Press, a division of Macmillan, Inc., 1985.

Bass, Bernard M. "Evolving Perspectives on Charismatic Leadership." In *Charismatic Leadership* edited by Jay A. Conger, Rabindra N. Kanungo and Associates. San Francisco: Jossey-Bass Publishers, 1988.

Beer, Michael, Russell A. Eisenstat, and Bert Spector. "Why Change Programs Don't Produce Change." *Harvard Business Review* (November-December 1990).

Bennis, Warren, and Burt Nanus. *Leaders*. New York: Harper & Row Publishers, 1985.

Bennis, Warren. *On Becoming a Leader*. Reading: Addison-Wesley Publishing Company, Inc., 1989.

Burns, James MacGregor. *Leadership*. New York: Harper Torchbooks, Harper & Row Publishers, 1978.

Clemens, John K., and Douglas F. Mayer. *The Classic Touch*. Homewood: Dow Jones-Irwin, 1987.

Conger, Jay A. *The Charismatic Leader*. San Francisco: Jossey-Bass Publishers, 1989.

Conger, Jay A., Rabindra N. Kanungo, and Associates. *Charismatic Leadership*. San Francisco: Jossey-Bass Publishers, 1988.

Conger, Jay A., and Rabindra N. Kanungo. "Toward a Behavioral Theory of Charismatic Leadership in Organizational Settings." *Academy of Management Review* Vol. 12 No. 4 (1987) pp. 637-647.

Conger, Jay A., and Rabindra N. Kanungo. "Behavioral Dimensions of Charismatic Leadership." In *Charismatic Leadership* , edited by Jay A. Conger, Rabindra N. Kanungo and Associates. San Francisco: Jossey-Bass Publishers, 1988.

Editors. "Ruthless Leaders." *Success* (June 1988).

Frankl, Victor E. *Man's Search For Meaning*. New York: Washington Square Press, 1963.

Holtz, Lou. " 'Do Right' with Lou Holtz." *The President*. The President's Association of American Management Association (November, 1988).

Iacocca, Lee, with William Novak. *Iacocca*. New York: Bantam Books, 1984.

Kotter, John P. *A Force for Change: How Leadership Differs from Management*. New York: The Free Press, a division of Macmillan, Inc., 1990.

Levinson, Harry, and Stuart Rosenthal. *CEO: Corporate Leadership in Action*. New York: Basic Books, Inc., 1984.

Levinson, Harry. "You Won't Recognize Me: Predications About Changes in Top-Management Characteristics." *Academy of Management Executive* Vol. 2 No. 2 (1988) pp. 119-125.

Louis, Meryl Reis. "Putting Executive Action into Context: An Alternative View of Power." In *Executive Power*, edited by Suresh Srivastva and Associates. San Francisco: Jossey-Bass Publishers, 1986.

Luthans, Fred. *Organizational Behavior*. New York: McGraw-Hill Book Company, 1985.

Meyers, Gerald C. *When it Hits the Fan*. Boston: Houghton Mifflin Company, 1986.

Morse, Michael Block. "Survivor Syndrome." *Success* (September 1987).

Nanus, Burt. *The Leader's Edge*. Chicago: Contemporary Books, 1989.

Nutting, Anthony. *Lawrence of Arabia*. New York City: Signet Books, 1961.

O'Neill, Joe. "Park's Leader Stands Tall Amid Trouble." *Tampa Bay Business Journal* (February 2-8, 1986).

Pritchett, Price. *After the Merger: Managing the Shock Waves*. Homewood: Dow Jones-Irwin, 1985.

Saffold, Guy S., III. "Culture Traits, Strength and Organizational Performance: Moving Beyond 'Strong' Culture." *Academy of Management Review* Vol. 13 No. 4 (1988) pp. 546-558.

Saskin, Marshall. "The Visionary Leader." In *Charisma Leadership* edited by Jay A. Conger, Rabindra N. Kanungo and Associates. San Francisco: Jossey-Bass Publishers, 1988.

Schweiger, David M., John M. Ivancevich, and Frank R. Power. "Executive Actions for Managing Human Resources Before and After Acquisition." *Academy of Management Executive* Vol. 1 No. 2 (1987) pp. 127-138.

Srivastva, Suresh, and David L. Cooperrider. "Introduction." In *Executive Power*, edited by Suresh Srivastva and Associates. San Francisco: Jossey-Bass Publishers, 1986.

Stayer, Ralph. "How I Learned to Let My Workers Lead." *Harvard Business Review* (November-December 1990).

Walzer, Michael. *Exodus and Revolution*. New York: Basic Books, 1985.

Westley, Frances R., and Henry Mintzberg. "Profiles of Strategic Vision: Levesque and Iacocca." In *Charismatic Leadership*, edited by Jay A. Conger, Rabindra N. Kanungo and Associates. San Francisco: Jossey-Bass Publishers, 1988.

Wilkins, Alan L., and W. Gibb Dyer Jr. "Toward Culturally Sensitive Theories of Cultural Change." *Academy of Management Review* Vol. 13 No. 4 (1988) pp. 522-533.

Zaleznik, Abraham. "The Leadership Gap." *Academy of Management Executive* Vol. 4 No. 1 (1990) pp. 7-22.

Chapter 17, From Commitment to Sustained Effort

Bennis, Warren, and Burt Nanus. *Leaders*. New York: Harper & Row Publishers, 1985.

Blau, Gary J., and Kimberly B. Boal. "Conceptualizing How Job Involvement and Organizational Commitment Affect Turnover and Absenteeism." *Academy of Management Review* Vol. 12 No. 2 (1987) pp. 288-300.

Conger, Jay A. "Leadership: The Art of Empowering Others." *Academy of Management Executive* Vol. 3 No. 1 (1989) pp. 17-24.

Conger, Jay A., and Rabindra N. Kanungo. "The Empowerment Process: Integrating Theory and Practice." *Academy of Management Review* Vol. 13 No. 3 (1988) pp. 471-482.

Drucker, Peter F. *People and Performance: The Best of Peter Drucker on Management.* New York: Harper & Row Publishers, Inc., 1977.

Feinstein, Selwyn. "Charisma Is Costly in the Executive Suite." *Wall Street Journal* (March 22, 1989).

Ferris, Rodney. "How Organizational Love Can Improve Leadership." *Organizational Dynamics* (Spring 1988).

Frankl, Victor. *Man's Search For Meaning.* New York: Washington Square Press, 1963.

Geneen, Harold. *Managing.* Garden City: Doubleday & Co., Inc., 1984.

Horton, Thomas R. "Beyond Charisma." *The President.* The President's Association of American Management Association. (January, 1989).

Howell, Jane M. "Two Faces of Charisma: Socialized and Personalized Leadership in Organizations." In *Charismatic Leadership*, edited by Jay A. Conger, Rabindra N. Kanungo and Associates. San Francisco: Jossey-Bass Publishers, 1988.

Kahn, William A. "Psychological Conditions of Personal Engagement and Disengagement at Work." *Academy of Management Journal* Vol. 33 No. 4 (1990) pp. 692-724.

Kets de Vries, Manfred F. R. "Origins of Charisma: Ties That Bind the Leader and the Led." In *Charismatic Leadership*, edited by Jay A. Conger, Rabindra N. Kanungo and Associates. San Francisco: Jossey-Bass Publishers, 1988.

Levinson, Harry. "You Won't Recognize Me: Predictions About Changes in Top-Management Characteristics." *Academy of Management Executive* Vol. 2 No. 2 (1988) pp. 119-125.

Levinson, Harry, and Stuart Rosenthal. *CEO, Corporate Leadership in Action.* New York: Basic Books, Inc., Publishers, 1984.

Luthans, Fred. *Organizational Behavior.* New York: McGraw-Hill Book Company, 1985.

Myers, M. Scott. "Who Are Your Motivated Workers?" *Harvard Business Review* [reprinted in special *Harvard Business Review* series: "Motivation: Vol. I."] (January-February 1964).

O'Neill, Joe. "Park's Leader Stands Tall Amid Trouble." *Tampa Bay Business Journal* (February 2-8, 1986).

Peters, Tom. *Thriving on Chaos.* New York: Alfred A. Knopf, 1987.

Peters, Thomas J., and Robert H. Waterman Jr. *In Search of Excellence.* New York: Harper & Row Publishers, 1982.

Riggio, Ronald E., Ph.D. *The Charisma Quotient.* New York: Dodd, Mead & Co., 1987.

Thomas, Kenneth W., and Betty A. Velthouse. "Cognitive Elements of Empowerment." *Academy of Management Review* Vol. 15 No. 4 (1990) pp. 666-681.

Waterman, Robert H., Jr. *The Renewal Factor.* New York: Bantam Books, 1987.

Zaleznik, Abraham. "Real Work." *Harvard Business Review* (January-February 1989).

Chapter 18, After Zen, the Laundry

Campbell, Joseph. *The Power of Myth*. New York: Doubleday & Co., 1988.

Cullen, John B., Bart Victor, and Carroll Stephens. "An Ethical Weather Report: Assessing the Organization's Ethical Climate." *Organizational Dynamics* (Autumn 1989).

Fink, Steven. *Crisis Management*. New York: AMACOM, a division of American Management Association, 1986.

Gleick, James. *Chaos: Making a New Science*. New York: Penguin Books, 1987.

Peters, Tom. *Thriving on Chaos*. New York: Alfred A. Knopf, 1987.

Schnaars, Steven P. *Megamistakes: Forecasting and the Myth of Rapid Technological Change*. New York: The Free Press, a division of Macmillan, Inc., 1989.

Taubes, Gary. "The Body Chaotic." *Discover* (May 1989).

Epilogue

Bacon, Kenneth H. "Administration Weighs Plan on FDIC Stock." *Wall Street Journal* (November 28, 1990).

Harlan, Christe, and Wade Lambert. "Malpractice Insurers Worry Over Legal Work for Banks." *Wall Street Journal* (November 29, 1990).

Kesner, Idalene F., and Roy B. Johnson. "Boardroom Crisis: Fiction or Fact." *Academy of Management Executive* Vol. 4 No. 1 (1990) pp. 23-35.

Sahlman, William A. "Why Sane People Shouldn't Serve on Public Boards." *Harvard Business Review* (May-June 1990).

Suskind, Ron. "Some Banks Use Accounting Techniques That Conceal Loan Woes, Regulators Say." *Wall Street Journal* (November 29, 1990).